Total English

UPPER INTERMEDIATE

Students' Book with ActiveBook and MyEnglishLab
plus Vocabulary Trainer

eBOOK & LMS   VOCAB TRAINER

Araminta Crace
with Richard Acklam

B1+–B2

Contents

Contents

Contents

Contents

1 Read the text and match the parts of speech (a–l) with each <u>underlined</u> word or phrase.

According to (1) <u>the</u> ancient Greek historian Herodotus, (2) <u>in</u> the 7th century BC the king of Egypt, Psamtik 1, decided to conduct a (3) <u>scientific</u> experiment. Using his absolute power over his subjects, (4) <u>he</u> took two newborn babies and handed them to a shepherd, with instructions that they were to be (5) <u>brought up</u> in total isolation. Most importantly, no one was to speak in the babies' presence. Psamtik wanted to find out what language the children would speak if left to themselves. He thought that the language they produced would be the (6) <u>oldest</u> in the world – the original language of the human race. After two years, the shepherd heard the two children (7) <u>repeatedly</u> pronounce the word 'becos'. This was identified as meaning (8) <u>'bread'</u> in the language of the Phrygians, a people then living in central Turkey. From this experiment, Psamtik deduced that the Phrygian language (9) <u>must</u> be the first ever spoken. Nobody now believes Psamtik's (10) <u>conclusion</u> – a few commentators suggest that the infants (11) <u>were imitating</u> the sound of the shepherd's sheep, but no one since (12) <u>has had</u> any better success in discovering what man's very first spoken language was like.

a	Present Perfect	g	countable noun
b	Past Continuous	h	superlative
c	uncountable noun	i	adjective
d	phrasal verb	j	adverb
e	article	k	pronoun
f	preposition	l	modal verb

2 Find the grammar mistake in each sentence and correct it.

1 They've been to Brazil last year.
2 This cathedral built in 1590.
3 She's the person what told me I should study economics at university.
4 I was reading in my room when I was hearing a loud crash downstairs.
5 My grades this year are a lot bad than last year, unfortunately.
6 You work for IBM, aren't you?
7 If I'll have time, I'll paint my bedroom this weekend.
8 Can I give you a small advice?
9 He's always wanted to be teacher.

3 a Complete the word maps with words/phrases from the box.

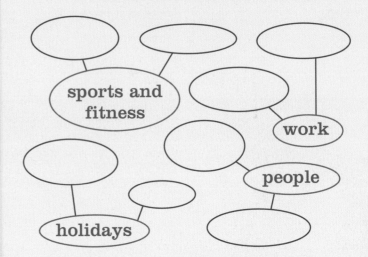

do aerobics souvenir application form
sense of humour take up a hobby
be promoted go sightseeing father-in-law

sports and fitness

work

people

holidays

b <u>Underline</u> the main stress in each word/phrase.

c Add three more words to each word map.

4 a Look at the dictionary extract from the Longman Active Study Dictionary. What does it tell you about each of the following: grammar, pronunciation and meaning?

sen·si·ble /ˈsensəbəl/ *adj* **1** showing good judgement: *a sensible decision* **2** suitable for a particular purpose, especially a practical one: *sensible clothes* – sensibly *adv*

b Complete the dictionary extracts by writing a definition for each one.

1 re·tire /rɪˈtaɪə/ *v* [I] _____:
  I'd like to retire before I'm 60.
2 a·broad /əˈbrɔːd/ *adv* _____:
  Did you go abroad for your last holiday?
3 get on with sb *phr v* [T] _____:
  I get on well with both my sisters.
4 pitch /pɪtʃ/ *n* [C] _____:
  The players ran out onto the pitch.

c Now compare your definitions with the definitions in a dictionary.

d Add the words/phrases above to the word maps in exercise 3a.

Lead-in

1 Look at the photos. Who are the people and how do you think they are connected?

2 Work in pairs. Choose three of the people from the box and take turns to describe them to your partner. Who is closest to you?

> partner   wife   husband   step-sister   half-brother
> sibling   colleague   soulmate   close friend
> neighbour   acquaintance

3 **a** Work in pairs. Look at the sentences and check you understand the meaning of the underlined phrases.

1 I come across as confident when you first meet me, but I'm shy really.
2 I often bump into old school friends when I'm out in my local area.
3 I didn't make a very good impression on my neighbours when I moved in.
4 I didn't see eye to eye with any of my siblings when I was growing up.
5 I keep in touch with almost all my friends from my first school.
6 I try not to 'judge a book by its cover' when I meet new people.
7 I prefer talking face to face, rather than on the phone or online.
8 I've never met anyone and just clicked with them immediately.

b Which sentences from exercise 3a are true for you? Give details.

1.1 First impressions

Reading

1 Work in pairs and look at the photo. What kinds of thing would you talk about to ...

- friends of friends at a party
- classmates in a new class
- colleagues in a new job
- neighbours in a new area

2 Read the 'Any Answers' website. How does each person feel about meeting new people?

Do you think first impressions are important? Most people think it takes about two minutes to make a judgement about someone when you first meet. I'm reading a book at the moment about first impressions. It says we make decisions about new people in a few seconds – that means we make a decision without even thinking. Our minds unconsciously say, 'I really like you' or 'I'll avoid you'.

How quickly do you think you make judgements about people? Do you have any advice on what to do or say when you meet new people? Any answers, please.

Ana, Spain. When a friend introduces me to someone at a party and I have to make small talk, I sometimes stumble over my words and start mumbling. I've watched more confident people and they always speak up. I read something about giving people compliments and asking questions. It's a good way to start a conversation; you can say something like, 'I really love your shoes! Where did you get them?' So, that's what I'm going to do next time I meet someone new. Also, feeling confident about what I look like helps me – so I always wear clothes that make me feel good.

Mark, Australia. I work in a big company and I meet new colleagues all the time. I like meeting new people and I'm quite confident, but in my experience people definitely form an instant opinion about you. Personally, I try not to be too judgemental, but I'm sure your unconscious mind takes over a bit! You need to think about the language you use, especially when you greet people. I always say, 'Hello, pleased to meet you.' I can't stand it when people you don't know are really informal and say something like, 'Hey, what's up?' I think it also sounds ridiculous when people are too formal and say, 'How do you do?'

Jelena, Poland. As I'm writing this, I'm nervous because I'm starting a new class tomorrow and I'm going to meet lots of new classmates. I think it'll be fine though. I know one person and I'm meeting her before the class. Also, most people are nervous in new situations. My parents always told me to treat people as you want them to treat you. You should never talk down to them or gossip about them. I'd like people to chat to me and be friendly, so I'm going to do that. I think it's also important to make eye contact and listen to people. You shouldn't talk about yourself all the time, boast about things or dominate the conversation.

3 Read the website again and answer the questions.

1. According to the book the writer is describing, how long does it take to make judgements about people?
2. What does Ana mention about saying nice things to people?
3. What does Ana say about the clothes she wears?
4. Does Mark think that people judge each other quickly or not?
5. What does Mark say about the formality of people's language?
6. What advice did Jelena's parents give her?
7. Does Jelena say it's good to talk about yourself a lot?

4 Work in pairs and discuss these questions.

1. How true do you think it is that we make very quick judgements about people when we first meet?
2. Do you think that your first impressions of someone you meet for the first time are usually correct or not?
3. What advice would you give to someone who is ...
   - worried about going to a party with lots of new people?
   - about to start a new job and wants to make a good first impression?

   Think about ...
   - what you say.
   - how much you speak or listen.
   - eye contact.
   - what you wear.
   - body language (e.g. bowing, shaking hands).

Grammar | overview (1): the present and future

5 Look at the underlined verbs in the sentences from the website. Match them with the uses (a–j) in the Active grammar box.

1 I'm reading a book at the moment.
2 Our minds unconsciously say, 'I really like you' or 'I'll avoid you'.
3 That's what I'm going to do next time I meet someone new.
4 I always wear clothes that make me feel good.
5 I work in a big company.
6 As I'm writing this, I'm nervous.
7 I'm going to meet lots of new classmates.
8 I'm meeting her before the class.
9 I think it'll be fine though.
10 Most people are nervous in new situations.

Active grammar

Use Present Simple for:
a) habits/routines
b) describing a state
c) things that are permanent/always true

Use Present Continuous for:
d) things that are happening now, at this precise moment
e) temporary situations that are happening around now
f) arrangements in the future

Use *will* + infinitive for:
g) unplanned decisions (made while speaking)
h) predictions based on what you think or believe

Use *going to* + infinitive for:
i) plans and intentions
j) predictions based on what you know or can see/hear now

We do not usually use state verbs in the continuous form (e.g. *like, think, want, need*).

See Reference page 19

6 Find the mistakes in the underlined verb tenses and correct them.

1 I enjoyed my first class and I'm sure I make some new friends.
2 He'll meet some new classmates after school in a café at 5.30.
3 She is always arriving early on the first day of a new course.
4 I've decided that I study harder this term than before.
5 My cousin lives with us at the moment – just for three years while he's at university.
6 I think I'm having a lot of homework to do this year.
7 We've got a really good teacher this term. I'm really liking her.
8 He'll listen to some music at the same time as studying right now.

7 a Work in pairs. Take turns to ask and answer questions about the topics below.

- accommodation
- family
- new people
- plans for the weekend
- meeting friends
- hobbies

b Tell the rest of the class about your partner.

8 Read the Lifelong learning box. Work in pairs and discuss the questions.

Reading skills: grammar in context

Texts contain a range of grammar that the writer has chosen for a particular reason. We can understand more about what we read by thinking about this choice of grammar.

1 Why do you think the writers chose to use the underlined grammar in these sentences?
   a) Our minds unconsciously say: 'I really like you' or 'I'll avoid you'.
   b) You should never talk down to them or gossip about them.
   c) I'd like people to chat to me and be friendly, so I'm going to do that.
2 What other verb forms could be used instead in each case?
3 What difference to meaning would those choices make?

Lifelong learning

Vocabulary | ways of speaking

9 Work in pairs. Find the verb phrases in the box in the website on page 8. Try to explain the meaning of each by looking at the sentences around the verb phrases.

> chat   gossip   make small talk   greet someone
> give someone a compliment   boast   mumble
> speak up   talk down to someone
> stumble over your words

10 a Choose the correct words in *italics*.

1 I spend at least an hour every day *chatting/making small talk* to friends on the phone.

2 People always respond positively when you *talk down to them/give them a compliment*.

3 'Hobbies' and 'the weather' are the best two topics when you have to *make small talk/boast*.

4 When I was a teenager, I *talked down/mumbled* a lot and people couldn't understand what I was saying.

5 I think it's particularly upsetting to hear people *mumbling/talking down* to elderly people.

6 I get nervous when I speak in public and I *stumble over my words/speak up*.

7 I make a point of always *mumbling to/greeting* my neighbours in the street.

8 *Boasting/Mumbling* about your possessions is worse than about your achievements.

9 I often can't hear people on my mobile and I ask them to *speak up/talk down*.

10 *Greeting/Gossiping* and talking about people behind their backs can be very hurtful.

b How true are the statements for you? Discuss with other students. Give reasons for your opinions.

Speaking

11 a 🔵 1.2 Listen to the conversation and answer the questions.

1 What is the situation?

2 Do you think that the two people make a good first impression on each other?

3 Which topics in the box do they talk about?

> hobbies   friends   work   study   travel
> the weather   clothes   where you live
> how you feel

b Listen again. Add one more phrase to each section of the How to... box.

How to... make a good first impression

Greet someone	*It's great to meet you.* *Hello, how are you?* *Nice to meet you, too.* *Fine thanks – and you?*
Try to find out what you have in common	*Have you done any Spanish classes before?* *Do you live near here?* *How did you get here today?*
Sound interested in the other person	*I know what you mean.* *Oh, really?* *Are you?*
Finish the conversation politely	*I'm sorry, I really must go. But it was great to meet you.* *Good to meet you. See you again soon.*

12 a You want to make a good impression on someone you haven't met before. Work in pairs and choose a situation from exercise 1. Prepare to have a conversation with them. Make notes about what to say for each section of the How to... box.

b Roleplay your conversation.

c Do you think you made a good impression on each other? How do you think you could improve your conversations?

1.2 Family ties

Grammar overview (2): the past

Can do express your opinion and manage a conversation

Listening

1 **a** Work in pairs. Look at the photo of the Boehmer family. What do you think they do?

b 🔵 1.3 Listen to an extract from a radio programme about the Boehmer family and answer the questions.

1 How many children are in the Boehmer family?

2 What is special about them?

3 How do they feel about what they do?

2 Listen again and answer the questions.

1 Why did Larry Boehmer start juggling?

2 How did his children become interested in juggling?

3 Where did the family first juggle for a public audience?

4 What is special about Casey Boehmer?

5 What does Larry believe about the skill of juggling?

3 **a** Look at the underlined phrases in audioscript 1.3 on page 162. What do you think they mean?

b Summarise the information in the radio programme using the phrases from the audioscript.

4 Work in groups. Discuss the questions.

1 From what you've heard about Larry Boehmer, how would you describe him?

2 What is an argument against doing what the Boehmer parents did with their children? Do you agree with this argument? Why/Why not?

3 Larry Boehmer says his 'children's talents aren't inherited; it's simply a matter of practice and persistence'. How far do you think that is true for different talents?

4 How do you think you would feel about working with a member of your family?

Grammar | overview (2): the past

5 **a** Look at the underlined verbs in the extract from the radio programme. Which are Past Simple, Past Continuous and Past Perfect Simple?

> It all started while Larry Boehmer <u>was working</u> as a pipeline worker for Shell Oil. His job <u>took</u> him away from his wife Judy and the four children they had at that time. He <u>had spent</u> the first few weeks sitting in his motel room between shifts, when one day, while he <u>was feeling</u> bored, he <u>decided</u> to take up a new hobby. Using a book, he <u>taught</u> himself to juggle. When he <u>had mastered</u> the basics, he <u>went</u> home and <u>showed</u> his children what he could do.

b Look at the Active grammar box and match the tenses (1–3) with their correct uses (A–C).

Active grammar

1 Use Past Simple ☐

2 Use Past Continuous ☐

3 Use Past Perfect Simple ☐

A to describe main events in the past

B to describe events and background information that happened before the main events in the past

C to describe actions that were in progress when the main events happened

See Reference page 19

6 Choose the correct words in *italics*.

A When Larry decided to teach himself to juggle, ...

1 ... he *had lived/was living* in a motel.

2 ... his family *wanted/had wanted* to learn to juggle, too.

3 ... he *took/had taken* a job with Shell Oil.

B When I arrived at the cinema, ...

4 ... my friends *were waiting/had waited* by the ticket office.

5 ... the film *had started/was starting* 15 minutes earlier.

6 ... I *bought/was buying* my ticket as quickly as I could.

7 a Complete the story with the Past Simple, Past Continuous or Past Perfect Simple form of the verb in brackets.

Before Peter and Kate Evans _had_ (have) children, they (1) _____ (hear) about home-schooling but (2) _____ (not think) about it as a serious option for their own family. They (3) _____ (live) in California when they (4) _____ (have) their first child and (5) _____ (start) to find out more about it. Both of them (6) _____ (work) full-time at that time, so they had to make some big decisions about their lives.

Thirty years later, Emily is a professor of mathematics at a top university, Jen is a lawyer specialising in family law and Heather is a professional pianist.

Emily says, 'When I (7) _____ (go) to university, I (8) _____ (realise) what home-schooling (9) _____ (give) me. Many students there (10) _____ (not know) how to think about things properly. We (11) _____ (learn) to process information – not just repeat other people's ideas. I am proud that all our careers are so different. While we (12) _____ (grow up), our parents were always very supportive; they helped us to build on our individual strengths.'

b Complete the sentences.

1 When I was studying for my exams, ...

2 When I left my last school, I ...

3 When I had finished my last exam, ...

4 When I look back at my education, I realise that ...

c Work in pairs and discuss your sentences.

Reading

8 Work in pairs and discuss the questions.

1 What are the advantages and disadvantages of being born first, middle or last in a family?

2 Do you think it is good to be an only child? Why/Why not?

9 Read the article above and choose the best summary.

1 It says which type of child it is best to be (i.e. first born, middle born, last born or an only child).

2 It gives advice to parents about dealing with each type of child.

3 It describes possible career consequences according to the position in the family.

4 It advises children how to cope with their position in the family.

WHO comes first?

A child's place in the family birth order may play a role in the type of occupations that will interest him or her as an adult, new research suggests. In two related studies, researchers found that only children – and to a certain extent first-born children – were more interested in intellectual, cognitive careers than later-born children. In contrast, later-born children were more interested in both artistic and outdoor-related careers.

These results fit into theories that say our place in family birth order will influence our personality, said Frederick T. L. Leong, co-author of the study and professor of psychology at Ohio State University. 'Parents typically place different demands and have different expectations of children depending on their birth order.'

'For example, parents may be extremely protective of only children and worry about their physical safety. That may be why only children are more likely to show interest in academic pursuits rather than physical or outdoor activities. An only child will tend to get more time and attention from their parents than children with siblings. This will often make them feel special

10 a Read the article again. Are these statements true (T) or false (F)? Explain why.

1 Only children and first-born children often follow similar types of career path. ☐

2 Parents usually expect different things from their first and last children. ☐

3 There are no disadvantages to being an only child. ☐

4 Last-born children tend to take more risks as a result of their parents' attitude towards them. ☐

5 Middle children often get on well with many different types of people. ☐

b Work in pairs and give your own opinions on the statements in exercise 10a. Give examples from your own family and other families you know.

Vocabulary | making adjectives from nouns

11 Complete the table. Then check your answers with the article.

Noun	Adjective
intellect	(1) _____
art	(2) _____
(3) _____	jealous
(4) _____	lonely
responsibility	(5) _____
(6) _____	successful
frustration	(7) _____
skill	(8) _____

but the downside is that they may suffer from jealousy and loneliness when friends discuss their brothers and sisters and family life.'

The first-born is an only child until the second child comes along – transforming them from being the centre of attention, to then sharing the care of parents. Parents will also expect them to be responsible and 'set an example'. The change from being the focus of a family may be quite a shock and so shape the first-born's outlook on life. Therefore, first-borns may try to get back their parents' attention and approval by achieving success in their careers. It is true that first-borns are significantly more often found as political leaders than any other birth-order position.

Being the youngest in the family can sometimes be a frustrating experience, especially if the child wants to be taken seriously and treated like an adult. The last-born is more likely than the other birth-order positions to take up dangerous sports. This may be a sign of the last-born's rebellious streak – a result of being fed up with always being bossed about by everyone else in the family.

Middle children, however, have different issues. 'Middle-child syndrome' can mean feeling sandwiched between two other 'more important' people – an older sibling who gets all the rights and is treated like an adult and a younger sibling who gets all the privileges and is treated like a spoilt child. Middle-borns have to learn to get on with older and younger children, and this may contribute to them becoming good negotiators – of all the birth-order positions they are most skilful at dealing with both authority figures and those holding inferior positions.

12 Complete the sentences with the words from the table in exercise 11.

1 There's a lot of _____ involved in juggling.
2 My sister is very _____ . She can paint well and writes poetry.
3 I'm an only child, but I never felt _____ because I always had a lot of friends.
4 Parents have a big _____ to give their children the right start in life.
5 My brother is interested in _____ hobbies like playing chess, whereas I'm more physical.
6 I was always very _____ of my older sister for being much more beautiful than me.
7 Not being able to do things your older siblings do can lead to _____ and arguments.
8 I've wanted to be a _____ lawyer and make a lot of money ever since I was a child.

Speaking

13 **a** 🔊 1.4 Listen to three people. What are they talking about? Do they agree with each other?

b Listen again and complete the How to... box.

How to... manage a conversation

Find out what someone else thinks	Ask a direct question: *What do you _____ about that?* Reformulate someone's answer into another question: *So, you're the _____ child then?*
Interrupt to get your point of view across	Refer to someone's point and back up with your own example: *That's not the _____ that I had ...* Find similarities with someone else's point: *I think it's quite _____ .* *I suppose my sister ...*
Support what another person says	Comment on someone's point and back up with your own example: *That's quite _____ . I've got an older brother and ...* Agree with someone's point: *I _____ it must be the case for some ...*

Pronunciation | intonation: sounding tentative

14 **a** 🔊 1.5 We can show how tentative or sure we are about what we're saying by using different intonation. Listen again to four extracts from the conversation. Which ones convey more tentative statements and which are more confident? How can you tell?

b Listen to the extracts again. Then look at the underlined sentences in audioscript 1.4 on page 162 and repeat them with similar intonation.

15 Work in small groups and discuss the statements. Use the language from the How to... box.

1 Parents tend to be stricter with their first-born children.
2 Middle children have the worst time.
3 Youngest children are usually spoilt.
4 Only children tend to be self-sufficient and not need many friends.
5 We are attracted to people who are born in the same position within the family.

Reading

1 Work in groups and discuss the questions.

1 Do you have a mobile phone? How much do you use it? What do you use it for?

2 Do you know anyone who doesn't have a mobile phone? Why don't they have one?

3 Do you think mobile phones are generally a good or a bad thing?

4 Do you think it is appropriate for a child to have a mobile phone? If not, why not? If so, what do you think the minimum age should be? Why?

2 Read the article. Tick (✓) the six topics that are mentioned.

1 the number of young people who have a mobile phone ☐

2 when the first mobile phone was invented ☐

3 the reasons why young people want a mobile phone ☐

4 how parents feel about their children having a mobile phone ☐

5 mobile phones and noise pollution ☐

6 the amount of contact teenagers feel they need with their friends ☐

7 the effect of mobile phones on relationships ☐

8 some possible educational uses of mobile phones ☐

9 the effect of mobile phones on reading for pleasure ☐

10 the health risks of mobile phones to children ☐

3 Read the article again. Make brief notes about the ideas in exercise 2 it refers to.

4 Work in pairs and discuss the questions.

1 Which two facts in the article did you find most interesting? Why?

2 How important do you think mobile phones are for young people in your country?

3 How do you think mobile phones will change over the next five years?

4 How far do you agree that the use of mobile phones can be addictive and bad for your health?

Mobile mad

There are good reasons to be worried about children and mobile phones, reports Michael Fitzpatrick.

In Japan, where mobiles have been common among the young for some time and offer sophisticated services, sociologists see an alarming trend. 'Keitai culture', as the use of mobiles in Japan is known, is huge. In Tokyo, for example, a third of all four to 15-year-olds have a mobile phone. Over half of Japan's high-school students own one and many of them are Internet-enabled. Half the children polled recently said their lifestyle 'required' them to have a mobile phone and many said their parents 'forced' them to have one. 'My parents say if I go out, I have to take my phone so they can get in touch with me, wherever I am,' says 14-year-old Aya Oguri. 'I don't have to phone them all the time but I mustn't turn it off. I don't really mind as it makes me feel safe.'

An informal survey conducted on the Tokyo streets by *Japan Today* magazine, however, suggests that the nation's teens have other reasons for keeping hold of 'their best electric friend'. 'I need to keep in touch all the time. If I can't find my phone I feel really isolated from my friends,' says 16-year-old Asuka Maezawa. Emi Inoue, 17, agrees, adding, 'I can talk to my friends about gossip I don't want my parents to hear.' Another survey also revealed that about 22 percent said they talked at least ten times per day, while 45 percent said they used their mobile to send ten or more text messages each day.

Such a density of mobile ownership, especially among the young, has led to a new type of neurosis, say sociologists. Japanese teens, in particular, have become fanatical about being 'always available' and not wanting to lose touch, even for a day. 'Teenagers take advantage of every spare minute to touch base with their friends. It is not the content of the communication but the act of staying in touch that matters. Indeed, many become extremely uneasy if they can't be in touch with their peers countless times each day, fearing they are becoming socially isolated,' writes sociologist Hisao Ishii, author of *The Superficial Social Life of Japan's Mobile Phone Addicts*. 15-year-old Miki Nakamura backs this up when she says, 'I must have my phone with me all the time. I'm completely out of touch with the world without my phone and I go into a total panic.'

'If this trend continues,' adds Hisao Ishii, 'two things will probably happen. One is mobile phone addiction, where a person doesn't have the necessary skills to form and maintain relationships without the help of mobiles. The second: superficial communication may drive out genuine conversation. The act of contacting one another may become all that matters, leading to a deterioration in the quality of relationships. Indeed, the very fabric of society may be threatened.'

The sociologist Maiko Seki has also suggested that, 'children read books less and less as they are too busy playing with their technological tools.' As well as this, it may be that academic performance is being affected: 68 percent of children who responded to a DoCoMo survey who owned a mobile phone said they got poor grades at school. In addition to this, a recent UK government report has highlighted the increased health risks to children under 16 using mobile handsets. A leaflet sent to schools suggests that children below this age shouldn't have unlimited access to mobile phones and that they should be used only in emergencies.

Vocabulary | keeping in touch

5 **a** Work in pairs. Find the verb phrases from the box in the article and try to work out the meaning.

> to be in touch   to be out of touch
> to get in touch   to keep in touch   to lose touch
> to stay in touch   to touch base

b Discuss the questions.

1 Which pair of verb phrases has the same meaning?

2 Which two pairs of verb phrases have opposite meanings?

6 **a** Delete the wrong word in each sentence.

1 I stay in of touch with a lot of my friends by email.

2 Sadly, I've lost in touch with someone who I'd really like to see again.

3 I'm in the touch with several people from my primary school.

4 I am touch base with most members of my family at least once a week.

5 I hate being in out of touch with friends, even when I'm on holiday.

6 I use my mobile every day to be get in touch with friends and family.

7 I find it difficult to keep in touch base with all my friends as much as I'd like.

b Tick the sentences which are true for you and change the others to make them true.

c Compare your sentences with other students.

Grammar | obligation and ability

7 **a** Complete headings A and B in the Active grammar box with *Obligation – present* and *General ability – present*.

b 1.6 Listen to a teenager talking about her mobile phone and answer the questions.

1 Why did she get a phone?

2 How does she feel about it?

c Complete headings C, D and E of the Active grammar box with:

Ability in the past on one specific occasion,
General ability – past and
Obligation – past.

> **Active grammar**
> _____
>
> A _____
>
> *can, can't*
>
> B _____
>
> *have to, don't have to, must, mustn't, should, shouldn't*
>
> C _____
>
> *could, was able to, couldn't, wasn't able to*
>
> D _____
>
> *could, was able to, couldn't, wasn't able to*
>
> E _____
>
> *had to, didn't have to, should have, shouldn't have*

See Reference page 19

8 Rewrite the sentences using the words from the Active grammar box. Start with the words given. Sometimes there is more than one possible answer.

1 I think <u>it's a good idea</u> for me to do more exercise.

I think I …

2 I <u>had the ability to</u> read when I was only three.

I …

3 <u>It wasn't necessary</u> to wear a uniform when I was at school.

I …

4 <u>It is necessary to</u> turn your phone off in the cinema.

You …

5 <u>It wasn't a good idea to</u> apologise to her so late.

You …

6 When I spoke to her, <u>I had the ability</u> to make her understand the problem.

When I spoke to her, I …

7 When I was a child, <u>it was necessary</u> to eat things I didn't like.

When I was a child, I …

8 <u>It is forbidden to</u> use your phone during the performance.

You …

Pronunciation | connected speech (1)

9 **a** Look at the <u>underlined</u> words in the sentences (1–8) and follow the instructions.

• Tick (✓) the weak forms of modal/auxiliary verbs (e.g. *can/was*) and prepositions (e.g. *to*).

• Mark connections between a consonant sound and a vowel sound.

• Mark connections between a consonant sound and another consonant sound.

1 **A:** <u>Can</u> you hear what she's saying?
B: Yes, I <u>can</u>.

2 I <u>couldn't</u> phone them.

3 I <u>was</u> able <u>to</u> phone from there.

4 I know I <u>should've</u> been more careful.

5 I <u>wasn't</u> able <u>to</u> tell them where I <u>was</u>.

6 You have <u>to</u> phone me when you get there.

7 He had <u>to</u> get in touch with his boss.

8 **A:** <u>Could</u> you speak English when you were five?
B: Yes, I <u>could</u>.

b 🔘 1.7 Listen and check the pronunciation. Work in pairs and repeat the sentences.

Speaking

10 **a** Choose five of the points below to talk about. On another piece of paper, write one word (as a clue) for each point you chose.

• one thing you can boast about

• a person you should get in touch with soon

• one thing you like doing, but shouldn't do

• one thing you were proud you were able to do

• a person you should've made a good impression on, but didn't

• one thing you must do before the weekend

• one thing you could play/do well before, but can't do now

• a person you know you mustn't lose touch with

• one thing you didn't have to do, but you're pleased you did

• a person you had to speak to face to face, but didn't want to

• one thing you shouldn't have done, but did

b Work in pairs. Show your clues to your partner but don't say which piece of information each one refers to. Take turns to ask each other about each clue and find out what each refers to.

A: *You've written 'Alicia'. I know she's a good friend of yours and I think she lives quite far away. So, is she someone you should get in touch with soon?*

B: *No. Actually, I saw her last week.*

A: *OK, well, maybe she's someone you mustn't lose touch with?*

B: *Yes, that's right. She's moving to New Zealand soon and I really don't want to lose touch with her.*

1 🔵 1.8 Read and listen to Tim's girlfriend (Mandy) and his sister (Gill). Answer the questions.

1 Who is Gill's boyfriend?
2 Who has made Gill upset?

M: So, do you think Tim <u>takes after</u> his dad?

G: Well, I suppose so, in some ways.

M: How?

G: Well, I mean, they're both very stubborn.

M: That's for sure. It runs in the family.

G: But you know Tim really <u>looks up</u> to him. He always has, right from when we were kids and while we were <u>growing up</u>. I remember he used to always be <u>showing off</u> to him, trying to get his attention, one way or another.

M: And how about you?

G: Oh, I suppose I was always closer to my mum. She didn't have an easy time, <u>bringing us up</u>. Dad wasn't around much.

M: And how did you and Tim <u>get on</u>?

G: Oh really well ... except when he'd put spiders in my bed!

M: And how's life with you now?

G: Not bad. You know I'm <u>going out</u> with Kevin?

M: Oh yes? But, it's not so long since you <u>split up</u> with Max, is it?

G: Hey ... it's nearly six months, and anyway, I've known Kevin for ages, it's just that it's never seemed to be the right time before.

M: And, how's Sally?

G: Oh ... Sally. Well, we've kind of <u>fallen out</u>.

M: Really? Why? What happened?

G: Well, it's a long story but, in a nutshell, I told her something pretty sensitive about me and things going on at work.

M: Yes ...?

G: And then I found out she'd talked about it to some other friends.

M: Oh no!

G: Yeah, I was really upset about it.

M: Do you think you'll be able to <u>make up</u>?

G: I'm really not sure ...

2 **a** Work in pairs. From the context, think about the meaning of each <u>underlined</u> phrasal verb and write a short definition.

take after – to look or behave like someone in your family

b Check your ideas in a dictionary.

3 Find the mistake in each sentence and correct it.

1 How long have you and your girlfriend been going out with?
2 You don't get on your boss very well, do you?
3 We made it up after we both agreed how silly we had been.
4 I think our parents did a great job of bringing up us with very little money.
5 David really looks up to. He thinks you're amazing.
6 Who do you take them after in your family, your mum or your dad?
7 I wish you would grow out and start behaving like an adult!
8 John's fallen out his brother again. I think his brother owes him some money.
9 Why did he tell us how much money he earns? I hate it when people show on like that.
10 Why did you and Lorraine split it up? I thought you were quite happy together.

4 **a** Read the statements (1–5). Which are true for you? Change the others to make them true for you.

1 Of all the people in my family, I probably get on best with my dad because we're so similar.
2 I take after my grandmother in lots of ways. We both love travel and discovering new places.
3 In my opinion, couples should go out for at least two years before they get married.
4 If I have children in the future, I'll probably bring them up in much the same way that my parents brought me up.
5 I really look up to my grandfather. He's incredibly kind and always ready to listen to you if you have a problem.

b Work in pairs. Compare your answers and give details and examples.

Can do talk about past and present members of your family

1 a 🔊 1.9 Listen to Morgan talking to a friend about his family. Who are the people in the pictures?

b Listen again and complete the family tree opposite.

2 a Draw a diagram of a family tree going back to at least grandparents. You can either do a family tree for your own family, or you can imagine a different family.

b Work in pairs and take turns to describe your family tree to each other. While your partner listens, he/she should try and draw your family tree. Then, compare what he/she has drawn with your diagram.

3 a Choose two of the people in your family tree and prepare to talk about one from the present and one from the past. Think about the tenses and vocabulary you will use.

b Work in pairs. Discuss the people in your family tree.

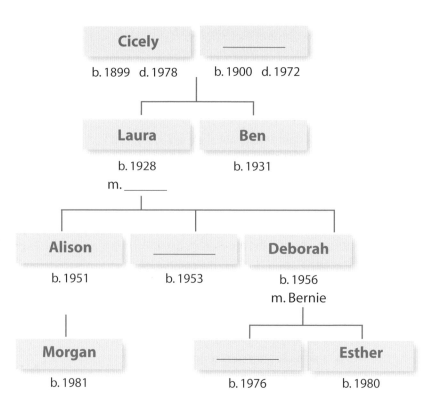

Cicely
b. 1899 d. 1978

_____
b. 1900 d. 1972

Laura
b. 1928

Ben
b. 1931

m. _____

Alison
b. 1951

_____
b. 1953

Deborah
b. 1956
m. Bernie

Morgan
b. 1981

_____
b. 1976

Esther
b. 1980

The present and future

We use the Present Simple for habits/routines:
*I always **have** a large coffee for breakfast.*

describing a state: *She **lives** in a flat.*

things that are permanent, or always true:
*Water **covers** about 70 percent of the world.*

We use the Present Continuous for things that are happening now, at this precise moment:
*I**'m waiting** for the bus at the moment.*

For temporary situations that are happening around now:
*He**'s using** his bike while his car is in the garage.*

For arrangements in the future:
*They**'re having** a meal together next Friday.*

We use *will* + infinitive for unplanned decisions (made while speaking): *I**'ll give** you a lift to the station.*

for predictions based on what you think or believe:
*I think Manchester United **will win**. They're always good.*

We use *going to* + infinitive for plans and intentions:
*I've decided I**'m going to apply** for university next year.*

for predictions based on what you know or can see/hear now: *He**'s going to fail** his exam.*

We do not usually use state verbs in the continuous form, e.g. *like, love, hate, think, believe, know, want, need.*

The past

We use the Past Simple to describe main past events and we use the Past Continuous to describe actions in progress when the main events happened:
*It **was raining** when I **went** to work.*

We use the Past Perfect Simple to describe events and background information that happened before main past events:
*As soon as I saw Mick, I knew I **had met** him before.*

Obligation and ability

We use *can/can't* to talk about general ability in the present. Use *could/couldn't, was/wasn't able to* in the past:
*I **can speak** Spanish and Portuguese fluently.*
*She **could read** by the time she was four.*

We use *couldn't* and *wasn't able to* to talk about ability in the past on one specific occasion in negative sentences:
*He **couldn't answer** the interviewer's questions.*

We only use *was able to* (NOT ~~could~~) to talk about past ability on a specific occasion in positive sentences:
*I **was able to explain** to him what the problem was.*

We use *have to* and *must* when something is necessary:
*You **must take** off your shoes before you come in.*

We use *don't have to* when something is not necessary:
*I **don't have to give** my homework in until next Friday.*

We use *mustn't* when something is prohibited:
*You **mustn't open** the machine before switching it off.*

We use *should/shouldn't* when something is/isn't the right thing to do:
*You **should apologise** to him immediately.*
*They **shouldn't close** the shops so early.*

We use *had to* when something was necessary:
*We **had to wait** in a queue for hours before they let us in.*

We use *didn't have to* when something was not necessary and there was a choice:
*I got a free ticket so I **didn't have to pay** anything.*

We use *should have* when something was the right thing to do, in your opinion, but you didn't do it:
*You **should have asked** me for a lift.*

We use *shouldn't have* when something was not the right thing to do, in your opinion, but you did it:
*He **shouldn't have worn** such casual clothes to an interview.*

Key vocabulary

Family/Relationships
partner   wife   husband   step-sister   half-brother
sibling   colleague   soulmate   close friend
neighbour   acquaintance
come across as   bump into someone
make a very good impression on someone
see eye to eye with someone
judge a book by its cover
talk to someone face to face   click with someone

Ways of speaking
chat   gossip   make small talk   greet someone
give someone a compliment   boast   mumble
speak up   talk down to someone
stumble over my words

Adjectives/Nouns
intellectual/intellect   artistic/art   jealous/jealousy
lonely/loneliness   responsible/responsibility
successful/success   important/importance
frustrated/frustration   skilful/skill

Keeping in touch
in touch   out of touch   get in touch   keep in touch
lose touch   stay in touch   touch base

Phrasal verbs (relationships)
take after someone   look up to someone
grow up   show off   bring someone up
get on with someone   go out with someone
split up with someone   fall out with someone
make up with someone

 Listen to the explanations and vocabulary.
ACTIVEBOOK

 see Writing bank page 150

1 Review and practice

1 Complete the sentences with the Present Simple or Present Continuous form of the verb in brackets.

She always _gets up_ (get up) late at the weekend.

1 I usually _____ (go) to the gym with a colleague after work.

2 Don't turn the radio off. I _____ (listen) to it.

3 It _____ (not/usually/rain) much in the summer here.

4 He _____ (play) tennis with his step-brother next Sunday.

5 _____ (the Moon/go) round the Earth?

6 She _____ (speak) four languages very well.

7 I _____ (not/know) how to play chess.

8 Jen is in London at the moment. She _____ (stay) at the Park Hotel.

2 Choose the correct words in *italics*.

A: Maria phoned while you were out.

B: Oh! I_'ll phone_/_'m going to phone_ her back now.

1 A: We haven't got any milk.

 B: Yes, I know. I_'ll get_/_'m going to get_ some now.

2 A: Patrick has studied really hard for his exam.

 B: Yes, I'm sure he_'ll pass_/_'s passing_ with distinction.

3 A: Have you been in touch with Anita recently?

 B: No, but I_'ll meet_/_'m meeting_ her after work on Friday.

4 A: Look at that broken glass on the floor.

 B: Yes, it_'s hurting_/_'s going to hurt_ someone.

5 A: It's Jane's birthday today.

 B: Is it? Oh, I_'ll get_/_'m getting_ her a present on the way home.

3 Find the mistakes in five of the sentences and correct them.

I broke my ankle while I ~~played~~ _was playing_ football.

1 The doorbell rang while I had watched television.

2 I didn't see Tom because when I got to the party, he left.

3 What were you doing when the clock struck midnight?

4 When I got home, I found that someone broke the kitchen window.

5 I realised someone followed me when I heard footsteps.

6 Diana didn't come because she was arranging to do something else.

4 Choose the correct words in *italics*. Sometimes both are possible.

When he was younger, my brother (could)/(was able to) play the guitar really well.

1 I _couldn't_/_wasn't able to_ sleep last night because it was so hot.

2 I _can_/_can't_ hear anything – she needs to speak up a bit.

3 She _could_/_was able to_ explain the answer very clearly this morning.

4 When I was a child, I _couldn't_/_wasn't able to_ understand why anyone liked coffee.

5 It was great that you _could_/_were able to_ finish the race so quickly.

6 He _can_/_could_ drive but he hasn't got a car at the moment.

7 I _couldn't_/_wasn't able to_ keep my eyes open during the whole film.

8 My grandmother _could_/_was able to_ walk for miles when she was in her eighties.

5 Complete the sentences with verbs from the box.

> had to   doesn't have to   didn't have to   should   ~~shouldn't~~   should have   shouldn't have   must   mustn't

You _shouldn't_ eat so many cakes and biscuits.

1 It was a great party – you _____ come!

2 It's a secret so you really _____ tell anyone.

3 The lift was broken so we _____ walk up the stairs.

4 He _____ get up early – he just likes it.

5 You're working too hard. You _____ take a few days off.

6 The bus came immediately so I _____ wait at all.

7 I'm so exhausted today. I _____ gone to bed so late.

8 You _____ take this medicine twice a day for the next ten days.

6 Find the wrong word in each sentence and correct it.

It's vital to _make_ ~~do~~ a good impression at a job interview.

1 I fell on with my flatmate when we disagreed about money.

2 She's never seen eye on eye with her boss.

3 It was the frustrated of the situation that made her shout at you.

4 He's a kind person but he comes up as a bit rude at times.

5 I make after my mother in both looks and personality.

6 He is full of jealous about his brother's sporting success.

7 I'm lucky because I have on really well with all my colleagues.

8 I can't stand it when he shows out about how much he earns.

Lead-in

1 Work in pairs and discuss the questions.
1 Where are the places in the photos?
2 Which would you most like to explore? Why?

2 🔘 1.10 Listen and answer the questions.
1 What gave Sonia the idea to travel?
2 Why did she go to Spain?
3 How did she feel when she first got to Guatemala? Why?
4 How did she feel later?

3 Listen again and complete the expressions in **bold**. Then work in pairs and check you understand the meaning of each one.
1 I began **to have** _____ **feet** and wanted to leave work.
2 I **went as an** _____ **traveller,** on my own.
3 I spent a month _____ **around** the town.
4 I was **bitten by the travel** _____ and wanted to explore lots of other places.
5 The first two months were difficult and I **experienced real** _____ **shock.**
6 I **was really** _____ and missed my family like mad!

4 Work in pairs and discuss the questions.
1 Why do you think people are bitten by the travel bug?
2 Do you ever have itchy feet? Give details.
3 How do you feel about exploring a place/country as an independent traveller?

Reading

1 Work in pairs and discuss the questions.

1 Look at the photos and read the title of the article. Where is this place and what do you think it's like?

2 Which things do you think you would find difficult in the jungle?

3 Which things would you most like to do when you return to 'civilisation' after a jungle expedition?

2 Read the article and answer the questions from exercise 1 about Charlotte Uhlenbroek.

3 Read the article again and write true (T), false (F) or not given (NG).

1 Charlotte looks and feels 'out of place' in the Savoy Hotel. T F

2 She had to climb tall trees without the use of ropes. F

3 The mosquito bites she had were the worst bites she's ever had. T

4 She cried because she couldn't stand the sweat bees on her face. NG

5 The film crew helped her to get the leeches off her leg. NG

6 She compares a tree with a tower block because there are so many living things in each tree. T

7 The water she used in the Congo was usually dirty. NG

8 When she gets home, she loves doing the cooking for her family. NG

4 Work in pairs and discuss this question. Would you like to go on a jungle expedition? Why/Why not?

BITTEN BY THE JUNGLE BUG!

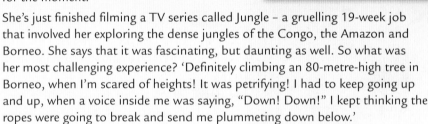

Sand flies, sweat bees, 80-metre-high trees.

Hell for most of us, yes, but all in a day's work for Charlotte Uhlenbroek. She moves as elegantly through the lounge of London's Savoy Hotel as she does through the Amazon jungle. But while she loves the adventure, she is also glad to be back in 'civilisation', at least for the moment.

She's just finished filming a TV series called Jungle – a gruelling 19-week job that involved her exploring the dense jungles of the Congo, the Amazon and Borneo. She says that it was fascinating, but daunting as well. So what was her most challenging experience? 'Definitely climbing an 80-metre-high tree in Borneo, when I'm scared of heights! It was petrifying! I had to keep going up and up, when a voice inside me was saying, "Down! Down!" I kept thinking the ropes were going to break and send me plummeting down below.'

And 'down below' was where the bugs were – clinging, stinging, sucking beasts. Apart from the usual mosquitoes, in the Amazon rainforest she was plagued by sand-fly bites. 'I've had some horrible bites but these really are the itchiest bites I've ever had. At one stage, I counted 70 bites on one arm,' she says. 'Just as annoying were the sweat bees in the Congo. They try to drink the sweat on your face and even the tears from your eyes. The most disgusting thing, though, was trying to pull the slimy leeches off your skin. The more I pulled, the more they stretched and the tighter their jaws clung to my leg. I kept shouting, "Get them off!" and the film crew kept saying, "Just a minute … this makes a really good shot!"'

Charlotte's journey into the heart of the world's most significant rainforests was an inspiring experience. 'The rainforest really is like a city. Each tree is like an urban tower block with hundreds of residents. If you knock it down, you cause just as much disruption and damage as if those residents were human. The jungle is extraordinary because although it only covers about 6 percent of the world, it contains over 50 percent of all known animal and plant species, plus lots more that are unknown, too.'

Back in London, what has she been enjoying since her return to 'civilisation'? 'I've been having lots of nice, long showers,' she says. 'In the Congo, the possibility of using up our water supplies was always a worrying thought. And I find that when I've been in hot, uncomfortable conditions for a while, the things I look forward to more than anything else are being with my family and enjoying my favourite meal.'

Grammar | Present Perfect Simple and Continuous

5 **a** Complete the rules (A–B) in the Active grammar box with *Present Perfect Simple*, *Present Perfect Continuous*, *Past Simple* or *Past Continuous*.

b Complete the examples (1–2) in the Active grammar box using the correct form of the verb *to live*.

Active grammar

A We use both the _P Simple_ and the _P Continous_ to talk about actions in the past which are finished and have no effect on the present.

*At one stage, I **counted** 70 bites on one arm.*

*A voice inside me **was saying** 'Down! Down!'*

B We use both the _Pp simple_ and the _Pp continous_ to talk about things which started in the past, but continue to the present, or are finished but have an effect on the present.

*She**'s just finished** filming a TV series called 'Jungle'.*

*I**'ve been having** lots of nice, long showers since I got back.*

C We can use the Present Perfect Simple when we focus on: the present result of the action; the finished action; or the number of times the action has been completed up to the time of speaking.

(1) *She _has lived_ in three different jungles.*

D We can use the Present Perfect Continuous when we focus on: the activity itself; the length of time; the repetition of the activity.

(2) *I _have been living_ in jungles for 19 weeks.*

---

see Reference page 33

6 Choose the correct words in *italics*.

1 I *went/have been* to the Brazilian rainforest in 2009.

2 She *bought/has bought* her plane tickets already. I saw them on her desk.

3 I *have visited/have been visiting* friends in Italy three times this year.

4 What *did you do/have you been doing* since I last spoke to you?

5 *Did you see/Have you seen* Jack this morning?

6 I'm learning Spanish at the moment. I *have started/started* classes three months ago.

7 I *have been going/went* to the same holiday resort every year since 2005.

8 I played games on my phone while I *have been waiting/was waiting* for the plane.

7 Find the extra word in six of the questions (1–8) and delete them.

1 Have you ever been ~~going~~ to a jungle?

2 Have you ~~been~~ decided where to go for your next holiday?

3 How long have you been studying English?

4 Where did you ~~been~~ go for your last holiday?

5 How much coffee have you already had ~~having~~ today?

6 ~~Did~~ have you ever had a bad insect bite?

7 What do you want to do today that you haven't done yet?

8 Where have you ~~lived~~ been living for the last year?

Pronunciation | connected speech (2)

8 **a** Look at the sentences (1–6) and follow the instructions.

- Tick the weak forms of auxiliary verbs (e.g. *have/been/was*) and prepositions (e.g. *to, for*).
- Mark connections between a consonant sound and a vowel sound.
- Mark connections between a consonant sound and another consonant sound.

1 A: Have you ever been to Brazil?
   B: Yes, I have.

2 I've always wanted to travel as much as possible.

3 What time did you get to the airport?

4 I've been learning English for three years.

5 A: Has she been working here for long?
   B: Yes, she has.

6 I was walking in the mountains when I fell and broke my leg.

b 🔊 1.11 Listen and check the pronunciation. Then repeat the sentences/exchanges in pairs.

9 Work in pairs. Take turns to ask and answer the questions from exercise 7. Ask each other questions to find out more information.

A: *Have you ever been to a jungle?*

B: *Yes, I have, actually.*

A: *Oh really? Where did you go?*

B: *I went to an amazing jungle area in the north-east part of Australia.*

Vocabulary | describing situations and feelings

10 **a** Find the adjectives from the box below in the article on page 22. Work in pairs and discuss what you think they mean. Use the sentences around the word to help you.

> fascinating   daunting   challenging   petrifying
> annoying   disgusting   inspiring   worrying

b All the adjectives from the box describe situations. How can you change the endings to make adjectives to describe feelings? Give examples.

11 **a** Complete the dialogue with the most appropriate adjective from exercises 10a and 10b.

A: Have you ever been camping?

B: Yes, and I hated it! I spent a week camping once and every night I was (1) _____ because it was so dark and I kept hearing animals. I even found putting up my tent quite (2) _____ . It's quite old and some of the bits were missing.

A: Are you scared of heights?

B: No, I'm not. I like being high up. I went up in a small aeroplane a few years ago. I was a little (3) _____ , but I found it really (4) _____ . I might even go parachuting one day.

A: How do you feel about eating food you've never tried before?

B: I'm not keen on eating meat I've never tried before. A friend of mine made me try snails recently. I was (5) _____ with him because he said they were bits of chicken. When I found out, I was nearly sick! They were really (6) _____ !

A: How would you feel about a job that involved working with animals?

B: I've just spent the summer working at a monkey sanctuary. You might not think monkeys are very interesting but they're (7) _____ when you get to know them. Some things were difficult – like catching them to give them medicine was pretty (8) _____ , but it was all very rewarding.

b Work in pairs and take turns to ask and answer the questions from 11a. Use the adjectives from exercise 10a.

12 Read the Lifelong learning box. Then look at the pairs of words/phrases below. From each pair, say how you might decide which word/phrase in each pair to use.

> interesting/fascinating   difficult/daunting
> to fall/to plummet
> get used to/become accustomed to

Choosing vocabulary

❗ Some words/phrases have very similar meanings to each other. When we choose which word to use, we need to think about why we are choosing that particular word/phrase, depending on …

1   general or precise meaning.

2   strength of meaning.

3   exact context and connotation.

4   more formal or informal situations.

*While I was running for the bus, I **fell** and hurt my knee.* (**plummeted** isn't usually used from such a low height.)

*Profits **plummeted** last year from £50 million to £10 million.* (**fall** isn't strong/dramatic enough here.)

Lifelong learning

Speaking

13 **a** 🔵 1.12 Listen to part of a radio interview with Oliver, who has been working/studying abroad. Which situation (1–5) is he talking about?

1   working in a monkey sanctuary for three months

2   studying English for six months

3   helping in a school in a village for six weeks

4   learning how to cook with a family for eight weeks

5   researching climate change for two months

b Listen again and answer the questions (1–5).

1   Where has he been living?

2   What has he been doing?

3   How does he feel about leaving?

4   What is he most looking forward to about going home?

5   What does he think he'll miss about the place?

14 **a** Work in pairs and imagine you have been doing one of the things from exercise 13a. Prepare to be interviewed about your experience. Think about the questions from exercise 13b and make some notes.

b Work with a different student and take turns to interview each other using the questions from exercise 13b.

Reading

1 **a** Work in pairs. Look at the photo. Where do you think this place is? What do you think it's like? Do you think a lot of tourists go there? Why/Why not?

b Read the website extract quickly and check your ideas.

2 Read the website extract again. Then summarise the …
- important beliefs of the Bhutanese people
- nature in Bhutan
- tourism in Bhutan.

Vocabulary | weather

3 🎧 1.13 Listen and decide which of these questions each of the three people are talking about.
1 What's the weather like in your country?
2 What's your favourite type of weather?

4 **a** Look at audioscript 1.13 on page 163. Write the <u>underlined</u> words in the correct category in the list below.
- cold *cool*
- sky *clear*
- windy
- rain *pours*
- warm/hot
- weather in general

b Work in pairs. Check you know the meanings of the words. Decide if each word is a noun, adjective or verb, e.g. *breeze* = noun. Find out what other forms there are, e.g. *breeze* (n), *breezy* (adj).

5 Work in pairs and discuss the questions.
1 How would you describe the weather in your area/country?
2 How would you like the weather where you live to be different?
3 How do you think this would improve your life?
4 Does the weather affect your mood? In what ways?

BHUTAN is a country of about 750,000 people in the eastern Himalayas. Visitors may be surprised how much culture, tradition and nature are all flourishing in this very private country. The Bhutanese believe that all forms of life, human and non-human, are precious and sacred. Because of this attitude, they live in harmony with nature and their environment remains pristine, with an astonishing variety of animals, birds and plants. The people live in harmony with each other too, with no discrimination of any kind.

In order to safeguard this rich natural environment and peaceful culture, Bhutan has adopted a cautious and controlled approach to tourism. In 2008, there were fewer than 21,000 tourists and this number is not expected to increase greatly. No independent travellers are permitted in Bhutan; all tourists must go on a pre-planned, prepaid, guided, package tour. However, if you make the effort and manage to get a visa and arrange a trip, you will certainly have a life-changing experience in this magical kingdom.

Pronunciation | connected speech: linking sounds

6 **a** We sometimes add sounds to link words that end in a vowel sound with words that begin with a vowel sound. Listen to the sentences (1–3). Which sound can you hear between each pair of words which are linked: /w/, /j/ or /r/?

1 The summer is generally hot.

2 You are often quite uncomfortable.

3 The sky is clear.

b 🌐 1.14 Listen and check. Then repeat in pairs.

Listening

7 **a** If you went on holiday to Bhutan, what would you like to know about in advance, e.g. the weather?

b 🌐 1.15 Listen to a question-and-answer session with an expert on Bhutan and some people who are considering a trip there. Number the topics (a–f) in the order you hear them.

a	special events/festivals	☐
b	the ideal time of year to visit	☐
c	food	☐
d	what to do there	☐
e	what to take	☐
f	organised trips	☐

8 Listen again and complete the notes.

TRIP TO BHUTAN

WHEN TO GO
Spring and autumn are the best seasons to go.
Don't go in winter because (1) _____ .
Don't go in summer because (2) _____ .

ACTIVITIES
Trekking is fantastic – amazing views and a lot of different (3) _____ .

CLOTHES
Don't forget to take: rain gear and good (4) _____ .
Also, for the sun: a hat and (5) _____ .
Don't bring (6) _____ or (7) _____ for trekking (it's all provided).

FOOD
One of the main ingredients used is (8) _____ .

FESTIVALS
The main reason for festivals is for people to (9) _____ .

FLAGS
The reason for the flags is for people to (10) _____ .

9 Work in small groups and discuss the questions.

1 Would you like to go to a remote place like Bhutan? Why/Why not?

2 Would you like to go on the organised trekking trips described in the listening? Why/Why not?

3 Have you been to any festivals or celebrations in your country or abroad which you particularly enjoyed? Give details.

Grammar | questions

10 Complete the questions (1–9) in the Active grammar box and then check your answers with audioscript 1.15 on page 163.

Active grammar

Direct questions

There are two main types of direct questions:

A *Yes/No* questions

(1) _____ *to carry all our equipment?*

(2) _____ *provide a guide?*

B *Wh-* questions

(3) *What activities _____ ?*

(4) *When _____ the best time to go?*

Subject questions are used when the question word (e.g. *who*) refers to the subject of the sentence.
When a *wh-* word replaces the subject in a question, we do not use the auxiliary verb.

(5) *Who _____ with the trekking group?*

Indirect questions

Use indirect questions when you want to be polite (e.g. when you don't know someone). Use the word order of positive statements. Use *if* or *whether* for indirect *Yes/No* questions.

(6) *Can you tell me what _____ ?*

(7) *Could I ask you what _____ like?*

(8) *Do you know _____ any interesting festivals at that time?*

(9) *I'd like to know _____ to take anything special.*

---

see Reference page 33

11 a Find the mistake in each question and correct it.

1 Where you are living at the moment?
2 He has ever been trekking before?
3 Who did give you those lovely flowers?
4 What time you be here tomorrow?
5 You having a holiday soon?
6 When this company was started?

b Make the questions in 11a indirect.

Can I ask you if you go on holiday every year?

1 Can you tell me _____ ?
2 Do you know _____ ?
3 Can I ask you _____ ?
4 Can you tell me _____ ?
5 Do you know _____ ?
6 I'd like to know _____ .

Speaking

12 Complete the How to... box with the headings below.

- Give details of personal experience
- Add extra information to illustrate further what you mean
- Use different words to make your description more precise

How to... add detail

You can make your speaking more specific and sophisticated by adding details in different ways.

A _____

*There is a lot of snow in winter, **which can make travelling difficult**.*
*You will need an assortment of clothes, **including good walking boots**.*

B _____

*It's **hot** in the summer, sometimes really **scorching**.*
*It can get **cool**, actually pretty **chilly**.*

C _____

***In my experience**, the best seasons to visit are spring and autumn.*
***I'd also recommend** warm clothes for the evenings.*

---

13 a Prepare to find out about two other types of holiday. Divide into two groups (A and B) and write questions using the notes below.

Group A: write questions about camel trips in Egypt.

Group B: write questions about bird-watching in Mexico.

Think about cost, location, what the area is like, accommodation, food, facilities, activities/organised tours. Think also about the types of questions you should ask.

b Now prepare the answers you're going to give. Think of ways of making them as detailed as possible using ideas from the How to... box.

Group A: read about bird-watching in Mexico on page 147.

Group B: read about camel trips in Egypt on page 149.

14 a Work in A/B pairs. Take turns to ask and answer questions.

b Which holiday would you rather go on? Why?

2.3 On the move

Grammar | modifying comparatives

Can do | express opinions about places and make comparisons

Vocabulary | verb phrases about moving/travelling

1 Work in pairs and match the underlined verb phrases (1–8) with the definitions (a–h).

C 1 My parents are Scottish but they emigrated to Australia.

A 2 My brother has lived abroad for ten years, so I don't see him much.

B 3 I've just moved house. Here's my new address.

G 4 My sister left home when she was 18 and went to university in York.

D 5 I spent a lot of holidays just roaming around the countryside, exploring.

F 6 After weeks of planning, we finally set off on our round-the-world trip.

H 7 We all cried when we went to see her off at the airport.

E 8 I'm off to the shops. Is there anything you need?

a to live in a foreign country

b to leave your house and go to live in another one

c to leave your country and go to live in another country

d to walk or travel, with no definite purpose

e when you are ready to go, or you're going to go somewhere very soon

f to leave at the start of a journey (especially an important, exciting or difficult one)

g when a young person leaves his/her parents' house and goes to live somewhere else

h to go to an airport, train station, etc. to say goodbye to someone who is leaving

2 Complete the questions below with the correct form of a verb phrase from exercise 1.

1 At what age do young people in your country typically leave home?

2 Do you like people to come and see you off (you) at the airport?

3 What time did you set off when you last went on holiday?

4 Which country would you move to if you lived abroad?

5 What would you miss if you emigrated?

6 How many times have you moved house in your life?

7 Where are you off (you) to after class today?

8 When was the last time you went to a new place and just roamed around without any clear direction?

3 **a** You are going to ask your partner the questions from exercise 2. First, predict what you think his/her answers will be.

b Work in pairs and ask the questions from exercise 2. How many answers did you predict correctly?

Reading

4 **a** Work in pairs. Look at the photos on page 29 and discuss the questions, giving reasons for your answers.

1 Where and when do you think photo A was taken?

2 In which country do you think photo B was taken?

3 Do you think the family in photo C are going on holiday or emigrating to another country?

b Work in pairs. Do you think the following statements are true or false?

1 In the late 1800s, a lot of people emigrated from the UK.

2 Over a million British people emigrate every year.

3 Spain is a popular destination for British people to emigrate to.

4 Most people who emigrate go back home after a year.

c Read the article on page 29 quickly and check your answers.

5 Read the article again and match the summaries (a–g) with the paragraphs (1–4). There are three extra summaries.

a The appeal of many places is the price of property, better wages and the good weather.

b For most people who emigrate, it's the best thing they've ever done.

c Many people find that the grass is not always as green as they had hoped.

d There is a trend in recent times for increasing numbers of British people to emigrate.

e It's very difficult to get a work permit for popular countries like Australia and Spain.

f Some people go abroad for about three years in order to earn and save money to go back with.

g Although emigrating can be hard, it can also provide people with greater job satisfaction.

6 Work in small groups and discuss the questions.

1 Have you ever lived abroad or are you living abroad now? If so, where did you go and what is/was it like? What do/did you miss? If not, would you ever consider doing so? Why/Why not? Where would you like to go?

2 Is it common for people to emigrate from your country? If so, where do they go and what are their reasons? Do you think they find what they are looking for?

ON THE MOVE!

¹ The last big wave of emigration from the UK took place towards the end of the 19ᵗʰ century. During this time, about 90,000 people per year were leaving to start new lives in places like Australia, New Zealand, Canada and the US. Today, the numbers are much bigger; every day, thousands of people are on the move and, either temporarily or permanently, setting up home abroad. Their move may be job-orientated or perhaps they think the grass is greener somewhere else. Whatever their reasons, it's clear that more and more people are stepping into the unknown and leaving their own country. In Britain alone, over 400,000 people make the move out of their country each year. In 2010, one survey revealed that almost three quarters of Brits have considered emigrating this year – that's an increase of 300 percent in five years. But where do they go and why? And do they 'live happily ever after'?

² Typically, a lot of people move abroad because of their jobs. They may find that their company is moving them overseas but many people make their own decision, believing they will have more successful careers abroad. Paul Derwin is a scientist who used to be based at a prestigious London university. He was dissatisfied, however, and felt that the opportunities he had were not nearly as good as he wanted and he decided to explore the possibilities California had to offer. 'Emigration is incredibly difficult, emotionally as well as practically,' he says. 'But after ten years here, I've got a far nicer life than before. I have a fantastic job and the recognition I wanted. People take my work much more seriously here. It would be difficult to give that up now.'

³ By far the most popular reason for emigrating, however, is the desire for a better quality of life. Destinations that place a greater value on leisure and have a more laid-back lifestyle were easily the most popular. People also look for places where the weather is sunnier and generally a lot warmer. Britain is famous for its bad weather especially during the dark and cold winter months. Southern Spain becomes very appealing when you think of the 320 days of sunshine a year. In 2008, over a million people emigrated to Spain and there are thought to be over one million Brits now living there. Cheaper property is another reason given for moving abroad. The cost of living in America, for example, is a bit lower than in Britain and often salaries are slightly higher. For all these reasons, it's not surprising that the top five most regularly chosen destinations for Britons to emigrate to are the US, Australia, New Zealand, Canada and Spain. The fact that most of these are English-speaking countries is obviously also a major factor for British people. Sue Riddell, a 30-year-old nurse from Birmingham, wants to emigrate to Australia with a group of friends. 'We're fed up of the conditions we work and live in,' she says. 'I went travelling to Australia after I left school and I loved it – the beaches, the fresh air, the sense of space. If I can, I'm going. And I don't know if I'll come back.'

⁴ Despite the fact that so many Britons move abroad, however, most of them go back home after only about three years. Often, living overseas is not quite as attractive as it first seems. Generally people emigrate because they think life is going to be a little better. They sometimes want to do this because they get certain feelings on holiday and they romanticise about what it would be like to live there. They tend to focus on the best aspects and think it will be nearly as good as this all the time, when often that is not the case. Making enough money and getting work abroad can be just as difficult as it is at home and people tend to find they miss family, friends and things they took for granted back home.

Grammar | modifying comparatives

7 **a** Look at the language in the Active grammar box and underline one example of each phrase in the article on page 29.

b Complete the Active grammar box with the headings (1–3).

1 Describing things which are the same
2 Describing a big difference
3 Describing a small difference

> ### Active grammar
>
> A _big diff_
> 1 *far, much, a lot* + comparative adjective/adverb
> 2 *by far, easily* + superlative adjective/adverb
> 3 *not nearly as* + adjective/adverb + *as*
> B _small diff_
> 4 *a little, a bit, slightly* + comparative adjective/adverb
> 5 *not quite as* + adjective/adverb + *as*
> 6 *nearly as* + adjective/adverb + *as*
> C _the same_
> 7 *(just) as* + adjective/adverb + *as*

see Reference page 33

8 Complete the second sentence so that it means the same as the first. Use three or four words (including the word in brackets).

Spain is much sunnier than Britain.

Britain isn't nearly as sunny as Spain. (nearly)

1 I find learning foreign languages far more difficult than my sister.
My sister learns foreign languages _much easier_ than I do. (much)

2 I'd prefer to live somewhere that is a bit drier than this.
I'd prefer to live somewhere that isn't _quite as wet as_ this. (quite)

3 I certainly haven't lived in a more expensive country than this.
This country is _easily the most exp_ place I've lived in. (easily)

4 I'm a bit more adventurous now than I was ten years ago.
Ten years ago I was _slightly less adven._ I am now. (slightly)

5 I've never lived in a place nearly as good as this.
This is _by far the best_ place I've ever lived. (far)

6 My lifestyle in Canada now is no better or worse than it was in England.
My lifestyle here in Canada is _the same as_ it was in England. (as) _as good as_

Speaking

9 **a** 🔊 1.16 Listen to the dialogue and decide which topics (1–7) the people are discussing.

1 Your hometown is by far the best place to live.
2 Being near your family is much more important than living in a warmer climate.
3 When it comes to the weather – the warmer, the better.
4 Living abroad is much more interesting than staying in your own country.
5 Integrating into a new culture is a lot easier than most people think.
6 Living abroad wouldn't be nearly as good as being on holiday there.
7 It's far better to go on holiday to a place where they speak your language.

b Listen again. Which phrases from the How to... box do you hear?

> ### How to... describe two things which change together
>
> *When it comes to language, **the more** practice, **the better**.*
> ***The more** time you spend abroad, **the easier** you'll find integrating ...*
> ***The more** you explore a country, **the more** you find out about it ...*
> ***The less** you know about a country, **the less** prepared you are.*
> ***The more** you practise the language, **the less** worried you'll be about integrating ...*

10 Work in small groups and discuss one of the statements from exercise 9a.

1 Match the underlined expressions with *go* with the definitions (a–j).

1 They <u>went to great lengths</u> to make the party a success.

2 We're <u>going away</u> for two weeks to stay with my cousin.

3 There's a lot of shouting next door. I wonder what's <u>going on</u>.

4 Which course have you decided to <u>go for</u>?

5 I totally trust Danielle. She would never <u>go back on</u> her word.

6 He <u>went down with</u> terrible flu the day before his interview.

7 He's decided to <u>make a go of</u> the new business for at least a year.

8 I've been <u>on the go</u> all day and I'm exhausted.

9 It <u>goes without saying</u> that we'll support you.

10 I've never been skiing before, but I want to <u>have a go</u>.

a   to happen

b   to catch an illness

c   to take a lot of time and effort

d   to choose a particular thing

e   to attempt to do something

f   to be clear without being said

g   to be very busy or working all the time

h   to not do what you've promised or agreed

i   to make something (e.g. a business or a marriage) successful

j   to leave your home and go to another place for a few days or weeks

2 Work in pairs.

Student A: say one of the definitions in exercise 1.

Student B: guess the correct expression.

A: *attempt to do something*

B: *have a go*

3 Choose the correct word in *italics*.

1 When I'm abroad I always *make/have* a go at speaking the language.

2 We're going *away/out* for the weekend. Could you look after our cat?

3 Don't worry. It goes without *saying/talking* that I'll meet you at the airport.

4 There's something going *down/on* in the city centre. It's full of people.

5 Although they argue a lot, they want to *make/have* a go of their marriage.

6 I promise I won't go back *with/on* what I've said.

7 Can you help with dinner please? I've been *on/off* the go all day.

8 Your teacher can't be here today. She's gone *off/down* with a bad cold.

9 I couldn't decide which kitten to go *away/for*. They were all gorgeous.

10 He went to *great/long* lengths to make sure he was totally prepared for the interview.

4 **a** Prepare to describe an experience using five of the expressions from exercise 1. Your experience could be true or you could make it up (you can use the photos below to help you). You should include one of the sentences below.

I've decided that I want a bit more adventure in my life.

I've always been fascinated by the idea.

I've never considered myself much of an explorer.

b Work in pairs and take turns to tell each other about your experiences.

Student A: don't say if your experience is true or not.

Student B: guess if it is true or false.

1 Work in pairs and discuss the questions.

1 Which of the holidays in the photos appeals to you most? Why?

2 What is the best holiday you've ever been on? Why?

2 **a** Look at the quiz. Match the questions (1–6) with the possible answers (a–f).

b For each question in the quiz, put the ideas in the boxes (a–f) in order according to how important they are for you.

c Do the quiz with as many different students as possible. When you're answering the questions, explain the reasons for the order you decided on. You can also add your own ideas, giving reasons.

3 **a** Read the descriptions on page 147.

• Which one do you think you are most like?

• Which one do you think each person you questioned is most like?

b Which students do you think would be the best travelling companions for you? Why? Which would be the worst? Why?

Who's your ideal travelling companion?

Are y... ...ep... a... who loves sleeping under the stars... ...home from home and all life's luxu... ...elling companion? And who is your... ...hell?

Do ... ... and find out.

anne.ferriera

1 W... ...oliday be?   c
2 W... ...your suitcase?   b
3 H... ...evening on holiday?   e
4 H... ...ys to be?   f
5 Y... ...our holiday?   a   d
6 ... ...home?   a

a   ...rts and crafts made by the locals
lots of photos   cheap ...tes and perfume

b   guidebooks   novels   suncream   penknife

c   package holiday with beach or pool
independent travel alone or with friends   exploring jungle or desert
sports and activities, e.g. skiing, scuba diving

d   being bored   spiders, mosquitoes, etc.
not being able to speak the language   getting robbed

e   in the hotel restaurant   in your tent   in local restaurants
in various bars and nightclubs

f   not more than a week   two weeks
at least three or four weeks   open-ended

ANG. PL

Present Perfect Simple and Continuous

We use the Present Perfect to talk about things which started in the past, but continue to the present, or are finished but have an effect on the present.

We use the Present Perfect Simple when we focus on: (a) the present result of the action, (b) the finished action, or (c) the number of times the action has been completed up to the time of speaking.

*Here look! The postman **has brought** you a letter.*

*I**'ve lived** here since last January.*

*She**'s sent** over 50 emails today.*

We use the Present Perfect Continuous when we focus on: (a) the activity itself, (b) the length of time, or (c) the repetition of the activity.

*They**'ve been having** such a nice time.*

*He**'s been playing** tennis for three hours.*

*I**'ve been telling** him for years to move to the country.*

We often use *for* (length of time) and *since* (starting point) to talk about the duration of the activity.

*I' ve worked in this office **for five years**.*

*She's been lying on her bed **since this time yesterday**.*

We often use *just/yet/already* with the Present Perfect.

Just means a short time ago. It usually comes between *has/have* and the past participle.

I've just seen Mariana.

Already shows that something happened sooner than expected. It usually comes between *has/have* and the past participle or at the end of the sentence.

I've already done the shopping.

Yet shows we expected something to happen before. It is used at the end of negatives and questions.

*Have you **finished** that email **yet**?*

Questions

There are two main types of direct questions.

Word order: question word + auxiliary verb (e.g. *are/ did/does*) + subject + main verb

Yes/No questions: *Are you going to Danka's party?*

Wh- questions: *Where did she learn to speak Spanish?*

Subject questions are used when the question word (e.g. *who*) refers to the subject of the sentence.

Word order: Question word + main verb + subject

***The teacher** told us to go.* → ***Who told** you to go?*

We use indirect questions when we want to be polite (e.g. when we don't know someone).

There are different ways of starting indirect questions (e.g. *Do you know ..., Can you tell me ..., Could you tell me ..., Is it OK if ..., I'd like to know ...*).

We use the word order of positive statements. We use *if* or *whether* for indirect *Yes/No* questions.

*Can you tell me **where the nearest bank is**?*

*Do you know **whether this bus goes to Oxford**?*

Modifying comparatives

For describing a big difference, we use:

far, much, a lot + comparative adjective/adverb: *I'm feeling a lot better today.*

by far, easily + superlative adjective/adverb: *This is **by far the best** café around here.*

not nearly as + adjective/adverb + *as*: *I can't play the piano **nearly as well** as Michael.*

For describing a small difference, we use:

a little, a bit, slightly + comparative adjective/adverb: *They've moved to a **slightly bigger** house.*

not quite as + adjective/adverb + *as*: *This exam wasn't **quite as hard as** the last one.*

nearly as + adjective/adverb + *as*: *My younger brother is **nearly as tall as** me.*

For describing things which are the same, we use:

(just) as + adjective/adverb + *as*: *This soup is **just as tasteless as** the other one.*

For describing two things which change together:

The more/less/comparative adjective/adverb ... , the more/less/comparative adjective/adverb

***The more** people who help, **the more** we'll get done.*

Key vocabulary

Exploring

have itchy feet   bitten by the travel bug
an independent traveller   experience culture shock
wander around   be homesick

Describing situations and feelings

fascinated/fascinating   daunted/daunting
challenged/challenging   petrified/petrifying
annoyed/annoying   disgusted/disgusting
inspired/inspiring   worried/worrying

Weather

cool   chilly   sub-zero temperatures   mild
scorching   pour   drizzle   shower/showery
breeze/breezy   clear   overcast   bright   changeable

Verb phrases about moving/travelling

emigrate   live abroad   move house   leave home
roam around   set off   see someone off   be off

Expressions with *go*

go away   go on   go for   go back on   go down with
have a go at   make a go of   be on the go
go without saying   go to great lengths

 Listen to the explanations and vocabulary.

ACTIVEBOOK

 see Writing bank page 151

2 Review and practice

1 Choose the correct words in *italics*.

Thanks for the party last week. I've *really enjoyed/ really enjoyed* it.

1 I've *written/'ve been writing* emails all morning.

2 I've *seen/saw* a really awful film yesterday.

3 My brother is in France. He's been there *for/since* a week.

4 She's very well-travelled. She*'s visited/ been visiting* more than twenty countries.

5 Billy's the nicest person I've *ever/already* met.

6 I live in a flat in London. I*'ve lived/lived* here for three years.

7 He*'s worked/been working* in the garden for hours and he's exhausted.

8 Would you like some coffee? I've *yet/just* made some.

2 Write sentences with the Past Simple, Present Perfect Simple or Continuous.

I/stand/at this bus stop/forty minutes

I've been standing at this bus stop for forty minutes. He has already phoned

1 He/already/phone me/three times this morning.

2 We/go/to India/three weeks last summer. We went to

3 I/just/see/a really fantastic musical. I've just seen

4 You/hear/the news/yet? Have y heard the news yet

5 I/decorate/the living room/all day. I've been decorating

6 I/know/my best friend/primary school. I've known

7 You/ever/read/the *Lord of the Rings* books? Have yo ever

8 How long/you/live/abroad? How long have u been living/ lived

3 Complete the direct questions for the underlined answers.

Where did you go on holiday last year?

I went to *Sardinia*.

1 How long have y had your motorbike?

I've had my motorbike *for a week and a half*.

2 What is she going at university?

She's going to study *engineering* at university.

3 _____? How tell r u

I think I'm about *1 metre 70 centimetres* tall.

4 Can u reach that box on the top shelf for me?

No, sorry, *I can't reach it.* I can only reach the second shelf.

4 Write indirect questions for the underlined answers with the words in brackets.

Can I ask you where you went on holiday last year? (you go on holiday last year)

I went to Rio de Janeiro for the carnival.

1 Can u tell me what time this shop closes? (this shop)

It closes at *half past five*.

2 I'd to know if . (can buy/theatre tickets here) I can buy tickets here

Yes, you can.

3 Would u mind tell me what time ? (you/finish your homework) u finished your homework

I'll definitely finish it by *12:00*.

4 Can you tell me what ist the most interesting country u ever visited ? (the most interesting country/you ever visit)?

I'm not sure – either *Japan* or *Russia*.

5 Choose the correct words in *italics*.

I want to get to work a bit earlier *than/as* yesterday.

1 My suitcase is *much/more* heavier than yours.

2 Tania got by far the *worse/worst* maths results in the whole class.

3 The exam wasn't nearly as difficult *than/as* I'd expected.

4 You're *easy/easily* the most helpful person I know.

5 You need to speak a lot *loud/louder* than that.

6 People are far more *friendly/friendlier* here than in my country.

7 Generally, it's *a/the* little chillier here than it is in my country.

8 She is just *as/more* talented as her sister at music.

6 Find the wrong word in each sentence and correct it.

1 We'll need an alarm because we're putting off setting very early in the morning.

2 He's desperate to go travelling. He's got really scratchy itchy feet.

3 I'd really love to make a go with off drama lessons.

4 I think I'm going down of a sore throat.

5 It's pouring with rain, so I'll give you a lift. That goes without speaking. saying

6 I experienced country culture shock at first and found it daunting living in a new place.

7 I'm really annoyed with Jane. I can't believe she went back to on her word.

8 It was lovely having so many people to see me away off at the station.

34

Lead-in

1 Work in pairs and discuss these questions.

1 What do you know about the places in the photos? What are they called? Have you visited any of them? If so, what were they like?

2 When do you think they were built?
- about 1653 AD
- about 1973 AD
- about 1200 AD
- about 1989 AD

2 **a** Three of the <u>underlined</u> adjectives in the questions (1–7) below are wrong. Correct them using the table and a dictionary.

Places	Buildings	Things	People	Clothes
ancient	old/new	old/new	old/young	old-fashioned
modern	modern	traditional	elderly	trendy
		second-hand	traditional (values)	fashionable
		modern		second-hand
		antique		traditional

1 Do you prefer <u>ancient</u> *antique* or modern furniture? Why?
2 Are you interested in wearing <u>fashionable</u> clothes? Why/Why not?
3 Does your country have <u>traditional</u> dress? If so, what is it?
4 Do you live in an <u>elderly</u> *old* building?
5 What do you think about using <u>second-hand</u> things?
6 Do you like visiting <u>antique</u> *ancient* ruins when you're on holiday?
7 In your country, do most <u>elderly</u> people live alone?

b Work in pairs and ask and answer the questions.

3.1 Heroes

Grammar Past Perfect Simple and Continuous

Can do tell a clear and engaging story

Reading

1 a Work in pairs and discuss the questions.

1 Do you have a favourite hero or heroine from: (a) a film, (b) a story/legend, or (c) real life?

2 What do you think makes these people heroic?

b Look at the film poster on page 37. Have you seen the film? If so, what did you think of it? If not, would you like to see it? Why/ Why not?

2 Read the blog entry below about *Avatar* and say which topics (1–6) are mentioned.

1 the writer's opinion of the film

2 technology used in the film

3 how much *Avatar* cost to make

4 the success of *Avatar*

5 future *Avatar* films

6 a particular hero in *Avatar*

3 Read the blog entry again and write true (T) or false (F). The writer says that:

1 *Avatar* was better than he expected. ☐ T

2 he is disappointed that the story is basically just about heroes and villains. ☐ F

3 Cameron worked on *Avatar* for several years in the late 1990s. ☐ F

4 part of Cameron's inspiration for *Avatar* was the film *2001: A Space Odyssey*. ☐ T

5 *Titanic* was the first film to make over $2 billion. ☐ T

6 he is irritated that 'heroes' is a theme of so many films. ☐ F

7 Sully is a hero because he decides to do what he thinks is right. ☐ T

4 Work in small groups and discuss the questions.

1 If you've seen *Avatar*, do you agree with the writer's opinion? If you haven't, has the blog entry changed your opinion about seeing the film?

2 How far do you agree with the writer's description of a hero?

Film heroes

As my regular readers know, I'm a fan of film director James Cameron. His older science fiction films, *The Terminator* and *Aliens* are brilliant, and *Titanic* is a classic in the true sense of the word. As you can imagine, I had been looking forward to the release of *Avatar* for a while before it came out. Although I must admit, I thought I'd be disappointed. I had heard so much about the film before I saw it ... but until I actually saw it, I couldn't understand what all the fuss was about. I was far from disappointed though – it was fantastic! The visual impact, with all the incredible special effects, is astounding throughout the whole film. And the plot has all the classic elements of a good story: love, war, 'goodies' and 'baddies'. The film tells an old story of heroes and villains; but the new technology and the director's vision bring the film into the 21st century with a bang.

Avatar was released in December 2009, but apparently the idea had started many years before that. Cameron wrote 80 pages of script for the film in 1994. After that, however, he decided not to make the film for many years, because at that time the technology wasn't available to do what he wanted with the film. Instead, he made several documentary films in which he practised using the latest visual effects and camera technology, perfecting his techniques that he would later use in *Avatar* in such a stunning way.

Cameron says that he had been thinking about making this kind of film way before he started writing the script. In fact, since he saw the epic film *2001: A Space Odyssey* in 1968, he had wanted to make a movie that 'would blow people's minds'. The film certainly caught the public's imagination and has had massive commercial success. *Avatar* broke several box office records during its release and became the highest-grossing film of all time, surpassing *Titanic*, which had held the record for the previous 12 years, and becoming the first film to reach over $2 billion. That's pretty impressive – to be the director of the two highest-grossing films ever!

While I was watching the film, I was thinking about the idea of a hero. I mean, not only is Cameron a bit of a hero for me, but so many films are about heroes in one way or another. In *Avatar*, the basic view of heroes and villains is very clear. In this case, the aliens are the heroes and the humans are the bad guys. It's interesting that one of the humans, Jake Sully, becomes a hero in the end too, when he realises that what he is doing is wrong. From that point on, he decides to do the right thing and help the aliens, even though this puts him in terrible danger. To my mind, the portrayal of a hero in this way adds another level to an already brilliant film.

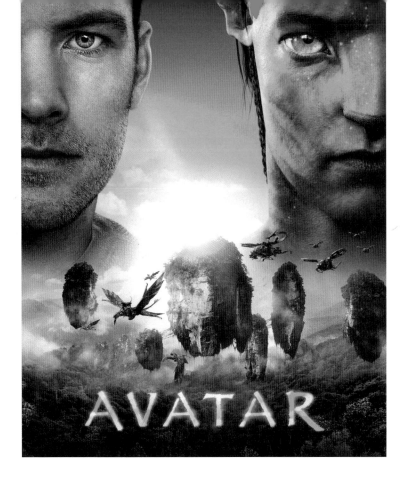

Vocabulary | time expressions

5 Find the expressions from the box in the blog entry on page 36 and look at the sentences around them. What does each expression refer to?

- a time before
- a specific time
- a time after
- actions at the same time

> until I actually saw it   throughout the whole film
> in December 2009   After that, he decided
> at that time the technology wasn't available
> since he saw the epic film   during its release
> for the previous 12 years   While I was watching
> From that point on

6 Choose the correct words in *italics*.

1   ~~While~~/*During* the summer, we travelled around seven European countries.

2   I changed schools when I was 12. *From that point on*/~~Throughout~~, I loved school.

3   I moved house last week. *For*/~~While~~ the previous few months, I'd lived with my parents.

4   The Great Fire of London happened ~~at~~/*in* 1666.

5   She was chatting *throughout*/*since* the whole maths lesson.

6   I left university last summer. ~~Until~~/*After that*, I got a job working in an advertising agency.

7   I met James last year. ~~After that~~/*Since then*, we've been seeing each other a lot.

8   China was ruled by emperors *until*/~~while~~ the beginning of the 20th century.

9   I had a great time when I was at university. *At that time*/~~Throughout~~, I was sharing a flat with four friends.

10 *While*/~~During~~ I was waiting for you, I finished my book.

Grammar | Past Perfect Simple and Continuous

7 **a** Complete the examples (1–4) in the Active grammar box with the correct form of the verbs *start*, *think*, *look* and *hear*.

b Check your answers in the blog entry.

c Complete rules A and B with *Past Perfect Simple* and *Past Perfect Continuous*.

d Work in pairs and look again at examples 1–4. Answer the questions.

1   In each example, what is the 'main event in the past' or the 'specified point of time'?

2   In which example, sentence 3 or 4, does the Past Perfect Continuous refer to an activity which happened 'up to and beyond a specified time'?

Active grammar

1   I *had heard* so much about the film before I saw it.

2   Avatar was released in 2009, but apparently, the idea *had started* many years before that.

3   I *had been looking* forward to the release of Avatar for a while before it came out.

4   He *had been thinking* about making this kind of film way before he started writing the script.

A   We use the **PP** to describe what happened before the main events in the past.

B   We use the **PPC** to describe activities that happened: over a period of time; up to a specified point in time; and up to and beyond a specified point in time.

see Reference page 47

8 Choose the correct words in *italics*.

1 I was disappointed when I saw the film because I *had read*/*had been reading* three good reviews about it.

2 I *had looked*/*had been looking* forward to seeing that film for ages before I finally got the DVD.

3 *Jurassic Park* came out in 1993. Before that, no film *had used*/*had been using* computer technology in that way.

4 They *had worked*/*had been working* on improving the technology for years before they made the film.

5 Before the first *Shrek* film in 2001, film-goers *hadn't seen*/*hadn't been seeing* such good animation.

6 I *had watched*/*had been watching* DVDs on my computer for years before I bought a new television.

7 Before you suggested going to see *Avatar*, I *had wondered*/*had been wondering* what to do this evening.

8 I *hadn't thought*/*hadn't been thinking* properly about what a hero was before I saw that film.

9 **a** Complete the sentences.

1 Throughout most of last year I _____ . For the previous few months, I …

2 The best year of my whole childhood was _____ . At that time, I …

3 I couldn't believe it when _____ . Before that, I …

4 One of the most important things to happen to me was _____ . Until then, I …

b Work in pairs and compare your sentences. Ask and answer questions and give more details.

Speaking

10 Work in pairs. Look at the photos and discuss the questions.

1 Do you think any groups of people who do particular jobs are modern-day heroes, e.g. firefighters, aid workers? Why?

2 Can you think of any famous people that you think are heroic? Give reasons.

11 **a** 1.17 Listen to Eben talking about a hero and answer the questions.

1 Is he talking about someone from 'real life', or someone from a film/story?

2 Do you agree that this person sounds like a hero? Why/Why not?

b Listen again and number the phrases in the How to… box in the order you hear them.

How to… engage your listener

Introduce what you are going to talk about in a general way	… many people have different definitions of what a hero is
Use rhetorical questions	… Now, what did he do?
Include details	… he was born in a mud brick house in the Kalahari.
Include your personal response	… I would think of people who do things that we can learn from.
Use a range of tenses and time expressions	He told me that his father had once explained to him that …

12 **a** You are going to talk about a hero. Choose one from the list and write notes about what you want to say. Use the ideas from the How to… box. Think about the tenses and time expressions you can use.

- a hero from a film, story or legend
- a modern-day hero (famous or not famous)

b Work in pairs. Take turns to talk about your hero.

3.2 Land of invention

Grammar	articles
Can do	talk about inventions and reach an agreement

Listening

1 **a** Work in pairs and discuss the questions.

1 What can you see in the photos?
2 What things do you associate with:
   (a) modern-day China, and (b) traditional China?
3 Do you know anything that was invented in China?

b 🔊 1.18 Listen to the radio programme. Do the speakers mention any of the things you talked about?

2 Listen again. Write true (T), false (F) or not given (NG).

1 China has over 3,000 years of history. `T`
2 China has been a major world economic power for centuries. `T`
3 Paper was made in China in around 1005 AD. `F`
4 The first paper was made of silk waste products. `T`
5 The wheelbarrow was invented by one person. `T`
6 The gun was developed by the Chinese in around the 10th century. ☐
7 The invention of cast iron had a huge impact on people's lives. `T`
8 Agriculture accounts for about 50% of China's economy. `F`
9 Rice, tea, cotton and fish are the major agricultural exports. `NG`
10 Iron production in China is a rapidly expanding business. `T`
11 The population of Shanghai is growing by 22% a year. `NG`
12 Production of industrial and consumer goods accounts for more than 50% of China's economy. `T`

3 Work in pairs and discuss the questions.

1 Have you been to China or do you live there?
2 If so, how far do you think the programme gives a fair description of both ancient and modern China? How would you describe China to someone who hasn't been there?
3 If not, from what you heard in the programme, in what ways do you think it is the same as, or different from, your country? Would you like to go to China? Why/Why not?

4 Read the Lifelong learning box. Work in pairs and discuss the questions.

1 Generally, how easy or difficult do you find understanding spoken English? Why do you think this is?
2 When you listened to the radio programme, which of the strategies in the box did you use?
3 Which strategies would be useful for you to use more?
4 What other strategies would you recommend?

Grammar | articles

5 Match the rules (A–N) in the Active grammar box with the examples in the box below.

> China   ~~an inventor~~
> ~~the simplest invention~~   cars
> the Himalayas   the Chinese
> a machine for making cast iron
> rice   the story I told you before
> the moon   the Republic of China
> wealth   ~~the gun~~   ~~the Yangtze River~~

Active grammar

We use the definite article *the* ...

A with inventions and species of animal. *the gun*

B with national groups. *the Chinese*

C with previously mentioned nouns. *the story i told ~ before*

D with superlatives. *the simplest*

E when we know which one we're talking about, OR it is the only one. *the moon*

F with names of places which are plural. *the Himalays*

G with names of countries with *States, Kingdom* or *Republic*. *the Republic of China*

H with names of rivers, oceans, seas and deserts. *the Yangtze River*

We use indefinite articles *a/an* ...

I with jobs. *an inventor*

J with singular countable nouns (mentioned for the first time or when it doesn't matter which one). *a machine*

We use no article (zero article) ...

K with most names of people and places. *China*

L when we make generalisations with plural nouns. *Cars*

M when we make generalisations with uncountable nouns. *rice*

N when we make generalisations with abstract nouns. *wealth*

See Reference page 47

6 Complete the sentences with *the, a/an* or – (zero article).

1 __The__ giant panda mostly lives in __–__ bamboo forests high in the mountains.

2 __the__ Yangtze River is 6,380 kilometres long. It is the third-longest river in __the__ world.

3 __–__ China covers __an__ area of almost six million square kilometres and is __the__ most populous country on Earth, having more than one billion people.

4 __The__ Chinese mainly speak Mandarin but there are over 150 other languages spoken in __the__ country.

5 I've got three Chinese silk dresses: __a__ red one and two black ones. I think I'll wear __the__ red one for my party.

6 Xiaolu Guo is __a__ famous Chinese novelist and film-maker. In 2009 she made __the__ film called *She, A Chinese*. __The__ film won the top prize at an International Film Festival.

7 __The__ umbrella was invented around 450 AD to protect __–__ people from sun and rain.

8 *Zong Zi* is __a__ dish made of __–__ rice and bamboo leaves and is traditionally eaten during the Dragon festival.

Pronunciation | connected speech: elision

7 a 1.19 In spoken English, some sounds almost disappear so we can't hear them. Listen to sentences 1–3 below and delete the sounds which have almost disappeared.

1 I went out for a delicious meal in a Chinese restaurant recently.

2 I think the giant panda is one of the most beautiful animals in the world.

3 I think that China sounds like a really interesting country and I'd love to visit it.

b Listen again and repeat the sentences.

8 Work in pairs and discuss how far each sentence from exercise 7a is true for you?

Vocabulary | materials

9 a Work in pairs and look at the photos (A–G). Which of the materials from the box below can you use to describe what each of the inventions is made of?

> glass   leather   metal   paper   plastic   porcelain
> rubber   wood   gunpowder

b Which of the words from the box below are fabric? Which are metal?

> bronze   cotton   denim   gold   iron   lycra   silk
> silver   wool

10 Think of five things you own. Work in pairs and take turns to describe the material each one is made of with words from exercises 9a and 9b.

My jeans are made of denim with a bit of lycra.

11 Match the underlined adjectives with their correct definitions (a–h).

1 I really like silk. It feels so <u>smooth</u>.

2 I can't wear wool. It's too <u>itchy</u> for my skin.

3 For the interview I wore a suit and my new <u>shiny</u> leather shoes.

4 I've got some new winter boots with <u>furry</u> insides.

5 Wear something <u>stretchy</u> for the gym class so you can move easily.

6 Be careful on the icy path. It's very <u>slippery</u>.

7 It was a very uncomfortable journey because the road was so <u>rough</u>.

8 This bed is too <u>soft</u> for me. I need a mattress that supports my back more.

a has an even surface

b has an uneven surface

c feels/looks like fur

d feels uncomfortable to wear because it irritates your skin

e isn't hard or firm, but is easy to press

f is slightly elastic

g has a bright surface

h is wet or difficult to hold/walk on

12 Think of an invention. Work in pairs and take turns to guess each other's invention by asking *Yes/No* questions. Ask questions which contain the materials or adjectives from exercises 9 and 11.

Is it made of plastic? Is it very shiny?

Speaking

13 a 🌐 1.20 Listen to two people talking about the inventions in the photos (A–G). Answer the questions.

1 What are they trying to decide?

2 What do they agree on?

b Listen again. Which of the phrases from the How to... box do you hear?

How to... reach an agreement	
Argue against someone's point	*If you take into account* what a negative influence it's had ...
	You can't really say that gunpowder is the most important.
	But then again, so is the lightbulb.
Concede a point	*Yes, that's a good point.*
	Communication, *yes, as you say* ...
	Birthday cards, *yeah, you're right.*
State an agreed point	*OK, paper it is.*
	Right, so we agree on the computer.
	So, that's decided: the lightbulb.

14 a Decide which invention you think is the most important. You can use the ideas in the photos or your own ideas.

b Work in small groups and try to reach an agreement on the most important invention. Use the language from the How to... box to help you.

(A) (B) (C) (D) (E) (F) (G)

3.3 The good old days?

Reading

1 a Work in pairs. In what ways do you think things nowadays are the same as or different from 20 years ago? Think about food, shops, music, travel, etc.

b Read the blog and discuss the questions.

1 Does the writer mention anything you talked about?
2 How far is your experience similar to the writer's?

2 a Work in groups.

Students A: read the comments on page 148.
Students B: read the comments on page 149.

b Work in pairs in the same group. Tell your partner about the comments you read. Say what (if anything) was written about the following topics: stereotyping, food, holidays, music, shops and language.

3 Work in A/B pairs and discuss the questions.

1 In what ways are Paul and Linda's opinions the same or different?
2 Whose opinion (Oliver's, Paul's or Linda's) is closest to your own point of view?
3 Do you think the old days really were 'the good old days'? Why/Why not?

Grammar | adjectives and adverbs

4 a Look at the underlined adjective below and choose the correct options for rules A and B in the Active grammar box.

Gone are the days when travelling meant finding new and different places.

b Look at the underlined adverbs and adverbial phrases in the sentences (1–10) and match them with the examples from the Active grammar box (a–i).

1 Recently, I took a trip around Europe with my family. ☐
2 I was truly saddened by what I found. ☐
3 When I asked for something in French, they generally answered me in English. ☐
4 I strongly disagree with almost everything you said. ☐
5 Far from being limited; the choice is almost endless. ☐
6 I read what you wrote with interest. ☐
7 To my mind your argument is wildly oversimplified. ☐
8 Latin American salsa is popular throughout the world. ☐
9 Many people speak English as a second or third language. However, in many cases, a new type of English has been created. ☐
10 Most people are embracing the new things that are being created all the time. ☐

Is the uniformity of globalisation here to stay? Is every high street in the world doomed to be the same? Is the English language killing other languages and taking over the world?

Recently, I took a trip around Europe with my family and it took my breath away to see how much everything has changed. I was truly saddened by what I found. It seems that gone are the days when travelling meant finding new and different places. Usually, I take change in my stride but it really upset me this time. Everywhere I went, I found the same things. I found towns with the same shops along their high streets. I found people wearing the same clothes, eating the same types of food and listening to the same types of music. When I tried out my language skills in shops and asked for something in French or Spanish or whatever, they generally answered me in English. In one or two of the places, I had to think hard to try and remember which country I was in.

What are your experiences of this? What do you think?

Posted by: Oliver, Brighton, UK – yesterday 15:35

Active grammar

Adjectives

A Adjectives are used to modify <u>nouns</u>/<u>verbs</u>.
B Position of adjectives: usually directly <u>before</u>/<u>after</u> the noun.

Adverbs

C Adverbs (and adverbial phrases) are used to modify verbs, adjectives and other adverbs.
D Position of adverbs:

Usually at beginning of a sentence

a) Connecting adverbs (which join a clause to what came before) *Nevertheless*, *Then*
b) Time adverbs (if the adverb is not the main focus of the message) *Tomorrow*, *Last year*

Usually in the middle of a sentence (before the main verb)

c) Adverbs of certainty and completeness *probably*, *nearly*
d) Adverbs of indefinite frequency *sometimes*
e) Adverbs of comment *stupidly*, *ignorantly*
f) Some adverbs of manner (if the adverb is not the main focus of the message) *quickly*, *rudely*

Usually at the end of a sentence

g) Adverbs of manner (also see f above) *slowly*
h) Adverbs of place *upstairs*, *in the corner*
i) Adverbs of time (also see b above) *this morning*, *a while ago*

see Reference page 47

5 For each sentence, decide if the <u>underlined</u> words are adjectives or adverbs.

1 She lives in a <u>lovely</u> village but it's quite a <u>lonely</u> place.
2 He's a <u>lively</u> child but can be a bit <u>silly</u> sometimes.
3 A: How are you?
   B: I'm <u>fine</u>, thanks.
4 Don't eat those mushrooms. They're <u>deadly</u>.
5 He can jump really <u>high</u>. I'm sure he'll do <u>well</u> in the competition.
6 I got up very <u>early</u> and caught the <u>early</u> train.
7 He's a really <u>friendly</u> dog but quite <u>ugly</u>!

6 Write the missing adverb or adverbial phrase in brackets in the correct place in the sentences. Two different positions may be possible.

1 I want to try the local food when I'm in Thailand. (definitely)
2 I spilt my coffee all over my new jacket. (accidentally)
3 I work in a really modern building. (on the 19th floor)
4 I went on a tour of six capital cities in Europe. (last month)
5 I'm quite shy about practising my English in shops. I'm going to try. (however)
6 My grandmother has been on an aeroplane in her whole life. (never)
7 The new building is designed to be both attractive and practical. (expertly)
8 I learned Spanish before I went travelling in Spain. (quickly)

7 **a** Choose the correct options for each pair of sentences.

complete/completely

1 **a** Do you think everywhere in the world is becoming _____ the same?
   b Do you think the passing of the 'good old days' is a _____ disaster?

late/lately

2 **a** Do you think it's a good thing that shops nowadays are often open _____ or all night?
   b What new shops have opened or closed down near you _____?

definite/definitely

3 **a** Do you think people should _____ try to speak the local language on holiday?
   b Do you think English as a 'lingua franca' has _____ advantages for global business and tourism?

b Work in pairs and ask and answer the questions from 7a.

Vocabulary | verb phrases with *take*

8 Look at the <u>underlined</u> verb phrases in the sentences (1–8). Work in pairs and try to explain the meaning of each one.

1 Is the English language killing other languages and <u>taking over</u> the world?

2 It <u>took my breath away</u> to see how much everything has changed.

3 Usually, I <u>take</u> change <u>in my stride</u>, but it really upset me this time.

4 We now <u>take it for granted</u> that anyone can eat sushi or spaghetti for dinner.

5 Many British people didn't <u>take to</u> the very spicy food introduced by Indian people.

6 I <u>took part in</u> some market research recently.

7 I found it hard to <u>take in</u> what you said about language.

8 A kind of 'global English' has <u>taken off</u> across the world.

9 Complete the sentences with the correct form of the <u>underlined</u> phrases from exercise 8.

1 Some people _____ that everyone can speak English.

2 I _____ a survey about a new shopping centre in the town centre.

3 That Indian restaurant has been _____ by new management.

4 The size of the new shopping centre _____ . It's enormous!

5 My Spanish really _____ when I spent three months living in Spain.

6 We introduced her to lots of new foreign food and she _____ it _____ .

7 I couldn't _____ everything he said, because my French isn't good enough.

8 I didn't _____ online shopping at first, but now I love it.

10 a Choose the correct words in *italics*.

1 To what extent are large chain stores *taking off/taking over* your high street?

2 Are you someone who hates change or do you usually *take it in your stride/take your breath away*?

3 Why do you think English has *taken for granted/taken off* as a kind of 'lingua franca'?

4 Do you find it easier to *take in/take part in* spoken or written information in another language?

5 Can you think of something which you *took to/took over* immediately?

b Work in pairs. Ask and answer the questions from 10a.

Pronunciation | speech units

11 🔊 1.21 Listen to a short talk about shopping. Which of these ideas does the speaker mention?

> small, local shops   chain stores   <u>large supermarkets</u>
> shopping centres   <s>good service</s>   fresh food
> crowded shops   rude shop assistants

12 a We usually divide our speech into logical parts. Between each part, we pause slightly to make it easier for the listener to follow what we're saying. Listen again. Mark // in the places you hear a pause.

> I really like the town where I live // and I think one of the main reasons is that, // in terms of shopping, // there's a lot of variety. // The main street has many different types of shops/ Some of them are run by local people and they have been there for a long time/ I like going into these shops/because you get very good service/ They're always very helpful and friendly. Also, if you're buying food, like vegetables, meat or fish, for example/ the food is always fresher, tastier and cheaper than in the large supermarkets/ There's one large supermarket in the main street, which is very convenient for lots of the basic things you need to buy./ I'd say that I'm very lucky/because there's such a good variety of shops in walking distance of where I live. I have a mixture of local shops and large supermarkets/ and therefore, I have the best of both worlds.

b Look at the places you have marked //. How many times does the pause happen ...

- at the end of a sentence?
- between clauses linked by *and, but* or *because*?
- before and after a phrase which adds extra information?

Speaking

13 a Write a short paragraph describing your opinions about shopping, restaurants or language learning. Mark the places where you are going to pause slightly.

b Work in pairs. Take turns to read out your paragraph.

1   **a**   Read the rules about making nouns. Then look at the examples and write some more examples of your own.

Rules	Examples
-er/-or is used to make nouns from verbs (often for a person who does an activity or for a thing which does a particular job)	*write → writer* *invent → inventor* *open → bottle-opener*
-ist is often used to make nouns from nouns (often for jobs, for people who play musical instruments and for holders of particular beliefs)	*journal → journalist* *piano → pianist* *social → socialist*
-(t)ion/-sion is one way of making nouns from verbs	*invent → invention* *pollute → pollution*
-ness is one way of making nouns from adjectives	*happy → happiness* *weak → weakness*
-ibility/-ability is one way of making nouns from adjectives	*visible → visibility* *inevitable → inevitability*
other common endings for nouns are: *-ment, -ity, -hood, -ship*	*excite → excitement* *product → productivity* *mother → motherhood* *friend → friendship*

b   Work in pairs. Take turns to test each other on making nouns.
Student A: *product*
Student B: *productivity*

2   Complete the sentences with the correct noun form using the word in brackets.

Electricity is the most important *invention* ever. (invent)
1   My boss really is the best _employee_ I've ever had. (employ)
2   She spent most of her _childhood_ in Scotland. (child)
3   Lots of money doesn't always lead to _happiness_. (happy)
4   Wait until the _supervisor_ arrives. She'll know what to do. (supervise)
5   The job offers a lot of _flexibility_ in terms of working hours. (flexible)
6   We need to improve _communication_ between departments. (communicate)
7   My cousin is a very talented _violinist_. (violin)
8   There has been a _reduction_ in the number of trains in service. (reduce)
9   Vegetables are important for a child's growth and _development_. (develop)
10   The crowd was full of _excitement_ as the fireworks started. (excite)

3   One noun in each group is wrong. Find and correct it.

1   involvement, arrangement, <u>producement</u>, replacement
2   friendship, partnership, membership, <u>enjoyship</u>
3   b<u>r</u>otherhood, emplo<u>y</u>hood, manhood, neighbourhood
4   type<u>writist</u>, pianist, phy<u>s</u>icist, scientist
5   forgetfulness, readiness, forgiveness, <u>modernness</u>
6   alteration, donation, <u>develoption</u>, admission

4   **a**   Work in small groups. You're going to write short stories. Each sentence in each story must contain a noun from exercise 1a. Follow the instructions below.

1   Each person in the group starts by writing the first sentence of a story on a piece of paper. Don't forget to include a noun from exercise 1a. Then pass the paper to the next student.
I was full of happiness as I left the house that morning.

2   The next student should read the sentence and continue the story with another sentence (again, containing a noun from exercise 1a). Then pass the paper to the next student.

3   Continue until everyone has written at least three sentences in each story.

b   Prepare to read out your stories. Divide your story into speech units and mark the places where you can pause slightly.

c   Take turns to read out your stories. Which is the best story in your group?

3 | Communication

1 Work in pairs and discuss the questions.

1 What was your most/least favourite subject at school? Why?

2 Which do you think are the three most important subjects to study at school? Why?

3 Are there any subjects you had to give up before you wanted to? Why?

4 Are there any subjects you wish you'd studied harder? Why?

5 Do you think it's important to do vocational subjects at school, e.g. mechanics, cookery? Why/Why not?

6 Do you think it's important for students to do languages, sport, music and drama at school? Why/Why not?

2 **a** 🔊 1.22 Listen to Karl telling a short anecdote about 'My school days' and answer the questions.

1 Are his school days 'the best days of his life'?

2 Apart from English and maths, what other subject does he think is really important?

3 What job is he doing now? Does he like it?

4 What is 'one of the biggest lessons' he has learned?

b Complete the sentences to make them true for you.

1 Looking back, I wish I'd ...

2 Now I'm older and wiser, I realise ...

3 It's only with the benefit of hindsight that I now realise ...

4 One of the biggest lessons I've learned in life is ...

c Work in pairs. Compare your answers to questions 1–4 above.

3 **a** Prepare to tell a short personal anecdote on 'My school days'. Choose one or more of the questions from exercise 1 to speak about and write a short anecdote, including plenty of extra, personal details.

b Think about where you will pause in the anecdote when reading aloud.

4 Work in small groups. Take turns to tell your anecdotes to each other, making sure you speak clearly and pause in the correct places.

Past Perfect Simple and Continuous

We use the Past Perfect Simple to describe events that happened before the main events in the past.

Form: *had* + past participle
*I'd just **finished** my lunch when the doorbell rang.*

We use the Past Perfect Continuous to describe activities that happened over a period of time, up to a specified point in time, and up to and beyond a specified point in time.

Form: *had* + *been* + verb + *-ing*
*Before they came here, they **had been living** in Australia.*

Articles

We use the definite article *the*:

– with inventions and species of animal: *the giant panda.*

– with national groups: *the British, the Ancient Greeks*

– with particular nouns when we know which one we're talking about OR it is the only one: *the sun, Can you turn off the light, please?*

– with superlatives: *Russia is the biggest country.*

– with previously mentioned nouns: *Would you like an apple or a banana? The banana is very ripe.*

– with names of places which are plural: *the Netherlands*

– with names of countries with states, kingdom or republic: *the United Kingdom*

– with rivers, oceans, seas: *the Mediterranean Sea*

– to specify which one we mean: *What did you do with the book I lent you?*

We use the indefinite article *a/an*:

– with jobs: *a teacher, an engineer*

– with singular countable nouns (mentioned for the first time or when it doesn't matter which one): *I'd like an apple.*

We use no article (the zero article):

– with most streets, villages, towns, cities, countries, lakes, mountains: ***Oxford Street, Italy, Mount Fuji***

– when we make generalisations with plural nouns: ***Cats** make very good pets.*

– when we make generalisations with uncountable nouns: ***Coffee** is very expensive in this country.*

– when we make generalisations with abstract nouns: ***Accommodation** is difficult to find.*

Adjectives and adverbs

Adjectives are used to describe nouns. They usually come directly before the noun.
*I live in a really **beautiful** city.*

Adverbs (and adverbial phrases) are used to modify verbs, adjectives and other adverbs. The position of adverbs in a sentence can vary, depending on the main focus of the message.

Position of adverbs

Usually at the beginning of a sentence:

connecting adverbs (e.g. however) and time adverbs (e.g. tomorrow), if the adverb is not the main focus of the message.
***Tomorrow**, I'm going to start doing some gardening.*

Usually in the middle of a sentence (before the main verb):

adverbs of certainty and completeness (e.g. *probably*), adverbs of indefinite frequency (e.g. *often*), adverbs of comment (e.g. *stupidly*), some adverbs of manner (e.g. *quickly*), if the adverb is not the main focus of the message.
*I think I'll **probably** go and see Jane later.*

Usually at the end of a sentence:

adverbs of manner (e.g. *silently*) (see above), adverbs of place (e.g. *beside*), time adverbs (e.g. *a while ago*) (see above).
*She threw her bag down **beside the sofa**.*

Many adverbs end in *-y*, but some words ending in *-y* are adjectives not adverbs.
(e.g. *friendly, lively, lonely, silly*)

There are also many adverbs which do not end in *-y* (e.g. *late, fast, fine, hard, high, well*).

Sometimes the adjective and adverb have the same form (e.g *fast, hard, fine, early, daily*).
*He worked really **hard**.*
*This chair is too **hard**.*

Key vocabulary

Age
modern   ancient   antique   traditional   second-hand
elderly   old-fashioned   trendy   fashionable

Time expressions
while   during   throughout   at that time   in (2010)
from that point on   since   after that   until
for the previous (few months)

Materials
glass   leather   metal   paper   plastic   porcelain
rubber   wood   bronze   cotton   denim   gold   iron
lycra   silk   silver   wool

Describing objects
soft   stretchy   shiny   smooth   rough   furry
slippery   itchy

Verb phrases with *take*
take over   take off   take to   take in   take part in
take your breath away   take it for granted
take it in your stride

 Listen to the explanations and vocabulary.
ACTIVEBOOK

 see Writing bank page 152

3 Review and practice

1 Six of the sentences (1–8) have a missing word. Find the sentences and write the word in the correct place.

1 We had walking for twenty minutes when it started to rain.

2 Today I bought that leather bag that I seen online.

3 When I got to the party, Jack already gone home.

4 I went back to my hometown after fifteen years and found that it had changed a lot.

5 While Christina sitting on the bus, someone stole her gold watch.

6 The doorbell rang and I hadn't even got dressed!

7 Someone finally answered the phone after I'd waiting for ten minutes.

8 As soon as I saw her at the party, I realised I met her before.

2 Complete the sentences with the Past Perfect Simple or Continuous form of the verbs in brackets.

1 I _____ (work) on the report for five days when she told me it wasn't necessary.

2 What _____ (you/do) before I arrived? You looked so hot!

3 It wasn't until I got home that I realised that someone _____ (steal) my wallet.

4 They _____ (think) about moving house for the previous five years before they actually did it.

5 I was embarrassed because she arrived before I _____ (wrap up) her birthday present.

6 _____ (you/learn) the guitar for a long time before you gave up?

7 I _____ (run) for about five minutes when I tripped and broke my leg.

8 _____ (you/read) the book before you went to see the film?

3 Put *a/an* or *the* in the sentences if necessary.

1 She lives in Alexandra Road. It's not far from antiques shop.

2 People say that British are reserved.

3 I'm not sure, but I think I'd like to be architect when I grow up.

4 Don't forget your sun cream. Sun is very strong today.

5 Leisure time is increasing for most people in Europe.

6 We stayed at very nice hotel in Barcelona.

7 That was one of best books I've read for ages.

8 Shall we sit in garden for a while?

4 Complete the pairs of sentences with the correct adjective and adverb.

quiet/quietly

a Could everyone be _quiet_ during the exam?

b You're speaking too _quietly_. I can't hear you.

1 **bad/badly**

a I fell and hurt myself quite _____ .

b The pollution is very _____ in this part of town.

2 **careful/carefully**

a Don't worry. He's a very _____ driver.

b You really need to do your homework more _____ .

3 **perfect/perfectly**

a Your pronunciation is absolutely _____ .

b Petra speaks English almost _____ now.

4 **good/well**

a How _____ can you play the guitar.

b He is a very _____ tennis player now.

5 Choose the correct word in *italics*.

I was only slightly (*late*)/*lately* for the class.

1 The new shopping centre is *enormous/ enormously*.

2 I couldn't believe it. The exam was *incredible/ incredibly* easy.

3 He drove frighteningly *quick/quickly* along the motorway.

4 I can't go out until I've *complete/completely* finished my homework.

5 I thought the meal would be cheap but it was *surprising/surprisingly* expensive.

6 I'm absolutely *certain/certainly* that you'll take to the new teacher.

6 Find the mistake in each sentence and correct it.

My grandfather lives in a home for ~~ancient~~ people.
elderly

1 I don't usually wear wool because I find it too stretchy.

2 When I first visited Rome, it took my head away.

3 She's got all the most fashion clothes.

4 I've decided to take part of a writing competition.

5 I've been working in a café while the summer.

6 I like going to second-time shops and buying old clothes.

7 It's too much information to take on at once.

8 I broke my leg last year. While then, I haven't played football.

4

Lead-in

1 Work in pairs and discuss the questions.

1 Which of the jobs in the box below can you see in the photos?

> journalist   firefighter   social worker   nursery nurse
> surgeon

2 What do you think each job in the photos involves?

3 Which of the jobs would you most/least like to do? Why/Why not?

2 **a** 🔵 1.23 Listen and match each person with the correct jobs from exercise 1.

b Listen again and explain the meaning of the phrases from the box below.

> a change of career   a labour of love   a career path
> to take a year out   job satisfaction

3 Work in pairs and think of a job which fits each quality from the box below.

> be good with figures   be a people person   be a good listener
> have a 'can do' attitude   work well in a team   have an eye for detail
> get the best out of other people   be good at using your own initiative
> be able to meet tight deadlines   keep calm under pressure

4 **a** Underline the phrases from exercises 2b and 3 you think apply to you. Write a short paragraph about your qualities and give examples.

b Work in pairs. Take turns to read your paragraph and explain why you chose each phrase.

Reading

1 Work in pairs and discuss the questions.

1 What can you see in the pictures?

2 How do you think 'work' has changed over the last 1,000 years? In what ways do you think it is the same?

3 What do you think the title of the article means?

2 Read the article quickly. What does it say about question 2 above?

WORK

the daily grind we just can't do without

Work may sometimes seem like hell, but when people haven't got it, they miss it. They miss it, they want it and perhaps they even need it. Everyone wants to be valued and it seems to me that a salary is proof that you matter.

I've been doing some informal research on this topic and some jobs are better than others when it comes to how valuable they are to us. Housework and voluntary work tend to be seen as non-jobs. In this work-centred culture of ours, a 'proper job' means paid employment. Being paid for a job is better for our self-esteem. Of course, people would also prefer work to be useful and interesting, as well as paid. But you don't have to enjoy your job to get psychological benefits from it. According to some experts, achieving unenjoyable tasks during our work actually contributes to a sense of well-being. The obligation to be in a particular place at a particular time, working as part of a team towards a common goal, gives us a sense of structure and purpose that people find difficult to impose on themselves. The workplace has also taken over from the community as the place of human contact. Work often functions as a social club, an information network, an informal dating agency and a marriage bureau.

Genuine workaholics are uncommon, but I think that many people are job addicts without realising it. When people can't work for whatever reason, they show similar signs to real addicts who are deprived of their 'fix' – they become irritable and lethargic. Among newly retired men in particular, death rates increase significantly in the first six months after leaving employment. For most of their lives, their personality, self-esteem and status have been defined by work; without it, research shows that they lose their appetite for life. I don't think that life was always so driven by employment, however. Work in the pre-industrial age was task-oriented not time-structured, and focused not on money but on the tasks necessary for survival. Whole communities worked together so there was less division between work and 'free time'. The Industrial Revolution radically changed how people worked. Suddenly, work was no longer structured by seasons, but by the clock. From that point on, work became separated from the rest of life, and began to provide money rather than food and goods.

More recently, the revolution in Information Technology has again changed the nature of work and employment. The workplace itself may become redundant. Apparently, 3.5 million employees in the UK now work from home, keeping in touch via email and phone. Many employers say that working 'remotely' improves productivity, as workers are happier and waste less time commuting. There are disadvantages too, however, as workers lose touch with the workplace and the people there. It's clear to me that people will have to accept that the nature of work has changed and will continue to do so. After all, we managed to accept the nine-to-five working day and there is no reason why we can't accept a different way of working, too. This piece was written at home in the country during bursts of hard work interspersed with periods of inactivity. Perhaps that's the natural work-rhythm to which we are going to return?

3 Read the article again. Write true (T) or false (F).

1 Being paid to work makes many people feel better. ⊤

2 Non-paid work is just as good as paid work in terms of increasing self-esteem. F

3 Doing tasks you don't enjoy at work is always bad for your mental health. F

4 Most people find it difficult to find a purpose to the day without work. T

5 The social aspect of work is very important for the majority of people. T

6 People who work too much become irritable. F

7 When people retire, they sometimes feel less happy than when they worked. T

8 3.5 million workers in the UK work 'remotely'. T

9 One disadvantage of working from home is people feeling isolated. T

10 The writer is convinced that the work-rhythm of the future is a nine-to-five working day. ☐

4 Summarise the main argument of the article by completing this sentence. Work in pairs and discuss your sentences.

Although the nature of work has changed over the years, ...

5 Work in pairs and discuss the questions.

1 Do you agree that being paid for a job often gives people greater self-esteem? Why/Why not?

2 In what ways (if any) does your job increase your self-esteem? What other things (apart from work) do you think are important for increasing people's self-esteem?

3 Is it common for people to work from home in your country? If you don't work from home, would you like to? Why/Why not?

Vocabulary | work

6 Work in pairs and check you understand the meaning of the underlined phrases in the sentences below.

1 If you don't have to travel to an office, you waste far less time commuting.

2 Apparently, 3.5 million employees in the UK now work from home.

3 For many people, having a 'proper' job means having paid employment.

4 Doing voluntary work is a non-job and doesn't improve your self-esteem much.

5 Genuine workaholics are uncommon, but many people are 'job addicts' without realising it.

6 The workplace has also taken over from the community as the place of human contact.

7 A more natural work-rhythm might be mixing short periods of work with short periods of doing other things.

8 In our work-centred culture, people who do paid work have higher status than those who don't.

9 Many people have a nine-to-five working day.

10 Other people have a much more flexible working day.

7 a Find the mistakes in six of the sentences (e.g. a wrong word, an extra word or a missing word) and correct them.

1 Would you like to make voluntary work, e.g. gardening for old people?

2 Which do you think is more common in your country: a nine-to-five working day or a flexibility *flexible* working day?

3 Do you know anyone who you would describe as a workaholic? ✓

4 What do you think the disadvantages of working from ~~the~~ home are?

5 How far do you agree that a natural work-centred rhythm is a mixture of work and other activities?

6 ~~How far~~ do you agree that we live in a work-~~centred~~ cultural? *culture*

7 Do you think it's true that having a 'proper' job means having paid *for* employe~~ment~~?

8 How important do you think the workplace is as a social meeting place?

9 How do most people get to work in your country? What is your ✓ experience of commuting?

b Work in pairs. Take turns to ask and answer the questions from exercise 7a.

Grammar | futures (1)

8 **a** 🌐 1.24–1.27 Listen to four dialogues and answer the questions.

1 Why does each person want to change their work situation?

2 Has each person got any definite plans? What are they?

b Work in small groups. Have you been in similar situations? What did you do?

9 **a** Listen again and complete examples 1–5 in the Active grammar box.

b Write the headings (1–2) in the correct place (C and D) in the Active grammar box.

1 Imminent future (to say that something will probably happen very soon)

2 Certainty (to say that something is certainly going to happen in the future)

c Read examples 6–11 in the Active grammar box. What form of the verb comes after …

1 *be bound*, *be certain*, *be sure* and *be about*?

2 *be on the point of* and *be on the verge of*?

Active grammar

A **Predictions (to make predictions)**

1 *I think they ll offer Ania the job of departmental manager.*

2 *Dominic is gonna be assistant manager. I heard him talking about it.*

B **Plans and intentions (to express decisions, plans and intentions, arrangements)**

3 *I think I ll go to the library now.*

4 *I've decided I gonna to work.*

5 *I'm meet them at 10 o'clock tomorrow morning.*

C _____

6 *He's bound to get the job.*

7 *Lots of other people are certain to get those jobs before me.*

8 *It's sure to be really hard work.*

D _____

9 *I'm about to have dinner.*

10 *I'm on the point of leaving really.*

11 *I'm on the verge of collapsing with sheer exhaustion.*

---

10 Choose the correct words in *italics*.

1 I've decided. I'm definitely *about to apply/going to apply* for a new job next year.

2 She's *getting/'s bound to get* the job. She's got the right experience.

3 We're *on the point of meeting/'re meeting* after work at the café on the corner.

4 I'm *on the verge of asking/'m sure to ask* my boss if I can work from home as I can't stand commuting anymore.

5 You're *certain to get/'re getting* a good job if you get good exam results.

6 Oh, there's the personnel officer. In that case, *I'll talk/'m bound to talk* to her now before I go home.

7 I'm really nervous because *I'll have/'m about to have* the most important interview of my life.

8 He's working very long hours at the moment so he *won't be/'s sure to be* tired tomorrow.

Speaking

11 🌐 1.28 Listen to the first two conversations again and complete the How to… box with words from the box.

> coming   depends   idea   so   sure
> thinking   time

How to… talk about future plans

Express some uncertainty about future plans	*I'm _____ about leaving.* *I'm not _____ yet but I think I'll leave soon.* *One _____ is to do some voluntary work.* *It _____ on being accepted on the course.*
Refer to future times in a vague way	*I think I'll leave in the next month or _____ .* *I'm doing the exam in about three week's _____ .* *I'll probably start the course this _____ September.*

---

12 **a** Prepare to talk about your work/study/life plans for the future. Make notes about two things you're sure about and two things you're not sure about. Use the How to… box to help you.

I've decided I'm going to learn a new language but I'm not sure yet which …

b Work in pairs and tell each other about your plans. Are they similar or different?

see Reference page 61

Listening

1 **a** Look at the photos. Work in pairs and write two questions you'd like answered about what you can see.

b 🔵 1.29 Listen to a radio journalist talking about Nek Chand and the Rock Gardens. As you listen …

1 check if your questions are answered.

2 decide on an appropriate title for the story.

2 Listen again and complete the notes.

Chand's appearance
small, elderly, wrinkled face, silvery hair

His personality

1 _modest, creative, hi. working_

His father's job

2 _poor farmer_

Chand's first job (1958)

3 _gourment Rd inspector_

Inspiration for his gardens

4 _city Chand_

Reason for his secrecy

5 _gardon build on land owned by_
goverment

Materials used

6 _rubish from building sites, recyling_

After 18 years of work

7 _gourden was discovered, tourist attractc_

After one year of paid work

8 _gardon was open to public_

Number of visitors per day

9 _____

How Chand feels about his work

10 _mekes him happy_

3 Work in pairs and discuss the questions.

1 a What do you think of Nek Chand?

 b Would you like to visit the Rock Gardens of Chandigarh? Why/Why not?

 c Do you know anyone with an unusual talent, hobby or job?

2 a What types of materials and things can be recycled?

 b What are the arguments for and against recycling?

 c How much recycling of rubbish happens in your area? Do you think it's enough?

3 a Which environmental issues concern you most (e.g. recycling, pollution from cars, over-fishing, deforestation, etc.)?

 b Would you consider your lifestyle to be 'environmentally friendly'? Why/Why not? What could you change?

Grammar | Future Perfect and Future Continuous

4 Read the rules (A and B) in the Active grammar box below. Read the examples (1–3) and decide which are Future Perfect and which are Future Continuous.

> ### Active grammar
>
> 1 *Tomorrow morning, he'll **be doing** the same as he's doing today.*
> 2 *Soon, Chand **will have spent** half a century working on this garden.*
> 3 *He **won't have finished** the garden by the time he retires.*
>
> **A** We use the Future Perfect to describe something which will/won't be completed before a definite time in the future (with common time phrases e.g. *by this time next week …, by the end of next month …, within the next year …, by the time you …*).
> Form: *will/won't + have + past participle*
>
> **B** We use the Future Continuous to describe something in progress at a definite time in the future (with common time phrases, e.g. *at 6.00 tomorrow …, this time next week …, a year from now …, when you're 21 …*)
> Form: *will/won't + be + present participle*

see Reference page 61

5 Complete the sentences with the Future Perfect or Future Continuous form of the verbs in brackets.

1 By this time next week, he ___have___ (finish) his art project. *won't finished*
2 I'm sorry I can't come. I __will be__ *playing* (play) football tomorrow afternoon.
3 My boss won't be at work at 5:30 p.m. She *will* __be gone__ (go) home already.
4 Between 10:00 and 12:00 tomorrow I _will_ *be* __have__ (have) a meeting so I'll phone you after that.
5 I hope you __will have__ (finish) making dinner by the time I get home. *finished*
6 I can't wait! This time next Friday, we __are going__ *will be* (lie) on a beach in Australia! *laying*
7 This article says that when you're 50, you _will_ __have__ *spent* (spend) a total of 16.7 years asleep.
8 Don't phone between 7:00 and 7:30 because I _____ (have) my piano lesson. *will be having*

6 Work in pairs and ask and answer the questions.

1 What do you think you will be doing …
  a … at 2.00 p.m. this Saturday?
  b … exactly one month from now?
  c … this time next year?
  d … when you're 65?
2 What do you hope you will have done …
  a … by this time next week?
  b … by the end of this year?
  c … within the next five years?
  d … by the time you retire?

Vocabulary | verb phrases about time

7 Work in pairs and look at the <u>underlined</u> verb phrases. Read the whole sentence and try to work out the meaning of each one.

1 At first, Chand <u>spent time</u> making walls and paths and buildings.
2 Many people find that they <u>waste time</u> doing nothing when they could do something useful.
3 He <u>made time</u> to do a bit more every day after work and every weekend.
4 Whenever he wasn't at work and he <u>had time to spare</u>, he worked on this huge project.
5 They paid Chand to <u>work full-time</u> on the project.
6 I had to <u>kill time</u> before the tour, so I walked around the shops for a while.
7 We'll <u>save time</u> if we go by taxi instead of walking.
8 It was a long, boring journey, so I <u>passed the time</u> by reading.
9 We wanted to see the Rock Gardens, but we went to lots of other places and eventually <u>ran out of time</u>.
10 He didn't rush his work, but <u>took his time</u> with each sculpture and they were beautiful.

8 **a** Complete the sentences below with the correct form of an appropriate verb phrase from exercise 7.

1 I _____ at work by only checking my emails three times a day.
2 I hate ~~wasting~~ time at work, so I always plan my day very carefully.
3 In my job, I ~~spent~~ a lot of _time_ travelling to other countries.
4 I always arrive at work early, so I have time to spare before everyone else arrives.
5 At the moment, I ~~work full-time~~, but I'd prefer to work three days a week.
6 I kill time on my journey to work by playing games on my mobile phone.
7 I always ran out of time in exams because I spend too long on the first question.
8 When I go to an art gallery, I like to take time and not rush around.
9 I think it's important to make time to do exercise at least five times a week.
10 When I'm waiting for a plane, the best way to pass the time is to go shopping.

b Work in pairs and say which of the sentences from exercise 8a are true for you. Give details.

Listening

9 🔊 1.30 Listen to two people talking and decide which questions (1–8) they talk about.

1 How good do you think your 'work/life balance' is?
2 Do you 'work to live' or 'live to work'? Why?
3 How often do you work/study late either at the office/school or at home?
4 How good are you at organising your time?
5 Are you someone who wastes a lot of time?
6 What do you think it's important to make time for?
7 Have you ever done any voluntary work in your spare time?
8 What's your favourite way of spending your free time?

10 Listen again and complete the How to... box.

How to... make your point in a confident way

The _fact_ is I have a really busy work schedule.

I _really_ do.

Believe me, I know, it's not easy, but I do think it's possible to improve it.

Without a _doubt_, I'd say that I 'work to live' and not the other way round.

Family and friends are the most important, for _sure_.

Pronunciation |
stress: sounding sure

11 **a** 🔊 1.31 When we want to sound sure, we often put more stress on certain words. Listen to the sentences from the How to... box. Which words are stressed?

b Listen again and repeat the sentences.

Speaking

12 **a** Work in small groups and choose three of the questions from exercise 9 to discuss. Before you discuss them, think about what points you feel sure about for each question. Then prepare how you are going to make your point confidently.

b In your groups, discuss the questions.

4.3 Dressed for business

Grammar	verb patterns: *-ing* forms and infinitives
Can do	discuss attitudes to clothes and the workplace

A

B

C

Getting dressed for the office doesn't mean leaving your personal style behind. But you don't want to find that your fashion sense has become a career killer – Jeremy Black tells us more.

It is clear that business wear has changed in the last few years – for both men and women. Even traditional businesses such as law companies have altered their dress codes from 'smart' to 'smart-casual'. Companies have seen that the more relaxed attitude to dress not only promotes comfort, but also encourages younger workers to stay. What is less clear, however, is what 'smart-casual' actually means. I hope to give you a few basic tips here. There are many factors involved: for example, the particular industry you work in, how much contact you have with the public and your position in the company. The seasons even have a part to play – what is acceptable in the summer might not be in the autumn or winter.

So, does 'smart-casual' mean you can come to work in tracksuit bottoms and sandals, or does it just mean that you don't have to wear a tie? First, let's look at colour. Fashionable colours for suits for both men and women this season are still the traditional grey, dark blue and black. You see someone wearing grey and it indicates a conservative, professional image; dark blue says you're trustworthy; and black always looks chic and classy. These colours don't have to look boring, however. Try wearing a shirt or blouse with a splash of colour. Pale blue, pink or lilac are better than loud colours like bright pink and dark red.

Of course, you don't always need to wear a suit. Men can go for a sports-type jacket, with a shirt or smart jumper. You can wear well-cut trousers made of wool, or a good pair of chinos. Women can wear trouser suits or skirt suits. You can also wear more fashionable trousers and a blouse, or a skirt and top. But be careful; avoid wearing baggy, loose clothes, very short skirts and lots of logos and patterns. If in doubt, go back to the suit. You need a similar attitude to jewellery, bags and other accessories: you should try to resist large, dangly earrings and huge, colourful bags. In short – remember to keep your whole style plain and simple.

Reading

1 Work in pairs and discuss the questions.

1 Which things in the box can you see in the photos?

> suit   tie   baggy T-shirt   earrings
> large logo   neat hairstyle   shiny shoes
> tattoo   piercings   uniform

2 In what work situations do you think each person's outfit/style would not be acceptable? Why?

2 Read the website. Which idea (1–4) best summarises the advice it gives?

1 How to look creative at work
2 How to look professional at work
3 How to look fashionable at work
4 How to look different from everyone else at work

JBell2 says: This is good advice, maybe, if you are a banker in New York. But I work for a film company in Los Angeles – and it's completely different in the media business. I don't know anyone at our company who wears a suit on a daily basis, and lots of people wear distinctive jewellery and things. I'd advise people to dress like your boss, then you can't go far wrong.

RubyRed says: I'm a receptionist for a Japanese export company and I see people look at my clothes all the time. I think the most important thing is to project a professional image by looking after the details: manicured nails, a neat hairstyle, shiny shoes, etc. And of course, it goes without saying that you should never have tattoos, piercings or any kind of over-the-top jewellery.

DanielM says: I don't think it's always easy to know what to wear at work – different companies have different ideas. I'd like my company to have a clearer 'dress code' so that you know every item that you can/can't wear. My top tip: I suggest keeping a smart outfit in a cupboard at work – that way you're always prepared for a surprise meeting.

3 Read the website again and complete each sentence with two words.

1 Employees in some law companies can wear clothes which are _more relaxed/casual_ than before.

2 Acceptable work wear is dependent on the industry, your position in the company and _how much contact u have with the_ [the person] _public_

3 If you want a professional image, you should choose a _traditional grey_

4 If you want to add colour to your look, you shouldn't choose _pale_. [blue dark pink blue likes]

5 You will look more professional if you wear well-cut clothes, not _baggy_ clothes.

6 The advice from JBell2 is to copy what _the boss_ is wearing.

7 RubyRed says that _looking after clothes_ are important if you want to look professional.

8 DanielM advises people to be ready to dress up by keeping a _smart outfit_ at work.

4 Work in small groups and discuss the questions.

1 What experience do you have of 'dress codes' at work?

2 Which of the tips in the readers' comments do you think is the most useful? Why?

3 Look again at the second sentence of the article. In what ways do you think that someone's 'fashion sense' could become a 'career killer'?

Grammar | verb patterns: -ing forms and infinitives

5 a Look at the verbs in **bold** in the sentences (1–7) in the Active grammar box and choose the correct underlined words.

b Write the verbs in **bold** in the correct place (A–E) in the Active grammar box.

Active grammar

1 I'd **advise** people _dressing_/_to dress_ like your boss.

2 I **suggest** _keeping_/_to keep_ a smart outfit in a cupboard at work.

3 I **hope** _giving_/_to give_ you a few basic tips here.

4 You **see** someone _wearing_/_to wear_ a grey suit.

5 I **see** people _look_/_to look_ at my clothes all the time.

6 **Try** _wearing_/_to wear_ a shirt or blouse with a splash of colour.

7 You should **try** _resisting_/_to resist_ large, dangly earrings.

verb + -ing

A _suggest_, avoid, carry on, practise

verb + infinitive with to

B _hope to_, agree, arrange, want

verb + object + infinitive with to

C _advise_, allow, encourage, persuade

verb + object + -ing or infinitive without to (usually with a change in meaning)

D _see_, hear, notice

verb + -ing or infinitive with to (usually with a change in meaning)

E _try_, regret, remember, stop

6 Work in pairs. Look at the underlined parts of each sentence and say what the difference in meaning is.

1 a I saw him sitting at his desk, working on the new report.

b I saw him sit at his desk and turn on his computer.

2 a I heard her talking to her boss – she seemed quite angry.

b I heard her talk to her boss and explain the whole situation to him.

3 a I noticed him eating his lunch as I walked past his desk.

b I noticed him eat three bananas before the meeting.

7 Choose the correct words in italics.

1 a I tried _wearing_/to wear a suit to work to see if I felt more professional.

b I tried _wearing_/_to wear_ that skirt, but it's too small for me and I couldn't get it on.

2 a You should remember _going_/_to go_ to the hairdresser regularly.

b Do you remember _going_/_to go_ to the hairdresser recently?

3 a I regret _telling_/to tell you that we're not offering you the job.

b I regret _telling_/to tell her about my tattoos.

4 a I stopped _buying_/_to buy_ expensive clothes when I lost my job.

b On my way home from work, I stopped _buying_/_to buy_ some new shoes.

see Reference page 61

8 Complete the second sentence in each pair, so it has the same meaning as the first. Use between two and four words including the word in brackets.

As a rehearsal, I gave my presentation in front of a mirror.

I _practised_ giving my presentation in front of a mirror. (practised)

1 'Why don't we go shopping together?' she said.

She _____ shopping together. (suggested)

2 'Go on! Buy the pink shirt! It looks really good,' she said to me.

She _____ the pink shirt. (persuaded)

3 I made an attempt to speak to her on the phone, but she was out.

I _____ to her on the phone, but she was out. (tried)

4 'OK. I'll give you a lift to work,' he said.

He _____ me a lift to work. (agreed)

5 I used to work here ten years ago.

I _____ here ten years ago. (remember)

6 'If I were you, I'd speak to your boss about it,' he said to me.

He _____ to my boss about it. (advised)

7 I drove the long way to work so I wouldn't get stuck in traffic.

I drove the long way to work to _____ stuck in traffic. (avoid)

8 I saw it all. He stole paper from the office cupboard yesterday.

I _____ paper from the office cupboard yesterday. (saw)

9 'You really should get a job in advertising,' she said to me.

She _____ a job in advertising. (encouraged)

9 **a** Complete the sentences (1–4) to make them true for you.

1 At work, someone once suggested …

2 In terms of clothes for an interview, I would always advise someone …

3 On the way here, I saw …

4 Recently, I arranged …

b Work in pairs. Take turns to compare and discuss your sentences.

Speaking

10 **a** 🔊 1.32 Listen to Marc. Which of the things from the box does he mention?

> what to wear at work/school   uniform at work/school
> using English for work/study   morale in the workplace
> the importance of punctuality at work/school
> 'fitting in' at work/school/another country

b Listen again and answer the questions.

1 What were Marc's aims in learning English?

2 Did his aims change?

3 How did he feel about his English?

11 **a** Work in pairs. Read the Lifelong learning box and add some more ideas for the questions (1–3).

b Discuss the questions.

English for work, study and travel

1 In what ways do you want to use English for work, study or travel?
e.g. to socialise with clients, to understand textbooks, to communicate with other students, …

2 What are your aims for your English?
e.g. to sound like a native speaker, to understand spoken English better, …

3 In what specific ways could you improve your English for work, study or travel?
e.g. do a course in EAP (English for Academic Purposes), …

Lifelong learning

12 **a** Choose one of the topics from exercise 10a to talk about. Make brief notes to prepare what you're going to say.

b Work in small groups and take turns to talk about your topic. Do you have similar ideas and opinions?

4 | Vocabulary | Collocations with prepositions

1 Choose the correct word in *italics* which collocates with the <u>underlined</u> adjectives.

1 I'm <u>interested</u> *of/in/about* training to be an architect.
2 Nek Chand is very <u>modest</u> *of/for/about* his achievement.
3 A lot of people are <u>afraid</u> *of/at/for* losing their jobs.
4 I'm really <u>worried</u> *about/from/on* my interview tomorrow.
5 I'm <u>keen</u> *about/on/in* doing some voluntary work in a prison if possible.
6 This job is very <u>similar</u> *of/for/to* my last one.
7 You look <u>different</u> *to/from/of* your sister, don't you?
8 Marc is really <u>good</u> *about/in/at* tennis. He always beats me.
9 I'm <u>proud</u> *of/about/for* passing all my exams this year.
10 My uncle has been <u>passionate</u> *about/of/for* jazz all his life.

2 Complete the sentences below with prepositions from the box which collocate with the verbs in **bold**.

> about   of   for (x3)   from   in (x2)   on (x2)

1 Are you going to **apply** _____ that job at the café?
2 He **resigned** _____ his job last month to travel round the world.
3 My colleague **insisted** _____ paying for the meal.
4 You must make sure you **prepare** _____ your interview properly.
5 Do you **believe** _____ things like astrology and horoscopes?
6 Would you **complain** _____ slow service in a restaurant?
7 I usually **pay** _____ things by credit card.
8 I'm not sure what we'll do tomorrow. It **depends** _____ the weather.
9 Have you **succeeded** _____ finding a job yet?
10 The interview procedure **consisted** _____ a series of group tasks.

3 Find the mistakes in eight of these sentences and correct them.

1 She is totally passionate for salsa dancing.
2 She insisted about helping me with the washing-up.
3 I'm worried about my driving test tomorrow.
4 The exams consist for three different sections.
5 He is always really modest of his success.
6 His mood often depends of how much sleep he has.
7 I believe in being honest with everybody.
8 He succeeded for upsetting everyone in the room.
9 They are keen about coming to the concert this weekend.
10 You must be really proud about your exam results.

4 Work in pairs. Choose three of the adjective + preposition collocations from exercise 1 and three of the verb + preposition collocations from exercise 2. Take turns to test each other.

A: *complain ...*
B: *... about*

5 **a** Complete the sentences with the correct prepositions.

1 ... is thinking _____ applying for a new job soon.
2 ... is keen _____ rock music.
3 ... is passionate _____ football.
4 ... is similar _____ his/her father.
5 ... is very different _____ his/her brothers and sisters.
6 ... is good _____ sport.
7 ... always pays _____ things in cash.
8 ... is worried _____ things a lot.
9 ... is proud _____ himself/herself for a particular achievement.

b Work in groups. Ask and answer questions to find someone who matches the things from exercise 5a. When you find someone, ask for more details.

4 | Communication

1 Work in small groups and discuss the questions.

1 How do you feel about interviews?

2 Do you get nervous? Why/Why not?

2 **a** Work in pairs. Look at this list of things that can happen at job/university interviews. Decide which you think are positive (P) or negative (N).

1 I was slightly late for the interview. ☐

2 I wore fairly casual clothes. ☐

3 I panicked and couldn't think clearly. ☐

4 I showed them that I was enjoying talking about myself. ☐

5 I wasn't very well prepared for the interviewer's questions. ☐

6 I maintained eye contact with the interviewer. ☐

7 I talked quite negatively about my previous experience. ☐

8 I didn't have any questions to ask the interviewer. ☐

9 I let myself visibly relax. ☐

10 I remembered to switch off my mobile phone. ☐

11 I didn't find out exactly what the job/course involved. ☐

12 I couldn't remember everything I wrote on my application. ☐

b Work in pairs and discuss. Have you experienced any of the situations above? What happened?

3 **a** 🔵 1.33–1.35 Listen to parts of interviews with three different candidates and answer the questions.

1 Is each interview for a job or for a place on a university course?

2 Which of the things in exercise 2 apply to each candidate? (There may be more than one for each.)

b Complete the interviewer's sentences.

1 Thank you for _____ for the job and coming to the interview today.

2 I'd like to ask you _____ your experience.

3 You say you've worked in an _____ before. Tell me about that.

4 I'm Peter Manning and I'll be _____ you today.

5 Can I start by asking you about your _____ for applying for the course?

c 🔵 1.36 Listen and check your answers.

4 **a** 💿 1.35 Listen to Karema's interview again. In order to sound interesting and enthusiastic, does she use ...

1 intonation which is quite flat, or which rises and falls a lot?

2 pauses or no pauses between groups of words?

b Work in pairs. Look at audioscript 1.35 on page 167. Take turns to roleplay Karema's interview and to practise sounding interesting.

5 **a** Work in pairs. Choose one of the adverts on page 148 and prepare to roleplay an interview.

Interviewees: make notes about ...

• any relevant experience and qualifications you've got.

• qualities that make you a suitable person for the course/job.

• your plans for the future.

• any further questions you'd like to ask.

Interviewers: make notes about ...

• how to start the interview.

• questions to ask about relevant experience and qualifications.

• questions to ask about personal qualities that make the candidate a suitable person for the course/job.

• questions to ask about plans for the future.

• how to finish the interview.

b Work in pairs and roleplay the interview.

c Change roles. Prepare and then roleplay another interview.

d Would you give your interviewee the job/place on the course? Why/Why not?

Futures (1)

We use *will* to talk about a decision made at the time of speaking. We often use *I (don't) think*.

I don't think I'll have anything to eat.

We use *be going to* to talk about a plan or intention (but no details have been decided).

I'm going to study law, but I'm not sure where yet.

We use the Present Continuous to talk about a future arrangement (when details have been decided).

I'm meeting Sonia after my interview in the café.

We use *will* to make predictions based on what you know/believe. We often use *think, hope, believe*, etc.

I think Ben will be the new school president.

We use *be going to* to make predictions based on what you can see/hear now.

Be careful! You're going to fall off that chair!

To say that something is certainly going to happen in the future, we can use *be bound/certain/sure* + infinitive.

He's bound to phone you when he's on the train.

To say that something will probably happen very soon, we can use *be about* + infinitive, *be on the point of* + *-ing* and *be on the verge of* + *-ing*.

He's on the verge of leaving the club completely.

Future Perfect and Future Continuous

We use the Future Perfect for things which will/won't be completed before a definite future time. We often use it with time phrases with *by*, e.g. *by that time, by tomorrow*.

Form: *will/won't* + *have* + past participle

She won't have finished her essay by Friday.

We use the Future Continuous to talk about something in progress at a definite time in the future. We often use it with time phrases which specify the time e.g. *at 9:30 p.m., this time tomorrow*.

Form: *will/won't* + *be* + verb + *-ing*

Don't phone me tonight. I'll be watching the football.

Verb patterns: *-ing* forms and infinitives

Some verbs are followed by particular structures. The following are some of the most common ones for each.

verb + *-ing* *enjoy, avoid, imagine, consider, finish, miss, practise, involve, carry on, suggest*
Does the job involve working in the evenings?

verb + infinitive with *to* *want, seem, offer, decide, hope, afford, agree, arrange, promise, refuse, manage*
He offered to give me a lift into town.

verb + object + infinitive with *to* *persuade, convince, encourage, allow, advise*
I encouraged her to work as hard as she could.

verb + object + *-ing* OR verb + object + infinitive without *to* (usually with a change in meaning) *see, hear, notice*

Verb + object + *-ing* generally implies we see/hear an activity/action in progress.
I noticed you washing your car earlier.

Verb + object + infinitive without *to* generally implies we see/hear the whole of an event/action.
I heard you slam the door three times.

verb + *-ing* OR verb + infinitive with *to* (usually with a change in meaning) *remember, regret, try, stop, go on*
I stopped talking to Sam. (I was talking to Sam and then I stopped.)
I stopped to talk to Sam. (I stopped what I was doing and started talking to Sam.)

Key vocabulary

Jobs/Phrases about jobs
journalist   firefighter   social worker
nursery nurse   surgeon   a change of career
labour of love   career path   take a year out
job satisfaction

Personality traits for jobs
good with figures   a people person   a good listener
a 'can do' attitude   work well in a team
an eye for detail   get the best out of other people
good at using your own initiative
able to meet tight deadlines   keep calm under pressure

Work
work from home   commute   paid employment
voluntary work   workaholic   workplace
work-rhythm   work-centred culture
nine-to-five working day   flexible working day

Verb phrases about *time*
spend time   waste time   make time   kill time
have time to spare   work full-time   save time
pass the time   run out of time   take your time

Collocations with prepositions
interested in   modest about   keen on   consist of
passionate about   good at   proud of   afraid of
worried about   similar to   different from   apply for
resign from   insist on   prepare for   believe in
complain about   pay for   depend on   succeed in

Listen to the explanations and vocabulary.

ACTIVEBOOK

see Writing bank page 153

4 Review and practice

1 Choose the correct words in *italics*.

1 A: Why are you turning on the TV?
   B: I*'ll watch/'m going to watch* the football.

2 A: What would you like to eat?
   B: I think I*'ll have/'m having* a cheese sandwich.

3 A: Wow! Look at those black clouds!
   B: Yes, I think it*'ll rain/'s going to rain*.

4 A: Have you seen John recently?
   B: No, but I*'ll meet/'m meeting* him at six.

5 A: Where is Eva?
   B: Oh, she*'ll be/'s being* late. She always is!

6 A: Have you finished your exams?
   B: No, but by this time next Friday,
      I*'ll finish/'ll have finished* them all!

7 A: What time can I come round?
   B: Come after seven because before that
      I*'ll be doing/'ll have done* my homework.

8 A: How many times has she been to Italy?
   B: After this holiday, she*'ll be/'ll have been* there
      four times.

2 Rewrite the sentences using the prompts.

1 I'm sure she'll get the job.
   bound → _____

2 I'm going to resign from my job very soon.
   about → _____

3 They'll definitely take some photos.
   certain → _____

4 I'm going to shout at the neighbours very soon.
   point → _____

5 He's certainly going to buy the tickets today.
   sure → _____

6 She's going to tell him everything very soon.
   verge → _____

3 Find the mistakes in five of the sentences and correct them.

1 We encourage all students doing some voluntary work.

2 I've arranged visiting my grandparents on Saturday.

3 I couldn't avoid hitting the dog as it ran out in front of my car.

4 He considered to have a career in medicine but decided against it.

5 She persuaded me to stay up and watch the film.

6 My teacher suggested to learn ten new spellings every week.

7 I can't afford to go out for dinner very often.

8 He advised to have us an early night before the exam.

4 Choose the correct words in *italics*.

1 I remember *going/to go* to the park every day after school when I was a child.

2 I heard her *shouting/shout* my name once.

3 Please be quiet! Will you stop *talking/to talk* for a minute?

4 She broke the vase. I saw her *drop/dropping* it on the floor.

5 She tried *negotiating/to negotiate* a better deal on her salary.

6 I regret *informing/to inform* you that tonight's performance is cancelled.

7 He saw someone *running/run* a marathon go past his house.

8 She went on *becoming/to become* a very successful lawyer.

5 Complete the sentences using the words from the box. Three of the words cannot be used.

> career commuting deadlines flexible
> pressure save spare take voluntary

1 The journey was really quick so we had plenty of time to _____ when we arrived.

2 I want to work from home and stop spending two hours _____ to and from work every day.

3 In my spare time I do a lot of _____ work with deaf people.

4 You don't need to rush the report. _____ your time and do it as thoroughly as you can.

5 As a journalist, I'm always having to meet very tight _____ .

6 I used to work from nine to five, but now I have a much more _____ working day.

6 Choose the correct words in *italics*.

1 My flatmate always complains *with/about* the noise when I'm listening to music.

2 I'm so pleased that I succeeded *in/of* passing my driving test first time!

3 I'm not sure if I can come tonight. It depends *of/on* what time I finish work.

4 I haven't prepared *for/about* my test tomorrow. I'm sure I'm going to fail.

5 She's so different *with/from* her sister. They have completely opposite personalities.

6 The flat consists *of/in* a kitchen, a large living room and three bedrooms.

Lead-in

1 Work in pairs and discuss the questions.

1 What is happening in the photos?
2 In what ways do you think the people are 'taking a risk'?

2 Which words in *italics* are not possible?

1 Moving abroad without a job can be a bit of a
   risk/*gamble*/*hazard*.
2 You'll never get another *luck*/*opportunity*/*chance* like this.
3 We need this contract. There are a lot of jobs at *stake*/*risk*/*gamble*.
4 My one real *ambition*/*dream*/*belief* is to go to the North Pole.
5 If we don't go back now, there's quite a *big*/*substantial*/*vast*
   risk that we'll get caught in a storm.
6 For some people, doing something that no one else has ever
   done can become an *obsession*/*infatuation*/*all-consuming passion*.
7 They're *hardly*/*amazingly*/*incredibly* brave to walk across that tightrope
   without a safety net. What if they lost concentration?

3 🔊 1.37 Listen to someone talking about her attitude to risk.
Answer the questions.

1 Does she take risks at work, away from work or both?
2 What risky activities does she mention?

4 Work in small groups and discuss the questions.

1 When did you (or someone you know) last take a big risk?
2 What did it involve doing?
3 How did you (or he/she) feel before/during/afterwards?
4 Would you (or he/she) do something like that again?

Reading

1 a Work in pairs and discuss the questions.

1 Do you like to spend a lot of time on your own? Why/Why not?

2 Do you prefer working in a group or on your own? Why?

3 Do you prefer team or solo sports?

b Look at the woman in the photos. What challenges do you think she encountered?

2 Read the article and tick (✓) the topics mentioned.

1 Ellen's achievement ☑

2 her family background ☐

3 her feelings about being alone ☐

4 the qualities a solo sailor needs ☑

5 the costs of the voyage ☐

6 her charity work ☑

7 her future plans ☑

One woman's determination

Ellen MacArthur is possibly the greatest sailor Britain has ever produced. In 2005, at the age of 28, she risked everything and broke the record for sailing solo around the world, encountering terrible storms for much of the 44,000-kilometre journey. She finally completed her voyage in 71 days, 14 hours, 18 minutes and 33 seconds, breaking the existing record by 33 hours, set the previous year by Frenchman Francis Joyon.

Ellen's boat was 23m long and 15m wide, with a cabin no more than 2.5m by 1.5m. It contained a bunk, a table, navigational equipment and a tiny kitchen. That was it. No toilet (just a bucket) and no shower. She put up with this discomfort and isolation and never complained or got lonely. She said her boat was all the company she needed. The danger never seemed to bother her either; she just dealt with the risks. 'Often you don't know what's going to happen when there's a big storm coming so when you're actually in it, it's better,' she said.

Although Joyon broke the record again two years later, Ellen's achievement is still incredibly impressive. She is only the second person ever to sail solo non-stop around the world on a multi-hull boat. And four men, all great sailors, have tried and failed to match the feat of Joyon. Ellen, who is just 1.6m tall, was the first to succeed. It is a common misconception that size and muscle is all that matters. Single-handed sailing is really all about the mind. You need to be able to focus on the job completely, deal with things alone and have incredible levels of self-discipline and determination. Ellen probably wouldn't have survived, let alone broken the record, if she didn't have such extreme mental toughness. She also has her critics, however, who say that if previous sailors had had modern equipment, many of them would've broken records, too. It's speculation, however, and the fact is that it was Ellen who actually did it.

Nowadays, Ellen puts her mental and physical energy into different ventures. She continues to work for her charity, *The Ellen MacArthur Trust*. The charity takes young people sailing to help them on their way to recovery from cancer and other serious illnesses. Their challenges are clearly different from Ellen's challenges. But if she hadn't endured such tough experiences herself, she wouldn't understand nearly as much about what these young people have to face. In Ellen's words, 'I face challenges out on the water, but these are challenges that I choose to do. They, on the other hand, don't have this luxury. They battle against something harder than many of us could ever imagine and they do it with the biggest smiles on their faces.'

In 2009, Ellen decided to give up competitive sailing and put her efforts into saving the environment. While sailing, she realised the extent of the trouble facing the planet and set up *Team Ellen* to campaign for a more sustainable future. 'My life at sea has opened my eyes to things I did not expect – things which once I had learnt I could not ignore. This is why at present I am focusing on this,' she said. Would she go back to the sailing if she had the chance? 'If I manage to communicate what I have learned about the environment, I'll be the first person off to sea again! I miss the long periods at sea hugely, but for now I feel I have something more important to do.'

3 Read the article again. Write true (T), false (F) or not given (NG).

1 There were difficult weather conditions for a lot of Ellen's voyage. **T**
2 The record that Ellen broke was set in 2005. **F**
3 She found the lack of facilities in her boat very difficult to cope with. **NG**
4 Ellen held the record for two years. **F**
5 According to the article, mental strength is more important than physical strength in solo sailing. **T**
6 Some people have been critical of Ellen's achievement. **T**
7 Ellen thinks teenagers with cancer have similar challenges to her. **F**
8 She learned about environmental problems when she was sailing. **NG**

4 Work in small groups and discuss the questions.

1 From the article, what is your impression of Ellen MacArthur? In what ways do you think you are like her?
2 How would you feel about being alone on a boat like Ellen's for 71 days? What would you miss the most?
3 Which of Ellen's two projects, *The Ellen MacArthur Trust* or *Team Ellen*, interests you the most? Why?

Grammar | conditional structures (1)

5 **a** Complete the sentences (1–5) in the Active grammar box with *will*, *would*, *wouldn't* (x2) and *would've*.

b Match the sentences (1–5) with the correct rules (A–E).

Active grammar

B 1 _would_ she go back to the sailing if she had the chance?

C 2 *If previous sailors had had modern equipment, many of them* _would have_ *broken records, too.*

A 3 *If I manage to communicate what I have learned about the environment, I* _will_ *be the first person off to sea again!*

D 4 *If she hadn't endured such tough experiences herself, she* _wouldn't_ *understand nearly as much about what they have to face.*

E 5 *Ellen probably* _would not have_ *survived if she didn't have such extreme mental toughness.*

A We use the First Conditional: *if* + Present Simple/Continuous + *will/won't* to talk about future possibility.

B We use the Second Conditional: *if* + Past Simple/Continuous + *would/wouldn't* to talk about present or future imagined situations.

C We use the Third Conditional: *if* + Past Perfect Simple/Continuous + *would have/wouldn't have* to talk about imagined situations in the past.

We can use various Mixed Conditionals, e.g.

D *if* + Past Perfect + *would/wouldn't* to talk about imagined past conditions and the probable results in the present.

E *if* + Past Simple/Continuous + *would have/wouldn't have* to talk about situations that never happened because of conditions which are still true.

---

see Reference page 75

6 Find the mistakes in the sentences and correct them.

1 Before you go tomorrow morning, ~~do~~ *will* you phone me if you need anything?
2 What *would* you have done if a nearby boat hadn't picked up your distress call?
3 You ~~had~~ *would* feel a lot better about things if you took a risk and left your job.
4 She wouldn't have finish~~ed~~ the race if she wasn't such a determined person.
5 What *would* you like to do if you had some free time and money?
6 If I ~~didn't take~~ *had not taken* a year off to cycle across Africa, I wouldn't have met my wife.
7 If he ~~didn't have~~ *had not had* sailing lessons when he was young, he wouldn't be so confident in the water now.
8 If you~~'ll~~ *would* see John, ~~will~~ you ask him if he wants to come parachuting with us?

7 Choose the correct words in *italics*.

1 If he had the chance to sail around the world, he *will*/*would* do it.
2 If she *is*/*was* brave enough, she'd have a go at parachuting.
3 If he *took*/*'d taken* a risk by applying for the job, he'd have a better job now.
4 If I decided to campaign for something, it *would be*/*would have been* for the environment.
5 If he *had*/*'d had* to be alone for long, he'd hate it.
6 If I have more time, I'*ll*/*'d* go to the gym four or five times a week.
7 If I *will be*/*were* a different person, I'd like to be more self-confident.
8 If she'd had the opportunity when she was a child, she*'d like*/*'d have liked* to learn to swim properly.

Vocabulary | verb phrases about challenge

8 Work in pairs. Look at the <u>underlined</u> verb phrases and try to work out their meanings from the context.

1 She <u>risked</u> everything and sailed solo around the world.

2 She <u>broke the</u> existing <u>record</u> by 33 hours.

3 She <u>put up with</u> this discomfort and never complained.

4 The danger never seemed to bother her either; she just <u>dealt with</u> the risks.

5 You need to be able to <u>focus on</u> the job completely.

6 She <u>endured</u> tough experiences herself.

7 I <u>face challenges</u> out on the water.

8 They <u>battle against</u> something harder than many of us could ever imagine.

9 She decided to <u>put her efforts into</u> saving the environment.

10 She set up 'Team Ellen' to <u>campaign for</u> a more sustainable future.

9 **a** Choose the correct words in *italics*.

1 What challenges do you think Ellen *battles/faces* now?

2 How do you think Ellen was able to *put/face* up with all the discomfort during the trip?

3 What do you know about how Ellen *campaigns/battles* for the environment?

4 Why do you think Ellen *puts/campaigns* her efforts into sustainable living?

5 How do you think sailing helped the teenage cancer patients *focus/battle* against their illness?

6 How would you feel if you *broke/put* a record in sport?

7 Do you think you could *deal/endure* with the dangers of sailing round the world?

8 How do you think people *focus/endure* the experience of being alone for a long time?

9 What do you think about people who *deal/risk* everything to do something dangerous for fun?

10 Are you good at *dealing/focusing* on things or do you get distracted easily?

b Choose six of the questions from exercise 9a to ask and answer with a partner.

10 **a** Work in pairs. Read the tips in the Lifelong learning box and discuss the pros and cons of each one.

b Discuss the questions.

1 What other tips can you add to the Lifelong learning box?

2 What risks do you think you take in your learning at the moment?

3 What risks would you like to take more?

Taking risks

Lifelong learning

! In order to push your language learning to the next level, sometimes you need to take risks, challenge yourself and experiment with different ways of learning/practising English. You can ...

1 speak as much as possible inside/outside the classroom without worrying about mistakes.

2 read magazines/books etc., focusing on general understanding, not looking up unknown words in a dictionary.

3 watch TV/films without subtitles.

4 use new vocabulary and grammar in conversation, even when you're not completely sure it's correct.

5 write in English as much as possible without worrying about mistakes.

Speaking

11 ● 1.38 Listen to two people. What kind of risk is the man talking about?

12 **a** Choose three of these sentences and rewrite to make them true for you.

1 If I were a different person, I'd like to be more of a risk-taker.

2 If someone asked me to sail around the world with them, I'd do it.

3 If I had to be alone for a long period, I wouldn't mind at all.

4 If I have more time, I'll try to do more exercise.

5 If I could choose a characteristic, I'd like to be more courageous.

6 If I'd had the chance as a child, I'd have learned to play a musical instrument.

7 If I decided to campaign for something, I'd probably choose something to do with animals.

b Work in small groups. Compare and discuss your sentences.

Reading

1 Work in pairs and discuss the questions.

1 Which of these sports can you see in the photo?
- hang-gliding
- free running
- white-water rafting

2 How dangerous do you think it is? Do you think you would like to do it? Why/Why not?

2 Read the leaflets (A–C) quickly and match the titles (1–3) to each one.

1 Yorkshire Hang-Gliding Centre
2 The Challenge and Calm of Free Running
3 White-Water Rafting in New Zealand

3 Tick (✓) the information each text includes.

1 history of the sport   A ☐ B ☐ C ☑
2 information about who
  can do the sport   A ☑ B ☒ C ☑
3 rules about equipment
  required   A ☑ B ☐ C ☐

4 Work in pairs and discuss the questions.

1 Which of the sports do you think sounds the most dangerous?

2 Which would you most/least like to do? Why?

B **Experience** the exhilaration of free flight as you learn to fly with us. Look through our website and we will introduce some of the safety measures necessary as well as some of the incredible pleasures of this sport.

You have to do between 8–10 days training and then you can fly for hours at a few hundred feet or many thousands of feet ... the choice is yours. You learn not only how to take off, fly and land safely, but also to understand when you should stop flying. For example, you shouldn't continue when there is the possibility of a storm.

Apart from the glider itself, there are two pieces of essential equipment you will need. Firstly, you have to wear a helmet when you fly with us. You can wear any standard safety helmet, but we recommend one which does not cover your ears, as you should be able to hear the airflow in order to make judgements about your flight. The second piece of essential equipment is a harness and we have plenty of these for you to borrow.

A *Book individually to join a group of up to six other adrenaline-seekers for a two-hour experience you'll never forget!*

Prices from $45!

TERMS AND CONDITIONS – PLEASE READ

Restrictions: The Centre Management regrets that for safety reasons these participants must not take part in any rafting sessions ...
- any participants under the age of 14.
- any participants over 100 kg.
- any participants who are pregnant.

Clothing and equipment: The Centre provides the following pieces of equipment which all participants must wear: a helmet, a life jacket and a wet suit. In addition, you must bring the following with you: a spare set of clothes, a spare pair of trainers, a towel and a swimsuit to wear under your wet suit.

Spectator information: The café overlooks the course, so there are plenty of 'photo opportunities'.

Weather restrictions: Apart from lightning, we are not restricted by bad weather as you are going to get wet anyway!

C **It** is often known as 'Parkour' and it is an extreme sport that turns everyday urban landscapes into obstacle courses. It began in 1987 in Paris, where two teenagers started climbing up buildings, swinging around lamp posts and jumping over anything in their way. 25 years later, it's a global phenomenon with thousands of participants.

The philosophy is all about challenging yourself, while staying calm. That's why there are no competitions and no world records. You don't have to do any special training or have any special equipment. The whole idea is that anyone can do it.

There aren't any rules but you should understand a few basic principles. Most importantly, you must know how to land properly. You don't land flat on your feet; you should land on the ball of your feet and you mustn't forget to bend your knees. Basically, you land, you bend your knees, you roll, you stand up and you keep running.

A

B

C

Vocabulary | sport

5 **a** Which of the sports from the box can you see in the photos?

> white-water rafting   rock climbing
> horse-riding   off-road mountain biking
> rugby   free running   archery
> open-water swimming

b Which sports from the box collocate with *play, go* and *do*? Add three more sports to each group.

play	go	do

c Discuss the questions.

1 Which of the items of clothing and equipment in the box can you see in the photos?

> helmet   harness   swimsuit
> wet suit   life jacket   trainers
> goggles   mouth guard   gloves

2 What other things/equipment can you wear/use when you do sport?

6 Work in pairs. What is the difference in meaning between each pair of verb phrases?

1 to be competitive/to be addictive
2 to be a participant/to be a spectator
3 to win/to beat
4 to take part in/to train for
5 to be successful/to have a sense of achievement

7 **a** Complete the sentences with a correct word from exercise 6.

1 I like being a *spectator* at rugby matches.
2 I think dangerous sports are _____ and once you start, you want to do them all the time.
3 I think that if you're _____ in sport, it gives you confidence in other areas of your life.
4 I'd like to take _____ in a sporting event to raise money.
5 When I play a game, my aim is to _____ the other person.
6 I'd like to _____ for a marathon one day.
7 I think boys are more _____ than girls.
8 I get upset when my football team doesn't _____ a match.
9 Dangerous sports are good because you have a huge sense of _____ doing something you're frightened about.
10 I'd rather be a _____ in something dangerous like hang-gliding than just watch other people doing it.

b Choose four of the sentences from exercise 7a. Work in pairs. Take turns to say why they are/are not true for you. Give details.

Listening

8 **a** ◯ 1.39 Listen to someone talking about hang-gliding and answer the questions.

1 Did he do a lot of training?
2 Was he scared at all?
3 Would he like to go again?

b Listen again and write true (T) or false (F).

1 He arrived at the hang-gliding centre at about 8.00 a.m. ☐
2 The glider is taken into the sky by a plane. ☐
3 He was hang-gliding at about 2,000 metres up in the sky. ☐
4 When he steered to the left, he did it too gently. ☐
5 The instructor landed the glider very well. ☐
6 Next time, he wants to try hang-gliding without an instructor. ☐

9 Work in pairs and discuss the questions.

1 How do you think you would feel hang-gliding with an instructor or without an instructor?
2 Why do you think sports like this can be addictive?

Grammar | Advice and permission

10 a Look at the Active grammar box and audioscript 1.39 on page 167. Say which of the underlined sentences refer to …

1 advice in the present
2 advice in the past
3 permission in the present
4 permission in the past.

b Work in pairs. Look at the questions and decide why you might choose *can* and *could* for talking about permission in each one.

1 <u>Can</u> you go alone after doing a few flights with an instructor?
2 <u>Could</u> you do a really low flight?

Active grammar

Advice (present)

should/shouldn't (+ infinitive)

If I were you, I would/wouldn't (+ infinitive)

Advice (past)

should have/shouldn't have
(+ past participle)

If I were you, I would/wouldn't have
(+ past participle)

Permission (present)

can/can't (+ infinitive)

could/couldn't (+ infinitive)

are/aren't allowed to (+ infinitive)

Permission (past)

could/couldn't (+ infinitive)

were/weren't allowed to (+ infinitive)

---

see Reference page 75

11 a Complete the sentences in a logical way.

1 When you go rock-climbing, you should …
2 When I was a child, I wasn't allowed …
3 When I last did sport, I should have …
4 When you next go running, if I were you, I …
5 If you go horse-riding, if I were you, I wouldn't …

b Work in pairs and discuss your sentences.

12 Choose the correct words in *italics*.

One of the best things I did on holiday was to go white-water rafting. It was expensive and I (1) *shouldn't have done/shouldn't do* it really, but I'm really glad I did. I was a bit nervous when they said we (2) *shouldn't do/weren't allowed to do* it unless we signed something – it said we wouldn't hold the company responsible if we got injured or died! Apart from that, the company was very relaxed. In fact, I was surprised that we (3) *could choose/are allowed to choose* whether to wear a life jacket and a helmet! And we (4) *were allowed to wear/should've worn* anything on our feet, so I wore my trainers. I know you were thinking about going rafting and you (5) *can go/should go* definitely – but if I were you, I (6) *should wear/would wear* the life jacket and helmet. I really think safety equipment like life jackets (7) *aren't allowed to be/shouldn't be* optional. Luckily, we were all OK. Also, you (8) *should take/would take* a camera! I (9) *should take/should have taken* mine but I was afraid I would drop it in the water.

Pronunciation | connected speech (3)

13 a Read the <u>underlined</u> sentences in audioscript 1.39 on page 167 and do the following.

- Tick (✓) the weak forms of auxiliary verbs (e.g. *can/were*) and prepositions (e.g. *to, for*).
- Mark connections between a consonant sound and a vowel sound.
- Mark connections between a consonant sound and another consonant sound.
- Mark connections between a vowel sound and another vowel sound, with the added sounds /w/, /j/ or /r/.

b ● 1.40 Listen and check the pronunciation. Then repeat the sentences.

Speaking

14 a Prepare to talk about a sport or other activity. Make brief notes on…

- things you generally can/can't do.
- things you were/weren't allowed to do.
- things you should/shouldn't have done.
- advice you'd give to someone else about it.

b Work in small groups and take turns to talk about your sport/activity. Which would you most like to do? Which sounds the most dangerous?

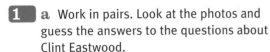

Grammar	emphasis
Can do	describe and choose films

Reading

1 **a** Work in pairs. Look at the photos and guess the answers to the questions about Clint Eastwood.

1 Is he a film star, a director or both?

2 Approximately how many films has he acted in?

3 When did his film career start?

4 What different types of films has he made (e.g. drama, comedy, etc.)?

b Read the information about Clint Eastwood and check your answers.

c Work in pairs and discuss the questions.

1 Have you seen any Clint Eastwood films?

2 If so, what did you think of them? If not, would you like to?

Listening

2 **a** ⏺ 1.41 Listen to two friends, Lidia and Paul, talking about two Clint Eastwood films and answer the questions.

1 Who enjoyed *Million Dollar Baby* more? *Paul brilliant*

2 What did Lidia think about *Gran Torino*? *great film*

3 Does Paul want to see *Gran Torino*? *yes defo*

b Listen again and answer the questions.

1 What is one important theme of *Million Dollar Baby*? *risk*

2 In what way does the Clint Eastwood character <u>not</u> take a risk in the film?

3 Who is the Clint Eastwood character upset about? *II not clear*

4 In *Gran Torino*, what kind of person is Walt? *bad tempered, bitter about the world*

5 Why is Walt's relationship with his young neighbour 'an emotional risk'? *decides to friend with hm*

6 Which areas of risk (a–d) do they mention in the conversation?

a becoming friends with someone and helping them

b getting close to someone, e.g. going out with someone, getting married, etc.

c working with someone and training them

d standing up and fighting for your rights or beliefs

3 Which of the areas of risk in question 6 above do you think is generally the most risky? Why?

Clint Eastwood was born in San Francisco in 1930. He is one of the most famous, versatile and longest-running movie stars ever. In his career, he has starred in over 55 films and directed over 30. He has received multiple awards for his acting and directing, including several Oscars and Golden Globes.

In his early films, in the 1960s, he often starred in westerns or 'cowboy' films like, *The Good, The Bad and the Ugly* (made in 1966). Then, in 1971, he directed his first film, a thriller called *Play Misty for Me*, which was a huge success. He continued to act, as well as direct, starring in films such as: *Dirty Harry* (a 1971 police drama), *Every Which Way But Loose* (a 1978 comedy), *The Bridges of Madison County* (a 1995 love story) and *Mystic River* (a 2003 thriller).

More recently, Eastwood's hit films include *Million Dollar Baby* (2004) and *Gran Torino* (2008). Both films are dramas in which the central characters regret their past mistakes and are given one last chance to redeem themselves. Eastwood starred in and directed both of them.

Grammar | emphasis

4 **a** Look at the ways of emphasising (A–C) in the Active grammar box and complete the sentences (1–7).

b Check your answers in audioscript 1.41 on page 167.

Active grammar

A   Add an appropriate form of *do*:

1   *I __do__ like Clint Eastwood.*

2   *She __does__ stay with him in the end.*

B   Add an emphasising word (*so* + adjective/adverb, *so* + *much/many*, *such a/an* + noun/noun phrase):

3   *There are __so__ many different themes running through the film.*

4   *I thought the whole theme of risk was __so__ interesting.*

5   *They're __such__ great films.*

6   *It sounds like __such__ an interesting film.*

C   Use the structure starting *It is/was …* :

7   *__It__ the film I've enjoyed most this year.*

see Reference page 75

5 Rewrite the sentences, adding *do, does* or *did* for emphasis. Change the form of the verbs where necessary.

1   She knows when the film starts. She does know

2   I sent you a message this morning. I did

3   They like dangerous sports. They do

4   He apologised for being late. He did

5   She needs some help with her homework. she does

6   I understand how you are feeling.

6 Complete the sentences with *so, such* or *such a*.

1   It's __so__ risky to buy a second-hand car from a stranger.

2   I think rock climbing is __such a__ dangerous sport.

3   There are __so__ many risks associated with smoking.

4   My sister does everything __so__ cautiously.

5   There are __such__ interesting characters in that film.

6   That film was __so__ much better than the first one.

7 Rewrite these sentences giving special emphasis to the <u>underlined</u> parts of the sentences by beginning each one with *It is …* or *It was …* .

1   He had always wanted <u>this job</u>.
    It was this job he had always wanted.

2   I went and saw <u>that new Clint Eastwood film</u> yesterday.

3   I asked if I could borrow <u>his new Mercedes</u>.

4   She really doesn't like <u>the words to their new song</u>.

5   He wants to study <u>sociology or psychology</u> at university.

6   He broke <u>the window</u> while he was playing with a ball.

Pronunciation | stress: emphasis (1)

8 **a** ● 1.42 When we use emphatic structures with *do/does* and *so/such*, we can also use stress to add emphasis. Listen to four extracts from the dialogue and mark the stressed words in the sentences (1–6).

1   I do like Clint Eastwood.

2   There are so many different themes in the film.

3   I thought the whole theme of risk was so interesting.

4   She does stay with him in the end.

5   They're such great films.

6   It sounds like such an interesting film.

b Listen again. Why does each person want to emphasise what they say?

9 **a** Work in pairs. Think of a film, an actor, or a place you both know and can talk about. One of you should be mostly positive and the other should be mostly negative.

b Prepare to persuade your partner to change his/her opinion by making a note of some points you particularly want to emphasise.

c Take turns to persuade each other. Were you successful? Why/Why not?

Vocabulary | phrasal verbs with *out*

10 Match the <u>underlined</u> phrasal verbs (1–8) with their meanings (a–h).

1 She <u>turns out</u> to be a very good boxer.

2 We never really <u>find out</u> what he's upset about.

3 I couldn't <u>work out</u> why his daughter never replied to his letters.

4 He's <u>fallen out with</u> his family and doesn't speak to them much.

5 They <u>gave out</u> a pair of 3D glasses to every member of the audience.

6 We had to walk along a dangerous road when we <u>ran out of</u> petrol.

7 Firefighters risk their lives when they enter buildings to <u>put out</u> large fires.

8 We need to <u>sort out</u> the problem with the safety equipment before you can start.

a give to each person

b stop being friends

c become, happen in a particular way

d extinguish, stop a fire or cigarette from burning

e discover, get information about something or someone

f put something in order, correct a mistake

g use all of something so there is none left

h calculate, find a solution to a problem

11 **a** Complete the sentences with the correct form of the <u>underlined</u> verbs from exercise 10.

1 Have you ever had to _____ out a fire? What happened?

2 When you want to _____ out about a piece of information (e.g. where you can go bungee jumping), what do you normally do?

3 Have you ever been in a car which has _____ out of petrol? What happened?

4 Have any friends of yours ever done anything strange and you couldn't _____ out why they had done it?

5 Have you ever met someone who _____ out to be very different than you imagined they were like at first? In what way were they different?

6 Have you ever _____ out with a good friend? If so, why? What happened?

b Work in pairs and ask and answer the questions.

Speaking

12 **a** 🌐 1.43 Listen to two people talking about the DVDs below. Which one do they decide to watch? Why?

b Listen again and complete the sentences in the How to... box.

How to... talk about which film to watch

Speculate about the general feel/look	*I like the* ___look___ *of Mystic River just **because** it's a bit mysterious.* *Judging **by the cover, it looks like** a romance.* *That **sounds a bit** ____ **to me.*** ***Sounds** like **it could** be intense.*
Talk about the actors/director/plot	*They're* ___both___ *such good actors.* *I have a hard time seeing him* ___as___ *a romantic lead.* *It's based **on a book and it's about** three brothers.*

---

13 **a** Look at the information and photos from two films on page 147 and prepare to talk about them.

b Work in pairs and talk about the two films. Which one would you rather watch? Why?

1 **a** Work in pairs and discuss the difference between …

1 a low-risk strategy/a high-risk strategy.
2 a long-term plan/a short-term plan.
3 a local phone call/a long-distance phone call.
4 a short cut to somewhere/a long way round.
5 a broad-minded person/a narrow-minded person.
6 saying a person is skinny/saying a person is slim.
7 saying a person is shallow/saying a person is deep.

b Work in pairs.

Student A: choose a word or phrase from exercise 1a. Describe a situation or person to illustrate it.

Student B: guess which word/phrase your partner is describing.

A: *It was a really good football match … They put a lot of players up front to try and score a lot of goals, which meant there weren't many players defending. In the end, they won, but the spectators were really nervous because it was a really …*

B: *… high-risk strategy!*

2 **a** Complete the table with the missing parts of speech.

Adjective	Noun	Verb
long	length	lengthen
(1) short	xxx	shorten
wide	width	(2) widen
broad	breadth	(3) broaden
(4) high	height	heighten
deep	(5) depth	deepen
low	xxx	(6) lower

b ◯ 1.44 Listen and check your answers.

3 Complete the sentences (1–10) with the correct form of words from the table above.

1 I know the length of this rug, but I don't know the __breadth/width__
2 The pool is quite shallow at this end, but do you know the __depth__ at the other end?
3 The average __height__ of a woman in the US is about 162cm.
4 They intend to __widen__ this road and make it four lanes instead of three.
5 This bed is very __low__ . It's almost like sleeping on the floor!
6 This skirt's too short. It needs __lengthen__ a bit.
7 If I go by car to work instead of by train, it __shortens__ my journey by about fifteen minutes which is great.
8 He has very __wide__ shoulders and is quite muscular.
9 I had a very high temperature this morning but it's __lowered__ considerably since then, luckily.
10 The artist's death _____ the value of his paintings and they are too expensive for me now.

4 Choose the correct words in *italics*.

1 We'd like to *expand*/*heighten* our business and start producing different kinds of kitchen equipment.
2 We have *grown*/*extended* the house at the back and now we have a much bigger kitchen.
3 It's a wonderful beach. It *stretches*/*expands* for miles.
4 It's quite a *distance*/*length* to the next petrol station.
5 If the city keeps *stretching*/*spreading*, our local forest will disappear.
6 They had a *broad*/*lengthy* conversation about the problems in the company.
7 You know that metal *contracts*/*shortens* when it becomes cooler, don't you?
8 This jumper seems to have *shrunk*/*reduced* in the wash!

5 **a** Work in pairs. Prepare to tell a story involving someone taking a risk of some kind. Include at least five of the words/phrases from exercises 1a, 2a and 4.

b Take turns to tell your stories. Which story involved the biggest risk?

Can do | participate actively in a debate

1 **a** Work in pairs. Which of the things from the box below can you see in the photos?

> oil rigs   wind farm
> solar panels   hydroelectric dam
> nuclear power station

b For the types of energy production in the box above, think of ...

1 any advantages for the area they might create.

2 any risks to health or the environment they might create.

2 🔵 1.45 Listen to part of a debate about a proposal to build a nuclear power station and answer the questions below.

1 Which two groups do the speakers represent?
• local government ✓←
• local business ✓
• local people ✓ ─
• environmental campaigners ✓

2 Is the first speaker for or against the proposal? What points does *for* he make? *cheaper energy, more jobs*

3 Is the second speaker for or against the proposal? What points does she make?

3 Listen again and complete the sentences in the How to... box with two words.

get a word in edgeways - who're [?]

> ## How to... make sure your point is heard
>
> | Interjecting | *Excuse me, if I could make* ~~a point~~ *there.* *I'd just like to* interrupt *for a minute.* |
> | Holding the floor | *If you could* let me *finish my point.* *I'm sorry but I haven't* ~~quite finished~~ |
> | Reformulating what you've just said | *What I* mean *you're introducing this by saying local people want this project.* *In* other words*, you are obviously for the whole project.* |

abrupt

4 **a** Prepare to have a debate about a proposal to build a nuclear power station in your area. Divide into groups of four (A, B, C and D) and make notes about three points that you want to make.

A You are representing the local government and you are <u>for</u> the proposal.

B You are representing local businesses and you are <u>for</u> the proposal.

C You are representing a local group of environmental campaigners and you are <u>against</u> the proposal.

D You are representing local people living in the area and you are <u>against</u> the proposal.

b Now work with representatives from each group and have the debate. Who is the most persuasive?

Conditional structures (1)

In conditional structures, the '*if* clause' can come first or second. When the '*if* clause' is first, we need a comma at the end of the clause.

We use the First Conditional for future possibility.

Form: *If* + Present Simple/Present Continuous + *will/won't*

*If you **ask** me, I'**ll be** happy to help you.*

We use the Second Conditional for present or future imagined situations and for giving advice.

Form: *If* + Past Simple/Past Continuous + *would/wouldn't* + infinitive

*If I **lived** in the country, I'**d do** a lot more walking.*
*I'**d buy** a good English–English dictionary if I **were** you.*

When less certain, we can use *might* instead of *would*.
*If I **had** more money, I **might take** a year off work.*

We use the Third Conditional to talk about imagined situations in the past.

Form: *If* + Past Perfect Simple/Continuous + *would have/wouldn't have* + past participle

*If I **had studied**, I **would have passed** the exam.*

We can use various Mixed Conditionals for imagined past conditions and probable results in the present.

Form: *If* + Past Perfect + *would/wouldn't* + infinitive
*If I **hadn't gone** to bed late, I **wouldn't be** tired.*

We can also use Mixed Conditionals to talk about situations that never happened because of conditions which are true.

Form: *If* + Past Simple/Continuous + *would have/wouldn't have* + infinitive

Advice and permission

For advice in the present, we use *should/shouldn't* (+ infinitive) and *If I were you, I would/wouldn't* (+ infinitive).
You shouldn't take *what he says so personally.*
*If I were you, I'**d take** the job.*

To give advice/criticism about the past, we use *should have/shouldn't have* (+ past participle) and *If I were you, I would/wouldn't have* (+ past participle).
You should have made *more of an effort to go.*
*If I were you, I **wouldn't have bought** so many clothes.*

To talk about permission in the present, we use: *can/can't* (+ infinitive), *could/couldn't* (+ infinitive) and *are/aren't allowed to* (+ infinitive). Choosing *could* instead of *can* shows that we are more tentative about what we are asking, or if we are not sure of the answer.
You can take part *after a two-hour training session.*
Could I borrow *your car this weekend?*
You aren't allowed to swim *unless you wear goggles.*

To talk about permission in the past, we use *could/couldn't* (+ infinitive) and *were/weren't allowed to* (+ infinitive)
*When I was a child, I **could stay up** late on Fridays.*
*They **weren't allowed to take** any photos.*

Emphasis

To emphasise what we're saying and make a point more strongly, we can add an appropriate form of *do*.
*I **do wish** you could stay a bit longer.*
*They **did enjoy** themselves very much.*

We can also add an emphasising word: *so* + adjective/adverb, *so* + *much/many*, *such* (*a/an*) + noun/noun phrase. We use *such a/an* with countable nouns and *such* with uncountable nouns.
*I was **so pleased** to meet your sister.*
*They are **such a nice couple**.*
*It was **such lovely weather**.*

We can use the structure starting: *It is/was ...*
It's *the kitchen I particularly like about that house.*

Key vocabulary

Risk/Achievement

risk   gamble   opportunity   chance   stake   ambition   substantial

Verbs and verb phrases about challenge

risk   break a record   put up with   deal with   focus on   endure   face a challenge   battle against   put your efforts into   campaign for

Sport

white-water rafting   rock climbing   horse-riding   off-road mountain biking   rugby   free running   archery   open-water swimming   helmet   harness   swimsuit   wet suit   life jacket   trainers   goggles   mouth guard   gloves   competitive   addictive   participant   spectator   win   beat   take part in   train for   successful   sense of achievement

Phrasal verbs with *out*

find out   run out (of)   turn out   work out   fall out (with)   give out   put out   sort out

Distances and dimensions

long/length/lengthen   short/shorten   wide/width/widen   broad/breadth/broaden   high/height/heighten   deep/depth/deepen   low/lower   contract   expand   extend   reduce   shrink   spread   stretch

---

Listen to the explanations and vocabulary.

ACTIVEBOOK

see Writing bank page 154

5 Review and practice

1 Match the sentence beginnings (1–8) with the endings (a–h).

1 If the cheque arrives today,
2 If I had more time,
3 If I had heard the weather forecast,
4 If I did more exercise,
5 If anyone spoke to me like that,
6 If I hadn't fallen in the race,
7 If I come to the party,
8 If I get my bonus at Christmas,

a I would be extremely angry.
b I wouldn't have gone walking in the mountains.
c I'll buy a new car.
d I would like to do a pottery class.
e I would probably start losing weight.
f I'm sure I would have won it.
g I'll put it straight in the bank.
h will you get them a present from both of us?

2 Complete the sentences with the appropriate form of the verbs.

1 What will we do if/taxi/not come/time?
2 If I/been born/year earlier,/I done/military service.
3 What would you do if/you/offer/better job?
4 If I/not home/11 p.m./my dad/be/really angry.
5 I/not/hired/a car/if I/known/expensive/it/going to be.
6 If she/work/hard/between now/the exams,/she/probably pass.
7 We/gone/the cinema/if we/able/find/babysitter.
8 If I/you,/I/go/long holiday.

3 Rewrite each sentence with the words in brackets so that the meaning stays the same.

1 I didn't want you to wait for me. (should)
   You ...
2 They let you in if you show some form of ID. (allowed)
   You ...
3 I don't think it was a good idea for you to get up so early this morning. (would)
   If ...
4 Photos are permitted if you don't use a flash. (can)
   You ...
5 It isn't a good idea to speak to the waiter like that. (should)
   You ...
6 My parents let me walk to school on my own when I was a child. (allowed)
   I ...

4 Find the mistakes in six of the sentences and correct them.

1 My brother is such competitive person when it comes to sport.
2 The participants did arrived on time despite the terrible traffic.
3 There were so much people who weren't wearing helmets on the ski slopes.
4 It's the job I found the most difficult of all.
5 Rock climbing is such incredibly addictive – I want to do it in all my spare time.
6 He has so much energy and spends a lot of time campaigning for good causes.
7 I do playing a lot of rugby even though it's quite dangerous.
8 It was so cold water that I was frozen by the end of the swim.

5 Choose the correct words in *italics*.

1 He managed to *endure/deal* a lot of pain during the three-day race.
2 We are very excited about plans to *spread/expand* the business in the next year.
3 I can't believe that you've never *won/beaten* your brother at tennis!
4 You need to completely focus *on/with* your driving throughout the whole test.
5 This skirt is too long for me so I'll need to *short/shorten* it a bit.
6 She put all her *efforts/battle* into her exams and got straight 'A' grades.
7 It's important to *stretch/shrink* your muscles after every training session.
8 I've decided I'm going to take part *with/in* the local football competition.

6 Complete the phrasal verbs with the correct form of the verbs from the box.

find   run   turn   work   fall   give   put   sort

1 This maths homework is so difficult. I can't _____ out how to do it at all.
2 I'd like to _____ out about the prices of your courses.
3 She's really upset because she's _____ out with her flatmate again.
4 I'm sorry about the problem with your bill. I'll _____ it out immediately.
5 We're _____ out of petrol. We need to stop at the next petrol station.
6 The party was a lot of work to organise but it _____ out really well in the end.
7 Before you go home, you need to make sure you _____ the barbecue out completely.
8 Can you help _____ out these forms to everyone?

The past

Lead-in

1 Work in pairs. Look at the photos and discuss the questions.

1 When do you think each photo was taken: the 1940s/1950s/1960s/1980s? What details make you think this?

2 What do you associate with each decade?

2 **a** Work in pairs and check you know the meaning of the underlined words in the sentences.

1 I get quite <u>nostalgic</u> when I look at old photos and <u>reminisce</u> about old times with my family.

2 There are two or three really <u>memorable</u> songs that immediately <u>take me back</u> to my younger days.

3 I have very <u>vivid</u> memories of my childhood after the age of ten, but before that I just have <u>vague</u> memories.

4 I've still got my first school bag, which I've kept as a <u>memento</u> of my days at primary school.

5 Whenever I go on holiday, I always buy at least one <u>souvenir</u> to bring home.

6 I'm quite a <u>forgetful</u> person, so I always write lists to <u>remind</u> me of things I need to do.

7 I usually <u>remember</u> someone's face, but their name is often <u>on the tip of my tongue</u> and I can't remember it.

8 I've got a terrible <u>memory</u> for new vocabulary, so I often use <u>mnemonics</u> to help <u>jog my memory</u>.

b Work in pairs. Take turns to choose four of the sentences from exercise 2a and make them true for you.

3 Work in pairs. Take turns to describe the happiest/most memorable time you had last year. What made it special? Describe it to your partner.

Reading

1 Work in pairs. Look at the photo of Mark Boyle and discuss the questions.

1 What can you see in the pictures?

2 Why do you think Mark started living in a caravan?

2 Think about which sentence(s) Mark would probably say. Then read the article and check your ideas.

1 I miss very little about my old life.

2 It was a good year but I'd like my old life back now.

3 Starting a new life was the most difficult thing I've done.

4 My new life is so good I want to live like this forever.

3 Read the article again and answer the questions.

1 How did Mark earn money before he lived in a caravan?

2 Why was he unhappy in his 'old life'?

3 How much did he pay for his caravan?

4 How did his feelings about cooking outside change?

5 Where did he get the soap for washing clothes from?

6 What does Mark say about friendship?

7 What did he decide at the end of the year?

4 Work in groups and discuss the questions.

1 Do you think that the changes Mark made in his life were sensible? Why/Why not?

2 What do you think you would find most difficult about what Mark did? Why?

3 Do you think you could ever change your life as radically as Mark did? Why/Why not?

4 What effect, if any, do you think his actions might have on changing people's attitudes to money?

A life without money

Mark Boyle gave up his job, his possessions and his money in order to live in an old caravan with absolutely no money at all. That might sound like a ridiculous idea, but Mark says, 'It's been fantastic. I never really knew how much stress and worry money brought to my life until I was free of it.' Before his new life, Mark used to have what most people consider a normal life. He was a successful businessman with a good job (managing a food company), a house and a girlfriend. But he was dissatisfied. He would constantly worry about money; about the way it creates problems, such as poverty, war and environmental destruction. After much thinking, he realised he wanted to change his life radically. He realised he couldn't just fight the world's problems, but that he wanted to do something about the causes — even if it was on a small scale, starting with his own life.

That's when he decided to take the radical step of living without money for a year. He managed to get a caravan from Freecycle — the website where people give away things they don't want for free. He parked his caravan on a farm, where in exchange for his work, the owners didn't charge him any rent. At first, many of life's basic chores were different and difficult for Mark. Soon, however, he got used to doing things in new ways. Food was the first essential. He found that there were four ways of getting food without paying: growing your own, foraging for wild food, bartering (giving people things in exchange for food) and using waste food from shops and restaurants. He then had to learn to cook outside, rain or shine, burning wood that he found in the local woodland. He felt rather overwhelmed by the cooking at first, but he quickly got used to it, and it became one of his biggest joys.

Mark found that even the simplest tasks, like having a shower or washing clothes, were incredibly time-consuming. For example, washing his clothes in a bowl of cold water, using liquid soap made by boiling some nuts on his stove, could take two hours or more. But, he got used to spending his time in this way and he says he never got bored; there was always something to do and something to learn about. He admits, however, that his new lifestyle had some repercussions on his personal life. He's single now and he knows that his prospects don't sound very appealing to possible girlfriends: no money, no car, no job, no hot water! But Mark says he's hopeful; although he may look a little scruffy at times and may not always be totally clean-shaven, he's quite good-looking and he has a nice personality!

People sometimes ask Mark what he has learned and he says the main thing is that 'friendship, not money, is real security'. They also ask him what he misses about his 'old' life and all he can think of are things like stress, traffic jams and electricity bills! Now, at the end of his year-long experiment, Mark is totally used to living without money. He is not only used to it, but he loves it, and has therefore decided not to go back to his 'old' life but to continue with his money-free life for good.

Grammar | *used to, be used to, get used to, would*

5 Look at the examples in the Active grammar box and complete the rules (A–D) with *used to*, *be used to*, *get used to* and *would*. You need to use one of them twice.

Active grammar

1 a *Mark **used to** have what most people consider a 'normal' life.*

  b *He **didn't use to** live in a caravan.*

2 a *He **would** constantly worry about money.*

  b *He **wouldn't** cook outside in his 'old life'.*

3 a *He quickly **got used to** cooking outside.*

  b *He **is getting used to** life without money.*

4 a *Now, Mark **is used to** living without money.*

  b *Soon he will **be used to** this life completely.*

A We use _____ (+ -*ing*/noun) to describe the process of becoming accustomed to a new situation (with things becoming more familiar and easier). Different tenses are possible.

B We use _____ (+ -*ing*/noun) to say when you have become accustomed to a new situation (and things are now familiar and easy). Different tenses are possible.

C We use _____ (+ infinitive) and _____ (+ infinitive) for repeated actions in the past which don't happen now.

D We use _____ (+ infinitive) only for states in the past.

see Reference page 89

6 **a** Choose the correct words in *italics*.

1 I *didn't use*/*wasn't used* to like cooking very much.

2 I'm getting used to *work*/*working* from home.

3 I'*m used to*/*used to* living on my own.

4 My family *would*/*were used to* always stay in a caravan for their summer holiday.

5 He *would*/*used to* have longer hair.

6 It's difficult to *get*/*getting* used to a different way of life.

b Work in pairs and take turns to explain what each sentence from exercise 6a means.

When the speaker was younger she didn't like cooking, but now she does.

7 There is one word missing from each sentence. Write it in the correct place.

1 I used play a lot of rugby at school.

2 I'm finding it difficult to used to my new boss. She's not very friendly.

3 You use to be so close to your brother when you were children?

4 When I was a child, we always have barbecues in the summer.

5 We slowly getting used to living in the country, but sometimes it feels a bit isolated.

6 We use to be vegetarian. It's only something we've started doing in the last couple of months.

8 Work in pairs and discuss these questions.

1 What did you use to enjoy doing when you were younger, but no longer enjoy? Why did you stop doing it?

2 How would you typically spend your summer holidays when you were a child?

3 What have been the biggest changes in your life so far? What were the most difficult things to get used to? Think about …

- home
- family
- work
- study

Vocabulary | appearance

9 **a** Read the article on page 78 again. What does Mark Boyle look like now? Do you think he looked the same ten years ago? Why?

b Put the words/phrases from the box in the appropriate categories in the table below.

> good-looking   scruffy
> clean-shaven   straight   muscular
> a bit overweight   elegant   fat
> slim   wrinkles   curly   chubby
> wavy   stocky   dyed
> going a bit bald   skinny   mousy
> round   tanned   spiky   beard

Hair	Face	Build	General
Spiky	clean-shaved	muscular	good-looking
going a bit bald	wrinkles	a bit overweight	elegant
wavy	round	fat	tanned
mousy	beard	slim	scruffy
curly	chubby		chubby
straight		tanned	
		stocky	

stubble
zero 15

c Add two more words to each column of the table.

10 **a** Choose the most appropriate words in *italics*.

1 He's got _dyed_/*tanned* black hair now, but it used to be blond.

2 She's _good-looking_/*muscular* enough to be a model.

3 She's got short, spiky hair and a _round_/*curly* face.

4 He used to have long, straight hair, but he's going a bit *stocky*/_bald_ now.

5 He's always been _clean-shaven_/*had wrinkles* so it's hard to get used to his beard.

6 She's very elegant, but her boyfriend looks quite _scruffy_/*spiky*.

7 He was a beautiful, *mousy*/*chubby* baby with wavy, blond hair.

8 She used to be a bit overweight, but she's too *slim*/*skinny* now.

b Look again at sentences 6–8 from exercise 10a. Do *scruffy*, *chubby* and *skinny* have a positive or negative connotation? When might they have a different connotation?

Pronunciation | consonant clusters (1)

11 **a** ⊕ 2.2 Listen to words beginning with two consonant sounds and write them in the correct place in the table below.

Two consonant sounds

sk-	sp-	st-	sl-
skinny			
sw-	sm-	sn-	sph-

b ⊕ 2.3 Listen to words beginning with three consonant sounds and write them in the correct place in the table below.

Three consonant sounds

scr-	str-	spr-	spl-	squ-
scruffy				

12 Listen to the words again and repeat.

Speaking

13 ⊕ 2.4 Listen to a woman describing the photos of Brad Pitt below. Do you agree with her opinion?

14 **a** Choose a famous person (e.g. pop star, politician, sportsperson, actor). Prepare to describe the appearance of the person, including your opinion.

b Work in pairs.

Student A: give your description and opinion about the person you chose but don't say the name.

Student B: guess who student A is describing and say if you agree with his/her opinion.

Ⓐ

Ⓑ

Ⓓ

Listening

1 Work in pairs. Look at the photos and discuss the questions.

1 Where and why do you think each photo was taken?

2 What places or situations does each photo remind you of? Why?

3 Do you take a lot of photos? If so, why and what situations/events do you usually take photos of? If not, why not?

2 Work in pairs. Which photos (A–D) do you think each of the following statements could be about?

1 It's from a typical family holiday.

2 It was probably taken in summer.

3 It shows a peaceful setting.

4 The photographer thought carefully about how to take the photo.

5 It shows an interesting cultural setting.

6 It shows a happy memory.

3 🔊 2.5-2.6 Work in pairs. Listen to two people talking about their photos. Answer the questions.

1 Which two photos are being described?

2 Why is each photo personally significant?

4 Listen again and answer the questions.

1 What two characteristics of Switzerland does Eben mention?

2 How did Eben feel about Geneva when he was a teenager?

3 How does Eben feel about Geneva as a place to bring up children?

4 What in particular does Eben say he wanted to share with his family?

5 When did Jeanette visit these gardens?

6 Why did Jeanette take photos of the gardens?

7 Why did Jeanette not make a Japanese garden when she came back to the UK?

8 Does Jeanette intend to make the garden in the future or not?

5 Work in pairs and discuss the questions.

1 How do you think Eben feels about not settling in Geneva as an adult with his family? How do you think you would feel about that?

2 How do you think Jeanette feels about not creating her Japanese garden? How do you think you would feel about that?

Grammar | wishes and regrets

6 **a** Read parts A and B in the Active grammar box and write the headings below in the correct place.

- Talking about plans that didn't come true
- Talking about wishes, regrets and things that didn't happen

b Read the Active grammar box again and complete the rules (1 and 2) below.

1 When we use *I wish/If only* + Past Perfect and Third Conditional sentences, *I had* is often shortened to _____ .

2 When we use Third Conditional sentences, *would have* is often shortened to _____ .

Active grammar

A _____

wish/if only + Past Perfect

1 **I wish I'd appreciated** it when I was a teenager.

2 **If only I'd appreciated** it when I was a teenager.

regret + clause/*regret* + *-ing* form

3 **I regret that** I didn't appreciate it when I was a teenager.

4 **I regret not appreciating** it when I was a teenager.

Third conditional: *if* + Past Perfect, *would/could have* + past participle

5 **If I'd settled** there, it **would have been** the ideal place to raise my children.

6 **I could have stayed** and finished university there **if I'd wanted**.

B _____

was/were going to + infinitive

7 **I was going to create** a Japanese garden when I came back to the UK.

would have + past participle

8 **I would have liked** to create a pool with carp in.

See Reference page 89

7 Find the mistakes in six of the sentences and correct them.

1 I wish I took more notice of my teachers at school. *[I had taken]*

2 If I would've had different advice, I would've started on a different career. *[had]*

3 I really regret that I didn't travel when I was younger. *[not travelling]*

4 I could bought myself a guitar if I'd had more money. *[have]*

5 If only I was thinking more about what career I wanted. *[had thought]*

6 I decided I'm going to be a doctor while I was still at primary school. *[was]*

7 I would've liked to study architecture but I became a designer in the end.

8 I regret not to learn the piano when I was younger. *[not learning]*

8 **a** Complete five of the sentences below to make them true for you.

1 I regret that I didn't go ... study at University new?

2 I would've liked to be ...more talent for

3 If I'd had more time, I could ...go around the world

4 I wish I'd taken more notice of ...of advice from my mum.

5 Last year, I decided I was ...

6 If I'd had different advice, I ...would have chose different route.

7 If only I'd thought more about ...

8 I deeply regret not saying ...goodbye to all my friends

b Work in pairs. Compare and discuss your sentences.

Pronunciation | intonation: wishes and regrets

9 2.7 Listen to three people talking about some personal memories. Answer the questions below.

1 What memory is each person talking about?

2 How long ago was the event/situation they are describing?

3 What does each person wish or regret?

10 **a** 2.8 When we are reminiscing about the past, or expressing wishes and regrets, we can sound nostalgic by using particular intonation. Listen to the sentences (1–6) from the extracts and decide ...

- generally, is the intonation high or flat?
- generally, do the people talk fast or with pauses?
- which words are stressed in each sentence?

1 It makes me feel really nostalgic about my childhood.

2 Oh, I would've liked to live there all the time.

3 Those were the days!

4 I wish I hadn't lost touch with so many of them.

5 It reminds me of one of the best times of my life.

6 I regret leaving that place in a way.

b Listen again and repeat the sentences.

Speaking

11 **a** 🔵 2.7 Listen again to the three people talking about personal memories and look at the How to... box. Number the sentences in the order you hear them.

How to... reminisce about the past

Talking about when things happened	*It doesn't feel that long ago.* *It reminds me of one of the best times of my life.*
Talking about feelings	*It brings back so many memories.* *It makes me feel nostalgic about my childhood.* *Those were the days!*
Talking about the clarity of the memories	*I can remember that place so clearly.* *I can picture it so well.* *It feels like last week.*

b Look at audioscript 2.7 on page 169 and <u>underline</u> three more phrases you like.

12 **a** Prepare to talk about something from the past which is personally significant for you. You can talk about your own photo, imagine one of the photos (A–C) is important for you or choose something from the list below.

- a memorable holiday from your childhood
- a place you wish you'd gone back to
- something you were going to do but didn't
- a day you spent with a close friend
- something you used to do regularly but don't do now

b Make notes on the questions below.

1 What vocabulary do you need?
2 What wishes or regrets can you express?
3 What plans did you make in the past?
4 Which phrases from the How to... box can you use?
5 How can you sound nostalgic?

13 Work in small groups and take turns to talk about your personal memories. Who sounded the most nostalgic?

Grammar	preparatory *it*
Can do	give a detailed reaction to a book

Vocabulary | feelings

1 🔊 2.9 Listen to eleven people and decide how they feel. Choose the correct emotion from the box for each person.

> confused   suspicious   uneasy   curious
> annoyed   excited   uninterested
> sceptical   optimistic   shocked   relieved

2 Complete the sentences with the most appropriate word from exercise 1.

1 She's very _____ that the police have dropped all the charges against her.

2 Our children are getting very _____ about our trip to Disneyworld next month. They keep asking when we're going.

3 Most of the people interviewed said they felt _____ about the idea of living near a nuclear power station.

4 Sam's _____ about selling his flat quickly. He's had lots of people come to see it since it went up for sale last week.

5 My sister's _____ with me because I borrowed her favourite jacket without asking her.

6 When I was learning to ski she gave me so many different pieces of advice that I just ended up totally _____ .

7 Environmental groups are _____ that the government is serious about tackling the problem of global warming.

8 I'm very _____ to know why Sarah got the job of marketing director. She's only been in the company a few months.

9 I'm afraid I'm fairly _____ in politics and politicians. They all seem to say the same things these days.

10 The fact that he didn't want to answer the police officer's questions made them _____ .

11 Julie's mother was quite _____ when they told her they were going to get married in June. They've only been together since November.

3 **a** Work in pairs. Choose six of the emotions from exercise 1. Try to remember the last time you felt each of them.

b Work in pairs. Take turns to tell each other why you had these feelings.

'A compulsive read, beautifully written ... with the same talent she displayed so brilliantly in *Hidden Lives*' Mary Wesley, *Sunday Express*

the memory box

margaret forster

Reading

4 **a** Work in pairs. Look at the cover of *The Memory Box* above. Discuss what you think the book might be about.

b Read an extract from the book on page 85 and decide who Susannah, Charlotte and Catherine are.

5 Read the extract again and answer the questions below.

1 'Susannah was apparently perfect, as the dead so often become.' (line 1) What do you think this means?

2 How did Catherine feel about what people said about her mother?

3 '... the existence of the memory box may have troubled my father from the beginning.' (line 10) Why do you think this might have been?

4 Catherine thinks she would have reacted differently to the memory box aged ten or fifteen. Do you think this is likely? If so, why?

5 Why do you think Catherine didn't want to think about her real mother as she was growing up?

6 How do you think Catherine felt when she first came across the memory box?

7 Find examples in the extract of five of the feelings referred to in exercise 1. Explain who has the feelings and what causes them.

6 Work in pairs and discuss the questions.

1 What kinds of things do you think Susannah might have left in the 'memory box' for Catherine?

2 What do you think the point of the memory box was?

3 How would you feel about making or being given a memory box?

Susannah was apparently perfect, as the dead so often become. She was, it seemed, perfectly beautiful, perfectly good and perfectly happy during her comparatively short life. They
5   said she met life with open arms, ever positive and optimistic. I do not believe a word of this. How, after all, could she be happy, knowing she was likely to die soon, when she was a mere thirty-one years old and I, her baby, was hardly six months old?

10   I have a feeling that the existence of the memory box may have troubled my father from the beginning. He didn't give it to me until my twenty-first birthday even though it had been in our house all that time. Charlotte knew about
15   it, of course, but neither she nor my father could bring themselves to mention it. I think they were both afraid of its significance. Also, I was a highly imaginative child and they simply didn't know how to introduce this memory box
20   into my life.

Now, however, their nervousness makes me curious. What exactly were they afraid of? Did they think I might be shocked, and if so why? At any rate, both of them were visibly on edge, almost guilty, when finally on the morning of my twenty-first birthday
25   they told me about it. It was clear they were relieved when I showed little interest in it. I said I didn't want to open it, or even see it.

This was a lie, and yet not a lie. The box did, in fact, make me curious even if I found I wanted to suppress the feeling. Aged ten, I don't think I would have been able to. I'm sure I would have been too excited at the thought that it might contain all sorts of treasures; and then around fifteen I'd have found it irresistibly romantic and
30   would have been ready to weep on discovering dried roses pressed between the pages of meaningful poems. But at twenty-one I was very self-centred; my curiosity was only slight and I could more easily deny it. In fact, I felt a kind of nausea at the notion of a dying woman choosing what to put in a box for me.

Nevertheless, there was no doubt that it forced me to think of Susannah. Growing up, I could hardly have thought of her less, wanting Charlotte to be my only mother. I was always furious if anyone referred to her as
35   my stepmother. However, Charlotte herself would try to calm me by pointing out that, whether I liked it or not, that was exactly what she was.

After Charlotte died, the hardest thing I had to do was go back into our old home. For a whole month, I was obliged to go there day after day until every bit of furniture, every object, every book and picture, every piece of clothing, every last curtain and cushion was sorted out and ready to be collected by all manner of people. This
40   was, of course, how I found the box, even though I very nearly missed it. My attention might not have been caught if it had not been for an odd-looking pink label attached to the parcel. On the label, written in ink which had faded but which you could
45   still read, was my own name – *'For my darling Catherine Hope, in the future'*.

Grammar | preparatory *it*

7 **a** Read the pairs of sentences below. Which sentence in each pair sounds clearer? Why?

1 a It was clear that they were relieved when I showed little interest in the box.

 b That they were relieved when I showed little interest in the box was clear.

2 a It was exciting to find the box at last.

 b To find the box at last was exciting.

3 a It was hard going back into our old home.

 b Going back into our old home was hard.

b Write the headings below in the correct place (A–C) in the Active Grammar box.

- The subject is an *-ing* form
- The subject is an infinitive expression
- The subject is a clause

Active grammar

We usually prefer to start a sentence with a preparatory *it* when:

A _____

1 *It was clear that* **they were relieved** *when I showed little interest in the box.*

2 *It seemed that* **she was perfectly beautiful,** *perfectly good and perfectly happy.*

B _____

3 *It was exciting* **to find** *the box at last.*

4 *It was important* **to introduce** *the box at the right time.*

C _____

5 *It was hard* **going back** *into our old home.*

6 *It was curious* **seeing** *how nervous they were.*

---

see Reference page 89

8 Make logical, complete sentences.

1 It's interesting
2 It's clear
3 It's no use
4 It was good of you
5 It seemed
6 It was a pleasure
7 It's worth
8 It's my intention

a to talk to her yesterday.
b to help me sort out all my photos.
c that if you read a lot, your reading skills will improve.
d getting books out of the library instead of buying them all.
e that every time I started reading in bed, I fell asleep.
f to talk about books you've read.
g to write a family tree of my whole family.
h trying to remember all that.

9 **a** Complete the statements below to make them true for you.

1 It's exciting ...
2 It's worth ...
3 It's my intention to ...
4 It's clear ...
5 It's good to ...
6 It seems that ...

b Work in pairs. Compare and discuss your statements.

Speaking

10 **a** ⊕ 2.10 Listen to someone talking about *The Memory Box* and what she thought of it. Was she generally positive or negative?

b Think of a book you've read (or a film you've seen). Make notes on ...

- the basic plot
- things you liked about it
- how it made you feel
- any criticisms you had.

c Work in small groups. Take turns to tell each other about the book (or film) you chose. Describe the plot, things you liked, how it made you feel and any criticisms you have.

11 **a** ⊕ 2.11 Listen to two students talking about reading. Look at the Lifelong learning box and answer the questions.

b Work in pairs and discuss the questions.

1 How far do you agree with what the two students were talking about?

2 What strategies have you used/would you like to use to improve your reading?

3 What kind of books do you enjoy most?

Extended reading

1 What three aspects of your English can you improve by reading a lot?

2 Why do students sometimes find extended reading in English frustrating?

3 How can you increase the speed of your reading?

4 Why is it sometimes a good idea to time yourself when you read something?

Lifelong learning

---

1 **a** Match the <u>underlined</u> expressions (1–8) with the meanings (a–h).

1 He's a bit of <u>a cold fish</u>.
2 She's <u>as hard as nails</u>.
3 He's <u>a pain in the neck</u>.
4 Her <u>heart's in the right place</u>.
5 He's <u>an awkward customer</u>.
6 She's <u>a real know-all</u>.
7 He's <u>a high-flyer</u>.
8 She's a bit of <u>a loner</u>.

a a very kind person who has the right feelings about something important
b very annoying, a nuisance
c someone who behaves as if they know everything
d someone who is extremely successful in their job/school
e someone who prefers to be on their own
f unfriendly person who seems to have no strong feelings
g a difficult person to deal with
h very tough or not caring about the effects of your actions on other people

b Match the pictures (A–E) with expressions from exercise 1a.

2 Cover exercise 1a. Then complete the sentences below.

1 She loved answering all the questions in class. She thought she was so clever. She was a real _____ .
2 She didn't like going out with friends and she spent most of the time at home in her room on the computer or reading. She was a bit of a _____ really.
3 They say he'll be a partner of the firm by the time he's 30. He's a real _____ .
4 I wish Caroline would stop coming into my room and borrowing my clothes. She's a pain _____ .
5 Brian's been asking about getting an increase in his salary. Will you talk to him about it? On the subject of money he's a bit of an _____ .
6 I know Steve is a bit loud and insensitive at times but honestly, his heart's _____ .
7 She had to go out to work from the age of 15 and has had quite a difficult life. As a result she's as hard _____ .
8 He never seemed to get excited about anything. All in all, he was a bit of a cold _____ .

3 **a** Think about people you know who you could describe with five of the expressions from exercise 1a.

b Work in small groups and take turns to describe the people you know. Say how you know them and what they are like. The other students should say which expression from exercise 1a is appropriate for each person.

4 Work in pairs and discuss the questions.

1 Which of the expressions do you have in your language?
2 Do you have expressions which are different but contain the same idea?

87

Can do give your opinions and justify your choices

A ***time capsule*** is a collection of things which are put in a box and buried underground.

They are usually intended as a method of communication with future people and to help historians of the future to understand about life during the time the capsule was made.

Objects which are put in a time capsule aim to show as much as possible about life at that time, for example, a newspaper, a coin, a photo, some clothes, a piece of technology, etc.

Time capsules are often buried to coincide with a public event, like the opening of a new building or a significant date, like 1st Jan 2000.

Time Capsule

Buried by George Howard

Chairman of

The British Broadcasting Corporation

on 17th November 1982,

not to be opened until 3982.

1 Read the information about time capsules above. What are they intended for and what do people put in them?

2 **a** 2.12 Listen to two people discussing what to put in a time capsule and answer the questions.

1 How many things do they want to put in the time capsule?

2 What two things in the photos (A–E) have they decided on so far? Why?

b Listen again and complete the sentences from the How to... box with *so that*, *since*, *because*, *to*, *as* and *in order to*.

How to... justify your choices

I think we should include a globe _____ they can see what the world looked like.

We should include a globe _____ , in 100 years' time, the world might look very different.

Jeans would be good _____ most people nowadays own at least one pair of jeans.

How about including a photo album _____ that could show someone's whole life?

In my opinion, we should include some typical clothes _____ show something about daily life.

Why don't we include a newspaper _____ show what was in the news?

3 **a** Work in small groups and choose five things to put in a time capsule. Give reasons to justify each of your ideas.

b Explain your choices to other groups. Which group do you think came up with the best idea? Why?

used to, be used to, get used to, would

We use *used to* (+ infinitive) for repeated actions and states in the past which don't happen now.

I **used to catch** the bus to work but now I go by bike.

I **used to have** blond hair.

She **didn't use to be** nearly so ambitious.

Did you **use to enjoy** travelling for your job?

! In negative and question forms, *use* is the infinitive form and does not finish with a *d*.

~~Did you used to have blond hair?~~

We use *would* (+ infinitive) for repeated actions (but NOT states) in the past which don't happen now.

When we were little, we **would dress up** and pretend to be kings and queens.

We **used to live** in Manchester.

(NOT ~~We would live in Manchester.~~)

We use *get used to* (+ *-ing*/noun) when we have become accustomed to a new situation (things are now familiar and easy). Different tenses are possible.

We**'re getting used to living** in a small village in the country, but it's still a little strange.

I'm sure she**'ll get used to the language** very quickly.

We use *be used to* (+ *-ing* form/noun) to say when we have become accustomed to a new situation (and things are now familiar and easy).

She's **used to being** her own boss.

I was **used to the warm climate** when I lived in Spain.

With *be*/*get used to*, the spelling is always with a *d*.

Wishes and regrets

To talk about wishes, regrets and things that didn't happen, we can use:

wish/*if only* + Past Perfect

I **wish I'd travelled** more when I was young.

If only I'd booked tickets two weeks ago.

regret + clause/*regret* + *-ing* form:

I **regret that I didn't tell** her how I felt.

I **regret not studying** harder when I was at school.

Third Conditional: *if* + Past Perfect + *would*/*could have* + past participle

I **would have invited** her to the party **if I'd seen** her.

If I'd thought of it before, I **could have booked** a table.

When we use *I wish*/*If only* + Past Perfect and Third Conditional sentences, *I had* is often shortened to *I'd*.

When we use Third Conditional sentences, *would have* is often shortened to *would've*.

To talk about plans that didn't come true, we can use:

was/*were going to* + infinitive

I **was going to** go but in the end, I was too busy.

would have + past participle

I **would've liked** to train to be a doctor.

Preparatory *it*

Sometimes the subject of a sentence is too long and complicated to sound natural at the beginning of the sentence. In this case, we usually prefer to start a sentence with a preparatory *it*. This can happen when:

... the subject is a clause

It's surprising <u>that so many people throw away perfectly good food</u>.

(Possible but less good: *That so many people throw away perfectly good food is surprising*.)

... the subject is an *-ing* form

It's worth <u>going to the doctor as soon as you feel unwell</u>.

... the subject is an infinitive expression

It's important <u>to listen carefully to all the instructions</u>.

There are some common fixed expressions which use preparatory *it*, for example: *It's no good ...*, *It's no use ...*, *It's worth ...*, *It seems that ...*

It's no good telling her anything – she's so stubborn.

It seems that everyone is booking expensive holidays at the moment.

Key vocabulary

Memory

nostalgic   memorable   forgetful   your memory   vivid memory   vague memory   memento   souvenir   mnemonic   reminisce   take me back   remind   remember   jog your memory   on the tip of my tongue

Appearance

Hair: straight   curly   wavy   going a bit bald   mousy   spiky   dyed

Face: wrinkles   clean-shaven   chubby   round   beard

Build: muscular   stocky   a bit overweight   fat   slim   skinny

General: good-looking   scruffy   elegant   tanned

Feelings

confused   suspicious   uneasy   curious   annoyed   excited   uninterested   sceptical   optimistic   shocked   relieved

Idioms to describe people

a cold fish   as hard as nails   a pain in the neck   (someone's) heart is in the right place   an awkward customer   a real know-all   a high-flyer   a bit of a loner

Listen to the explanations and vocabulary.

ACTIVEBOOK

see Writing bank page 155

1 Complete the text below with *used to* or *get used to* and the correct form of a verb from the box.

> have   be   finish   ~~teach~~   not understand

I recently went back to Cairo where I
(1) *used to teach* English as a foreign language in the early 1980s. A lot had changed. The area where I lived (2) _____ very quiet but it's much busier now. There are more modern buildings and bigger roads. I remember when I first arrived that it took a while to (3) _____ most of the shop signs, as they were in Arabic. Now a lot of them are in English too. Every evening we (4) _____ our classes at 9.30 p.m. and then all go out to a nearby club which had a great disco. I looked for the club but sadly it had gone. Cairo is a marvellous place and I really missed it when I came back to Britain. It took me ages to (5) _____ the different lifestyle.

2 Choose the correct words in *italics*.

1 I wish I *reminded/'d reminded* her to bring the photos.
2 I regret *to dye/dyeing* my hair. It looks awful.
3 I *am going/was going* to walk but it started raining.
4 If I'd known you were coming, I *'d have brought/'ve brought* that book to give you.
5 I regret that I *hadn't brought/didn't bring* back any souvenirs from my trip to Thailand.
6 I *could've phoned/could phone* you if I'd had your number.
7 I *would like/would've liked* to go to the theatre but we didn't have enough money.
8 If only I *wasn't/hadn't been* so suspicious when she told me what happened.

3 Rewrite the sentences starting with *It* so that the meaning stays the same.

1 To talk to you today was great.
  It …
2 That what we need is for someone to take charge is clear.
  It …
3 Finding out the name of the person you need to talk to is worth it.
  It …
4 Using mnemonics really helps me remember things, it seems.
  It …
5 Complaining to me about it is no use.
  It …
6 To give me your ticket was really kind of you.
  It …
7 To take part in a marathon for charity is my ambition.
  It …
8 That you don't want to go skiing is surprising.
  It …

4 Complete the sentences below with a word from the box. Three of the words cannot be used.

> muscular   vivid   scruffy   confused   bald
> sceptical   relieved   curious   clean-shaven
> vague   nostalgic

1 We were all very _____ when she arrived home safely at midnight.
2 What's happened to your beard? I've never seen you _____ before.
3 I've got really _____ memories of my childhood. I can remember every detail.
4 Monica is a very _____ person. She never believes anything people tell her.
5 Jim has become quite _____ in his arms and legs since he started going to the gym.
6 Looking through my old photo albums has made me feel really _____ .
7 You can't go to the interview in those _____ clothes. You need to look smart.
8 My father said I should go to university, but my brother told me it was a waste of time, so I was quite _____ about what to do.

5 Choose the correct words in *italics*.

1 Oh! I can't quite remember his surname, but it's on the *tip/top* of my tongue.
2 My sister was always a *bit/part* of a loner. Even as a child, she never seemed very interested in having friends.
3 My little brother is a real *ache/pain* in the neck. He keeps coming into my room and disturbing me when I'm trying to study.
4 This photo really *puts/takes* me back to when I was revising for my exams at school.
5 He's a kind person and his heart is in the *right/correct* place, even though he's a bit rude sometimes.
6 She'll be successful in business because she doesn't care about people's feelings. In fact, she's as *cold/hard* as nails.
7 They showed her photos to try to *jog/jab* her memory about what she was doing that day.
8 Tom seems to find fault with everything people do – everything is wrong. He's a really awkward *consumer/customer*.

Lead-in

1 Work in pairs and discuss the questions.

1 What can you see in each photo?
2 In what ways do you think they represent 'excess'?
3 In what other ways might people's lifestyles be described as 'excessive'?

2 **a** Work in pairs and discuss the meaning of the <u>underlined</u> words and phrases below.

1 When was the last time you bought something really <u>extravagant</u>?
2 Do you think spending €100 on one meal is <u>excessive</u>?
3 If you could take one <u>luxury</u> to a 'desert island', what would it be?
4 Do you ever order <u>extra-large</u> portions in restaurants?
5 Do you think you were <u>spoilt</u> as a child? Why/Why not?
6 When was the last time you bought something you thought was <u>overpriced</u>?
7 Do you think the idea of having a 'self-cleaning' house in the near future is <u>far-fetched</u>?
8 Do you know anyone who would go on a <u>spending spree</u> to cheer him/herself up?

b Work in pairs. Ask and answer the questions from exercise 2a. How many of your answers are similar?

7.1 Food for thought

| Grammar | quantifiers with countable and uncountable nouns |
| Can do | describe food and different attitudes to food |

Reading

1 Work in pairs. Look at the photo below and discuss the questions.

1 How does the picture make you feel?
2 Do you eat a lot of fast food? Why/Why not?
3 Do you think that fast food is healthy? Why/Why not?

2 a Read the article and answer the questions.

1 How many experiments are mentioned?
2 Did the experiments produce similar or different results?

b Explain what each phrase (1–6) means.

1 a considerably larger portion (line 15)
2 consume a lot of fat (line 20)
3 Weight gain was only one of the negative effects (line 30)
4 a fast-forward picture of your life (line 36)
5 possible short-term effects (line 42)
6 cause more harm (line 55)

c Work in pairs. Discuss the questions.

1 What do you think the experiments proved?
2 What implications do you think the experiments have for you, or anyone else you know?

SUPER SIZE ME

Fast food, otherwise known as junk food, is a huge passion for a large number of people across the Western world. Millions of adults and children feel they cannot live without hamburgers and chips. But what would
5 happen if you ate lots of junk food, every day? Would it seriously damage your health? These were the questions which led Morgan Spurlock, an independent film-maker, to do a radical experiment, which he made into a documentary film entitled *Super Size Me*.

10 The main basis of his experiment was that Spurlock promised to eat three McDonald's meals a day, every day, for a month. He could only eat food from McDonald's and every time an employee asked if he would like to 'super size' the meal, he had to agree. 'Super sizing' refers to the
15 fact that with this type of meal you get a considerably larger portion of everything. Instead of the normal burger, fries and a drink, you get an extra-large burger, extra-large fries and an extra-large drink for only a very small price increase.

Spurlock knew that by eating three McDonald's meals a day,
20 he would consume a lot of fat and a great deal of salt and sugar in each meal – much more than he needed. Before he started, three doctors certified that Spurlock weighed about 84kg and was in good health. Although both Spurlock and his doctors knew he would put on a bit of weight, and that
25 this diet was unhealthy, none of them were quite prepared for just how unhealthy it turned out to be. The changes in his body were horrifying. In the first week, he put on 4.5 kilos and by the end of the thirty days he had gained nearly 14 kilos, bringing his total weight to a massive 98kg.

30 Weight gain was only one of the negative effects, however. When all three doctors saw the severe damage to his liver, they all recommended stopping the experiment after 20 days. Spurlock continued to follow the diet, however, because he wanted to show people what this kind of diet
35 can do to you. Watching the film, you begin to realise that it could be a fast-forward picture of your life: in 30 days you get to see what could happen to you over 20 or 30 years of overconsumption. You're on a path to many long-term problems like heart disease, liver failure, high blood pressure,
40 diabetes, depression and more.

In another experiment, some scientists have also started to look at the possible short-term effects of a high-fat diet. Biological experts at Oxford University carried out an experiment on rats, comparing two groups of rats over ten
45 days; one group was fed a diet containing a little fat (about 7.5%) and the other a high-fat diet (with about 55% fat). The experiment produced some shocking results. Firstly, after just a few days, the rats' ability to exercise significantly decreased; they were less able to use oxygen to make the
50 energy needed to run around. Secondly, and perhaps even more appalling, after nine days the rats' short-term memory was damaged and they became less mentally alert; they took longer to complete a maze and made many more mistakes in the process than the rats on the low-fat diet.

55 Junk food is exactly what it says it is – junk. It will cause more harm to your body and your brain than good, both in the long and short term. That is the message that experiments like Spurlock's and the team at Oxford University are suggesting. Spurlock says that he hopes that the film
60 encourages people to take better care of themselves. He says, 'I'd love people to walk out of the movie and say, "Next time I'm not going to 'super size'. Maybe I'm not going to have any junk food at all. I'm going to sit down and eat dinner with my kids, with the TV off, so that we can
65 eat healthy food, talk about what we're eating and have a relationship with each other."' Food for thought indeed.

Grammar | quantifiers

3 Look at the <u>underlined</u> nouns in the examples (a–d) below and answer the questions.

1 Which are countable and which are uncountable?
2 What is the difference in meaning between *coffee* in sentences c and d?
3 Can you think of …
 • three more countable nouns
 • three more uncountable nouns
 • three more nouns that can be countable and uncountable.

a He ate three McDonald's <u>meals</u> a day, every day, for a month.
b He could only eat <u>food</u> from McDonald's.
c I'll have sausage, beans and a black <u>coffee</u>, please.
d If I drink <u>coffee</u> in the evenings, I can't sleep properly.

4 a Look at the quantifiers in **bold** in the Active grammar box and match them with the rules (A–C).

Active grammar

*Junk food is a huge passion for **a large number of** people.*

*He would consume **a lot of** fat and **a great deal of** salt and sugar.*

*One group of rats was fed a diet containing **a little** fat.*

***Some** scientists have started to look at the possible short-term effects.*

*You're on a path to **many** long-term problems.*

*His doctors knew he would put on **a bit of** weight.*

*After just **a few** days, the rats' ability to exercise significantly decreased.*

*What would happen if you ate **lots of** junk food every day?*

*I've decided not to eat **much** junk food any more.*

*The film gives us **a piece of** advice we should all follow.*

*Maybe I'm not going to have **any** junk food at all.*

A Used with countable nouns: _____, _____, _____

B Used with uncountable nouns: _____, _____, _____, _____, _____

C Used with both countable and uncountable nouns: *some, any, a lot of, lots of*

---

see Reference page 103

b Look again at the quantifiers in **bold** from the Active grammar box. Which group (a–c) does each quantifier belong to?

a greater quantity *a large number of*
b lesser quantity
c unspecified quantity.

c What is the difference between *few/a few* and *little/a little* in the sentences (1–4) below?

1 <u>Few</u> people think about the long-term effects of junk food.
2 <u>A few</u> friends of mine have decided not to eat junk food anymore.
3 There was <u>little</u> food and many people were hungry.
4 There is <u>a little</u> soup left if you'd like it.

5 Choose the correct quantifier in *italics*.

1 You haven't eaten *many/much* fries.
2 I only have *a few/a little* sugar in my coffee nowadays.
3 There isn't *much/a few* traffic in the city centre today.
4 She gave me a *piece/some* of paper with her address written on it.
5 He gave me *a few/some* really good advice.
6 I've got *lots/many* of bags to carry. Can you help me?
7 He's very lazy. He spends *a great deal of/a large number of* time doing nothing.
8 I'll just have one *bit/much* of toast, please.
9 There were only *a few/a little* shops still open when I went out.
10 I've spent a *much/lot* of time on this meal.

6 a Find the mistakes in six of the sentences and correct them.

1 Do you spend lot of time doing exercise?
2 How many sugar do you have in your coffee?
3 Have you given anyone a piece of good advice recently?
4 When was the last time you had bit of cake?
5 How many fruit do you usually eat every day?
6 How often do you use the Internet to get some information?
7 Do you keep a large number of money in your wallet?
8 When did you last buy a few new furniture?

b Work in pairs. Ask and answer the questions from exercise 6a.

Vocabulary | food and cooking

7 **a** Put the words from the box into the correct place in the word map.

> saucepan oven sweet bake cooker
> beef scramble bitter frying pan
> salty fry peach roast cabbage
> boil sour wooden spoon grill
> savoury parsley plate

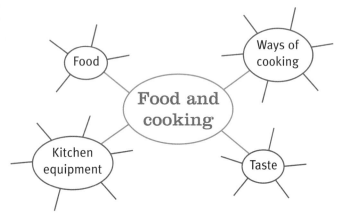

b What is the difference between the pairs/groups of words below?

1 a cook/a cooker
2 a vegetable/a vegetarian
3 a recipe/a dish
4 rare/raw
5 to stir/to beat
6 to slice/to chop/to grate

c Work in pairs and add at least two more words to each group in the word map.

8 **a** Choose the correct words in *italics*.

1 Sushi is a Japanese dish made with *raw/rare* fish.
2 *Beat/Stir* the mixture slowly every five minutes.
3 Ugh! This soup is much too *savoury/salty*.
4 First, you *slice/chop* the onion into cubes.
5 I don't eat many cakes and biscuits. I find them too *sweet/sour*.
6 Fill a large saucepan with water and *bake/boil* the pasta for ten minutes.
7 Macaroni cheese is my favourite *dish/plate*.
8 The *cook/cooker* has broken. I need to buy a new one.
9 In Britain at Christmas, it's traditional to *bake/roast* a turkey in the oven.
10 Oh no! I've put chicken in the soup and Diane is a *vegetarian/vegetable*.

Pronunciation | intonation: questions

9 ⊕ 2.13 Listen to two friends talking about a traditional meal. Do you think you would enjoy this meal?

10 **a** ⊕ 2.14 When we ask a question, we could be asking for information we don't know or checking information we think we already know. Listen to the questions (1–4) and decide which type they are. How can you tell?

1 What are you going to make?
2 How is it different from normal pancakes?
3 Oh, so, it's a savoury pancake?
4 Do you put it in the oven?

b Listen again and repeat the questions.

Speaking

11 Listen to the conversation again and complete the sentences from the How to... box using the words from the box below.

> careful sure because sounds first
> important then mean finally

How to... give and check instructions

Use sequence words	_____ , you make a pancake mix.
	_____ , you fry lots of pancakes.
	_____ , you bake it in the oven.
Give detailed instructions/ suggestions	**You must make** _____ it's not too thick.
	You should be _____ not to put too much spinach mix in one layer.
	The _____ **thing is** not to overcook it at this point.
Check instructions	**Is that** _____ there are lots of layers?
	So you _____ you pour the sauce over the whole thing?
	So it _____ **like** there are quite a lot of layers?

12 **a** Prepare to talk about your favourite dish. Think about ...

• how it is prepared.
• when you usually eat it.
• why you like it.

b Work in small groups and take turns to tell each other what the dish is and how to prepare/cook it. Ask and answer questions to check you understand or to find out more.

Listening

1 Work in pairs and discuss the questions.

1 What can you see in the photos (A–E)?

2 How do you think they are connected?

2 🔘 **2.15** Listen to the radio programme and answer the questions.

1 In what order are the items in the photos mentioned?

2 What three other items are mentioned?

3 Listen again and choose the correct words in *italics*.

1 The Giacometti sculpture was sold for *$104.3million/$140.3million*.

2 We *know/don't know* the name of the person who bought the sculpture.

3 *Action Comics* issue number 1 was published in *1938/1948*.

4 Someone sold *one/six* storm trooper helmet(s) at an auction.

5 One of Marilyn Monroe's dresses was sold for over *one/two* million dollars.

6 We *know/don't know* the name of the person who bought Michael Jackson's glove.

7 The piece of Elvis Presley's hair was cut in *1958/1968*.

8 Justin Timberlake's toast was bought by *an interviewer/a fan*.

9 Someone paid *$3,500/$5,300* for Scarlett Johansson's tissue.

4 Work in small groups and discuss the questions.

1 Do you know anyone who collects things (e.g. pop memorabilia, old magazines, stamps, etc.)? What do you think of this kind of hobby?

2 Have you ever visited an online auction site or a traditional auction? What do you think of these ways of buying and selling things?

Vocabulary | verb phrases about shopping

5 What is the difference in meaning between the underlined verb phrases in each pair of sentences?

1 a Lots of people <u>bid for</u> Justin Timberlake's toast.

b That bag is very expensive. Why don't you <u>haggle for</u> it?

2 a These boots were only £30. I think I <u>got a bargain</u>.

b I'd like to buy this T-shirt, but it's slightly marked. Could I <u>get a discount</u>?

3 a You can <u>get a refund</u> within 28 days if you are not completely satisfied.

b <u>Get a receipt</u> just in case you want to take the CDs back.

4 a I'd love to get a camera but I <u>can't afford it</u> at the moment.

b It'll cost £10 to take a taxi – <u>it's not worth it</u>. Let's walk.

6 **a** Rewrite the sentences (1–8) using the correct form of the underlined verb phrases from exercise 5.

1 I would never offer to pay for a celebrity item at an auction.

2 I'm very good at finding cheap, good things when I go shopping.

3 Sometimes I ask the shop assistant for money off the real price.

4 I'd like to buy a motorbike but I haven't got enough money.

5 If a new DVD player broke after only a week I'd ask for my money back.

6 I always try and negotiate a lower price with market traders.

7 It's too expensive to pay for a taxi when you could go by bus.

8 I always keep the paper they give you when I buy something.

b Work in pairs and say which of your rewritten sentences from exercise 6a are true for you. Give details.

Grammar | passives

7 **a** Read the example sentences in the Active grammar box and answer the questions.

1 Which of the verbs in **bold** are active and which are passive?

2 Why do you think the speaker would choose to use the passive (not the active) in each case?

b Check your answers with the rules (A and B).

Active grammar

1 *An original comic book **was bought** for $1.5million.*
*Someone **bought** an original comic book for $1.5million.*

2 *One of Michael Jackson's gloves **was bought** by 36-year-old Hong Kong businessman Hoffman Ma.*
*36-year-old Hong Kong businessman Hoffman Ma **bought** one of Michael Jackson' s gloves.*

Meaning

We use the passive when we want …

A to talk about actions, events and processes when who or what causes the action, event or process is unknown or unimportant. This is often the case in writing (or more formal speech).

B to put the focus of what is important at the beginning of the sentence and need to change the sentence to do so.

Form

verb *to be* + past participle

---

see Reference page 103

8 **a** Look at audioscript 2.15 on page 170 and underline all the examples of the passive that you can find.

b Read the rule of form in the Active grammar box and complete the passive sentences below with the correct form of the verbs in brackets.

Thousands of things *are bought* (buy) on online auctions every day. (Present Simple Passive)

1 The car _____ (clean) at the moment. (Present Continuous Passive)

2 The dress _____ (find) by chance at a second-hand sale last month. (Past Simple Passive)

3 The painting _____ (display) when I arrived at the auction. (Past Continuous Passive)

4 Some items _____ (buy) at auctions recently for incredibly high prices. (Present Perfect Simple Passive)

5 She bought a comic which _____ (published) in 1938. (Past Perfect Simple Passive)

6 Ridiculously high prices _____ (pay) for completely useless items. (Future Simple Passive with *will*)

7 The new shop _____ (open) by the mayor. (future with *going to*)

8 It seems that almost anything _____ (buy). (modals in the passive, e.g. *can*)

9 Rewrite the sentences (1–7), starting with the words given, to make them into more formal written news reports. Use the passive as appropriate.

'I heard that a Canadian businessman Jim Pattison bought John Lennon's Rolls-Royce car for $2.23 million.'

John Lennon's Rolls-Royce car was bought by a Canadian businessman Jim Pattison for $2.23 million.

1 'I'm sure that people are going to pay higher prices for comic books at next month's auction.'
Comic books …

2 'I heard on the news that an anonymous buyer has bought the Giacometti sculpture *Walking Man 1*.'
The Giacometti sculpture *Walking Man 1* …

3 'They said that someone paid over $104 million for the sculpture in an auction.'
The sculpture …

4 'In the future, I think they will sell Picasso's paintings for even higher prices.'
In the future, Picasso's paintings …

5 'Apparently, in 2001, they sold the white bikini that Ursula Andress had worn in the James Bond film *Dr No*.'
In 2001, the white bikini which …

6 'The American, Robert Earl, co-founder of Planet Hollywood bought the bikini for $61,000.'
The bikini …

7 'The singer George Michael bought John Lennon's piano, on which he had composed the song *Imagine*.'
John Lennon's piano, on which the song *Imagine* …

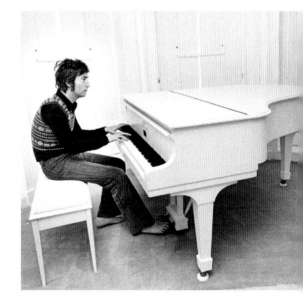

Speaking

10 Work in pairs. What would you do in each of the situations (1–4)? Why?

1 You have just been served a meal in a restaurant which is cold and very late to arrive.

2 You've ordered something online and when it arrives, you find it's faulty.

3 Your new washing machine is broken and some wet clothes are stuck inside it.

4 You have just arrived at your hotel on holiday. The brochure said there was a swimming pool, but it hasn't been finished.

11 ● 2.16 Listen to the dialogue and answer the questions.

1 Which of the situations from exercise 10 is it?

2 How does the customer feel?

3 What solution is offered?

12 Listen again and complete the How to... box.

> ### How to... complain about goods and services
>
> | Explain the problem | I'd just like to _____ about how long it took to deliver. |
> | | You _____ that delivery would be within three days but in the end, I waited two weeks. |
> | Apologise | Oh, I'm _____ sorry about that. |
> | | I can only _____ my apologies for that. |
> | | I do _____ for that. |
> | Request some action | I'm not prepared to accept _____ goods. |
> | | I'd be _____ if you could send a replacement. |
> | Offer a solution | We'll send someone to pick up the _____ TV as soon as possible. |
> | | I'll send out a _____ . |
> | | I can _____ you that we'll definitely stick to the appointment. |

Pronunciation | stress: emphasis (2)

13 ● 2.17 When we want to emphasise what we're saying, we can put more stress on particular words and use a higher range of intonation. Look at the underlined part of the conversation in audioscript 2.16 on page 171 and listen to two versions. What different effect does each version have on the listener? Why?

14 Work in pairs. Choose one of the situations in exercise 10 and take turns to roleplay.

Student A: explain a problem.

Student B: try to offer a solution.

Reading

1 Work in pairs and discuss the questions.

1 Do you have any pets? Did you use to have any pets when you were a child? If so, which ones? If not, why not?

2 What do you think are the main reasons why people keep pets? Do you think it is a good idea for children to have pets? Why/Why not?

3 What can you see in the photos?

2 Read the article quickly. Which of the things in the photos are mentioned?

PET HEAVEN?

In some parts of Europe and the US, many pet owners see their cat or dog as a member of the family. In the UK, owners spend an amazing £4 billion annually on keeping their pets fit, well and entertained. In one survey, it was found that up to 40% of owners said they bought gifts for their pets, including Christmas and birthday presents. Owners happily pamper their pets with increasingly lavish lifestyles, including toys, furniture, accessories, 'gourmet' food and other treats. There are also pet psychologists for those with problems, pet passports for those who want to travel and a whole range of services on offer. There are hundreds of retail outlets offering owners a vast array of products. But many pets have everything they could ever ask for (or bark for?). The question for many owners now is: what do you give to the pet that has everything? We asked some owners what their pet got for his or her last birthday …

Marion Dowdeswell and 'Pixie': Marion lives on her own in Edinburgh, UK, with her dog, Pixie. 'Pixie really is my best friend,' says Marion. 'He's such a lovely dog and my constant companion. I'd be lost without him, so I think I just treat him like I'd treat anyone I love.' For his last birthday, Marion bought Pixie a bed costing over £300. She admits that it was too much money to spend on an animal. 'I know it's a bit over-the-top,' she says, 'but he does love it!' Marion says she doesn't only indulge him on his birthday. Last week, she got a set of 'doggie boots' to keep Pixie's paws warm and stop him from slipping on wet ground. 'Probably a luxury, but why not occasionally?'

Sylvia and Brad Phillips and family and 'Beauty': The Phillips family from California, US, acquired Beauty three years ago when some friends emigrated. 'We didn't really know much about dogs then, and at first we didn't know how it would work out,' says Sylvia. 'But right from the start, she just made our family complete and the kids adore her. They're always finding new things to buy for her. She probably is spoilt but it's fun.' Last year, they got her a present they were really excited about: a necklace made of fake pearls which cost about $70. 'She doesn't really wear it because it seems to irritate her, but we took some great photos!' says Sylvia.

Claudette and Pierre Leroi and 'Mignon': Claudette and Pierre live in Paris with their Yorkshire terrier, Mignon. Because Mignon is a long-haired dog, Claudette says that it's necessary to take her to the hairdresser's regularly. 'I take her to the beauty parlour once a week to have her fur done. I don't think it's a luxury really.' Mignon has it washed and brushed and sometimes cut and even curled. On special occasions, like her last birthday, for example, Mignon had the fur from the top of the head pulled back and tied as a ponytail, while the rest of her fur was cut short. 'She looked so cute – like a little Barbie doll,' says Claudette. She gets the dog anaesthetised to do these things so that she stands still for long enough, but Claudette thinks it's worth it.

So, is this pet indulgence gone mad? Or is it simply spoiling a valued member of the family?

3 **a** Read the first paragraph again and write true (T), false (F) or not given (NG).

1 British owners spend £4 billion on their pets every year. ☐
2 One quarter of owners buy their pets presents. ☐
3 More pets than before have psychological problems. ☐
4 Some owners have a problem knowing what to buy for their pets. ☐

b Read the rest of the article. Which of the following apply to which pet (or none of them)?

1 his/her owner buys him/her clothes
2 his/her owner wants to make him/her look nice
3 he/she provides friendly company for his/her owner
4 his/her owner takes him/her on expensive holidays
5 his/her owner knows he/she is overindulgent
6 his/her owner takes him/her to the hairdresser
7 his/her owner buys him/her toys and dolls
8 his/her owner was ignorant about pets initially

4 Work in pairs and discuss these questions.

1 Do you think pets should be treated like a member of the family?
2 In general, what is the attitude to pets in your country?

Grammar | *have/get something done*

5 **a** Complete the examples (1–3) in the Active grammar box with *had*, *have* and *gets*. Check your answers with the article.

Active grammar

1 *I take her to the beauty parlour to _____ her fur done.*
2 *On her last birthday, Mignon _____ the fur from the top of the head pulled back and tied as a ponytail.*
3 *She _____ the dog anaesthetised so that she stands still at the hairdresser's.*

Form: *have* (or *get*) + object + _____

Meaning

A This structure can be used to talk about arranging for something to be done by somebody else.
B We can also use this structure with *have* or *get*, to talk about things that happen to us.
C and with *get* only (not *have*), to mean 'finish doing something'.

4 *I **had my bag stolen** on my way home from work.*
5 *She **got her fingers caught** in the car door.*
6 *As soon as I **get this essay written**, I'll take the dog out.*

b Complete the rule of form with the correct part of speech.

c Read rule A. In examples 1–3, was each of the things done by the dog's owner or the hairdresser?

d Read rules B and C. Then match each rule with examples 4–6.

see Reference page 103

6 Find the mistakes in six of the sentences and correct them.

1 I've never had my hair dye.
2 I've had my house broken into several times.
3 I never my house have decorated – I do it myself.
4 I haven't had my eyes testing for ages.
5 I've got a lot of things to get doing by this weekend.
6 I have dry-cleaned some of my clothes every month.
7 I really need to have my hair cut soon.
8 I'd like to get my photo took by a professional photographer.

7 Work in small groups. Discuss the questions.

1 Are any of the sentences from exercise 6 true for you? Tell another student and change the others so that they are true.

It's true I haven't had my eyes tested for ages. I think I should have it done soon because my eyes hurt when I use a computer.

2 What things do you have done regularly? Why? What things can you have done in your neighbourhood?

I have my car cleaned inside and out once a month! I know it's extravagant but I hate doing it myself.

HAND CAR WASH

Vocabulary | excess

8 **a** Look at the sentences below. What is the difference in meaning between the underlined words?

Having her hair done is a necessity not a luxury.

b Work in pairs and work out the meaning of the underlined words.

1 It's a bit over-the-top to spend £300 on a bed for a dog.

2 I think it's ridiculous to give gourmet food to dogs, as they don't appreciate it.

3 He has a lavish lifestyle with fast cars, expensive restaurants and numerous holidays.

4 She's a spoilt child whose parents give her anything she wants.

5 Have another piece of cake. Go on – you can indulge yourself once in a while!

6 I didn't feel well so I stayed in and pampered myself with food and lots of DVDs.

7 My grandmother used to spoil me all the time and buy me anything I asked for.

8 He treated me to the whole meal – I didn't pay anything.

9 **a** Choose the correct words in *italics*.

1 If I had a dog, I would *indulge/gourmet* him all the time with presents.

2 I think that sun cream is a complete *necessity/over-the-top* when you go on holiday.

3 I'm an only child, but luckily my parents didn't *spoil/treat* me at all.

4 Once in a while, it's great to go out for a *pamper/gourmet* meal in a top restaurant.

5 I like buying completely *indulge/over-the-top* presents for my friends on their birthdays.

6 On my last birthday, my friends *treated/pampered* me to a meal in an expensive restaurant.

7 After a stressful period like doing exams, I like to *pamper/gourmet* myself by having a massage.

8 I'm not interested in people who try to impress you with their *treated/lavish* lifestyles.

9 Having air-conditioning in your car is a *pamper/luxury* – it's expensive and you don't really need it.

10 I hate sitting in restaurants near *spoilt/lavish* children who don't behave properly.

b Work in pairs. Take turns to explain which of the sentences from exercise 9a are true for you.

Speaking

10 **a** Work in pairs. Read the Lifelong learning box and complete the three examples.

b Work in pairs and discuss the questions.

1 How do you feel about writing a 'study timetable'?

2 Do you ever set targets for yourself? Why/Why not?

3 What kind of treats and rewards do you think work best for you?

Timetables, targets and treats

! When you are studying, it is good to keep yourself focused and motivated by …

1 writing a 'study timetable', for example: _____

2 setting targets, for example: _____

3 giving yourself treats and rewards, for example: _____

Lifelong learning

11 Work in pairs and do the quiz. How similar or different were your and your partner's answers? Tell other students.

Luxury or necessity?
What can't you live without?

1 How often do you give yourself rewards for studying/working hard?
(a) every week **(b)** once in a while **(c)** never

2 Which of these things do you think is either an absolute necessity or a complete luxury?
(a) a television **(b)** a home computer **(c)** a microwave
(d) a mobile phone **(e)** air conditioning in your car

3 How often would you like to … ?
(a) buy a new bag **(b)** have a holiday **(c)** have a massage
(d) go out for dinner

4 When do you expect to receive presents?
(a) on your birthday **(b)** once in a while as a surprise
(c) on a regular basis
Do you like people spending a little or a lot of money on a present for you?
What kinds of presents do you most like getting?

5 When you go out to a restaurant, which would you prefer?
(a) tap water **(b)** bottled water **(c)** a hamburger **(d)** a steak
(e) to pay for yourself **(f)** the other person to pay for you

6 Which of these things do you prefer to either have done or do yourself?
(a) cut your hair **(b)** walk your dog **(c)** wash your car
(d) clean your house **(e)** decorate your house

1 a 🔵 2.18 Listen and match the people with items a–c below.

a Someone annoying

b Something to be proud of

c Something embarrassing

b Listen again and make brief notes about each story.

c Work in pairs. Take turns to retell each story.

2 a Look at audioscript 2.18 on page 171 and find a word to match each definition below.

1 a not usual or normal – *unusual*

   b very big

   c describing a way of speaking that sounds uninterested because it's on one note

2 a to sleep more than you had intended

   b to think or guess something is less than it is

   c a former employer

3 a to go back to studying again and learn new skills

   b to be able to speak two languages equally well

   c describing a company that has offices, factories, etc. in many different countries

b Look at the words from exercise 2a and write the appropriate prefixes in the table.

Prefixes	Meanings	Examples
mono	one/single	
	twice/two/every two	
	many	
	more than	
	less than	
	former	
	again	
	very	
	not	

c Read the rule below about hyphens. Then write one more example of your own for each prefix from the table in exercise 2b, e.g. *monolingual*.

> **Hyphens:** We use hyphens (-) with some prefixes, including *extra-* and *ex-*. Check in a dictionary if you are unsure.

3 a Complete the sentences (1–8) with the most appropriate word from the box below. Not all the words can be used.

> monologue monolingual bicycle biannual
> multimedia multi-purpose overtired
> overworked undercooked underpaid
> ex-girlfriend ex-husband reheat rewrite
> extra-small extra-strong uncomfortable
> unnecessary

I always feel slightly *uncomfortable* and silly wearing a hat.

1 The company holds a big _____ conference, so the next one will be in six months' time.

2 When you go camping, what you need is a good _____ knife that does everything.

3 You'll need to use some _____ packaging so that it doesn't get torn in the post.

4 Be careful that the food is hot all the way through and never eat _____ meat.

5 I think nurses are _____ especially considering the amount they get paid.

6 I've only studied English in my own country where the classes are all _____ .

7 The teacher has asked me to _____ my essay because I misunderstood the question the first time.

8 I still get on well with my _____ , even though I don't see her much nowadays.

b Listen and check your answers.

4 a Prepare a story using one of the ideas from exercise 1a. Use as many of the words from exercises 2a and 3a as you can.

b Work in pairs. Take turns to tell your stories. Ask questions to find out more information.

1 **a** Work in pairs. Look at the photos and add as many words as you can to each of the word maps below.

b Compare your word maps with other students.

clothes shop/ shoe shop

fitting room

hairdresser

scissors

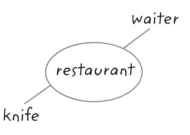

waiter

restaurant

knife

2 Which of the sentences (1–11) would you expect to hear in …

a a clothes/shoe shop   **b** a hairdresser's?   **c** a restaurant

1 I'd like to try these on, please.
2 I'll have the grilled tuna, please.
3 Just a cut and blow-dry?
4 I've got black in size 38, but not in 39.
5 Rare, please.
6 I'd also like some highlights done.
7 A bottle of the house red, please.
8 They look really nice on you. How do they feel?
9 I'd like to book an appointment.
10 We're offering all customers an Indian head massage.
11 We booked a table for two in the name of Morrison.

3 **a** Prepare to roleplay a situation from exercise 2. Divide into groups: (A) customers and (B) waiters/assistants. Follow the instructions below and think about vocabulary you may need and which questions to ask. Decide which are real questions and which you need for checking information.

Group A: Think of two problems to complain about and what action you want to request.

Group B: Think about which problems the customer may complain about, what action you can offer and how you could apologise.

b Work in A/B pairs and do your roleplay. Did you communicate your ideas clearly? Was the problem solved successfully?

Quantifiers

Countable nouns are words like *banana*, *hotel*. They can use a singular or plural form of the verb.

Uncountable nouns are words like *food*, *information*, *equipment*. They use a singular form of the verb.

Common uncountable nouns:

accommodation, advice, behaviour, bread, equipment, food, furniture, health, information, knowledge, luggage, news, research, salt, spaghetti, traffic, travel, trouble, water, weather, work

Common nouns which can be countable or uncountable:

chicken, chocolate, coffee, egg, glass, hair, iron, paper, room, space, time, wine

We can use *a/an* and quantifiers like: *some, any, a lot of, lots of, few, a few, many, a large number of* before countable nouns.

*There are **a few potatoes** left in the cupboard.*

We can use quantifiers like: *some, any, a lot of, lots of, little, a little, much, a piece of, a bit of, a great deal of* before uncountable nouns.

*There isn't **much time** before the film starts.*

Quantifiers which mean a greater quantity: *a large number of, a great deal of, many, much, a lot of, lots of*

Quantifiers which mean a lesser quantity: *a few, a little*

Quantifiers which mean an unspecified quantity: *a bit of, a piece of, some, any*

few/a few and *little/a little*:

Few and *little* (without *a*) are usually used to talk about more negative ideas, suggesting not as many or as much as you would like.

*She's got **few friends** and is quite lonely.*

*He's got **little money** and can't afford a new car.*

A few and *a little* are usually used to talk about more positive ideas, possibly suggesting 'better than nothing' or 'more than expected'.

*I've got **a few biscuits** left. Would you like one?*

*Could I have tea with **a little milk**, please?*

Passives

We can use active constructions when the subject is the person or thing that does the action.

*I **bought** a really fantastic table at an auction.*

We can use passive constructions …

– when who or what causes the action is unknown or unimportant.

– when we want to put the focus of what is important at the beginning of the sentence and need to change the sentence to do so.

We often use passive constructions in writing or in more formal speech. The passive is common in news stories, scientific and academic writing.

*The dog **was found** three days after it went missing.*

We also use the passive when the object of the active sentence is the main focus. Use *by* to say who did the action.

*The painting **was sold** by a wealthy businessman.*

We can use the passive in any tense and with modal verbs.

Form: *be* + past participle

*We **haven't been sent** the exam results yet.*

*They **will have been told** the news by now.*

*I **was being given** a massage when the phone rang.*

have/get something done

Form: *have* (or *get*) + object + past participle

We use the structure *to have* (or *get*) something done:

– to talk about arranging for something to be done by someone else: *I **have my hair dyed** once every six months.*

– to talk about things that happen to us or to describe an 'experience': *I **had my bike stolen** last week.*

There is another use of *get* (NOT *have*) + object + past participle which is used to mean 'finish doing something': *I need to **get my homework done**.*

Key vocabulary

Food and cooking

saucepan   frying pan   wooden spoon   oven
cooker   cook   plate   dish   recipe   sweet   savoury
bitter   salty   sour   rare   raw   bake   roast
scramble   fry   grill   boil   stir   beat   slice   chop
grate   beef   cabbage   parsley   peach   vegetable
vegetarian

Verb phrases about shopping

bid for something   haggle for something
get a bargain   get a discount   get a refund
get a receipt   be able to afford something   worth it

Excess

spoil someone   indulge someone   pamper someone
treat someone   go on a spending spree   luxury
necessity   over-the-top   lavish   gourmet   spoilt
extravagant   excessive   extra-large   overpriced
far-fetched

Prefixes

oversleep   undercooked   ex-boss   retrain
bilingual   multinational   unusual   extra-large
monotonous

 Listen to the explanations and vocabulary.
ACTIVEBOOK

 see Writing bank page 156

1 Choose the correct words in *italics*.

1 Could you give me *a few/some* information about train times please?

2 I've got *a piece of/a large number of* luggage to check in.

3 How *many/much* furniture have you got in your living room?

4 The news *is/are* always so depressing.

5 He's been doing *a little/a few* research into global warming.

6 There were only *few/a few* people there when I arrived.

7 I'd like *a bit of/many* toast with jam and an orange juice, please.

8 Can I give you *an/some* advice about revising for your exam?

2 Look at part of Tilly's diary below and imagine that today is Tuesday and it's 1:30 p.m. Write sentences about what she *had done*, *is having done* and *will have done*.

She had her living room decorated yesterday.

1 _____
2 _____
3 _____
4 _____
5 _____
6 _____
7 _____
8 _____

Monday

10:30 a.m. Decorator (living room)
Pick car up from garage (fit new tyres)
Delivery of new cooker (after 5 p.m.)

Tuesday

Haircut (& highlights) 9:15 a.m.
Carpet fitters (living room) – between
1 and 2 p.m.
Take watch to repair shop – don't forget!

Wednesday

Eye test (optician on High Street) 10:00 a.m.
Window cleaner (a.m.)
Don't forget to take coat to dry cleaners

3 Complete the sentences with the correct tense of a verb from the box in the passive form.

> catch   charge   deliver   employ   include   open
> repair   send

1 Service _____ in the bill so you don't need to leave a tip.

2 I _____ some flowers yesterday, but I don't know who they're from.

3 The goods that you ordered _____ next Friday.

4 My car broke down last week. It _____ at the moment.

5 Don't use the medicine if the packet _____ already.

6 It's unlikely that the robbers _____ .

7 I was annoyed because we _____ for a bottle of wine we didn't have.

8 She was sacked after she _____ by that company for over 15 years.

4 Choose the correct words in *italics*.

1 I don't really like cooked carrots. I much prefer them *rare/raw/roast*.

2 I've decided to bid *from/for/at* that table I told you about.

3 £60 is too much for that bag. It's really not *value/afford/worth* it.

4 I've decided I'm going to *treat/pamper/spoil* him to a meal for his birthday.

5 She spends a huge amount of money on her *spoilt/lavish/excessive* lifestyle.

6 The sound on this CD is really strange. Take it back and get a *discount/refund/receipt*.

7 Before you roast potatoes, you should *bake/beat/boil* them for ten minutes.

8 I think I'm addicted to cakes and biscuits and other *savoury/bitter/sweet* things.

5 Complete the sentences with the most appropriate prefix.

1 The children need an early night. They are _____tired and rather irritable.

2 It all took a lot longer than I expected. I _____estimated the time by several hours.

3 She talks in such a boring and _____tonous voice that I just fell asleep.

4 I've been a teacher for ten years, but I've decided to _____train as a computer technician.

5 We've decided to have a school reunion every two years and make it a _____ennial event.

6 The classrooms are extremely modern and have all the latest _____media equipment.

7 When you _____heat food, you need to make sure that you get it hot enough.

8 She's got a very _____usual name. I wonder where it comes from.

Lead-in

1 Work in pairs and answer the questions.

1 What do you think is happening in the photos?
2 What do you think the people all have in common?
3 What do you think they had to do to achieve their success?

2 Complete the sentences (1–8) with the words/phrases from the box.

> managed   succeed   achievement   high-achiever
> boasting   proud   have a go   give up

1 You know what they say, 'If at first you don't _____ – try, try, try again!'
2 I'm not sure that I'll be any good at ice-skating, but I'm going to _____ .
3 It was a hard match, but in the end they _____ to win by 3 goals to 2.
4 I nearly decided to _____ learning to drive after I failed my test four times.
5 I'm really _____ of myself for graduating in medicine with top marks.
6 Getting a certificate at the end of the course gave me a real sense of _____ .
7 She's always talking about herself and _____ about winning everything.
8 He's a _____ and wants to do really well in everything he does.

3 Work in pairs and discuss the questions.

1 When did you last achieve something special?
2 What did you do? How did you feel?

8.1 Lead or follow?

Grammar	*It's time, I'd rather, I'd better*
Can do	describe how you behave in different situations

Reading

1 Work in pairs and discuss the questions.

1 Is leadership a natural-born talent or a learned skill?
2 What qualities does a successful leader need?
3 In what different situations do people need to work together as a group?
4 Does every group need a leader? Why/Why not?

2 Read the company web page and match the questions from exercise 1 with the correct paragraphs (A–D).

3 Read the web page again. Write true (T), false (F) or not given (NG)?

1 Being able to work in a group is one of the most important life skills. ☐
2 Groups of people doing social activities generally don't need leaders. ☐
3 Members of leaderless groups often stop attending. ☐
4 Antonio Carluccio thinks he is a natural-born leader. ☐
5 Good leaders are often slightly afraid of their role. ☐
6 Good leaders should do more work than the other group members. ☐

Are YOU a successful leader?

The Successful Leadership Trust – our company specialises in training you to be a successful leader for whatever situation you're in.

A ...?

Almost nothing we do in this world is done in isolation. At work or at play, you'll find yourself in groups, working with other people: your team at work, a meeting with colleagues, your family, a holiday with friends, a group of students working together, a day out walking in the mountains, a group of neighbours wanting to make changes. It is now recognised that being able to work successfully with other people is one of the major keys to success, partly because we need to do it so often.

B ...?

In almost every situation where you're in a group, you will need a skilled leader. All groups need leaders and all successful groups have good leaders.

Groups without leaders or with weak leaders almost always break down. Members of a leaderless group often begin to feel dissatisfied and frustrated. Time is wasted and the tasks are not achieved. There are often arguments and tensions between people as there is nobody to keep the goals clear. Some personalities dominate and others disappear. Often group members begin not to come to meetings in order to avoid more disharmony.

C ...?

Some people are natural leaders. The celebrity chef, Antonio Carluccio says, 'True leaders are born and you can spot them in kitchens. They're people who combine toughness, fairness and humour.' Although a lot of people agree that there are some natural-born leaders, most people now recognise that leadership can also be taught. Our professional and experienced staff can train almost anyone how to be a successful leader. Good leaders don't make people do things in a bossy, controlling way. You can learn how to involve everyone, encouraging the whole group to work towards a common goal.

D ...?

Our training courses use activities and techniques to develop a range of qualities which are necessary to be a good leader. Self-confidence is vital and being able to overcome your own fears about being a leader. Successful leaders also need to be calm and intelligent. They need to be able to work out good strategies and make sound judgements under pressure. Lastly, and probably most importantly, good leaders need to be sensitive, sociable and be able to get on with a wide range of people. Good leadership is essentially the ability to influence others and good leaders allow all members of the group to contribute.

4 Work in pairs and discuss the questions.

1 How far do you think it is true that people can be trained to be good leaders?

2 Do you like doing things in a group, on your own or with one other person? Why?

3 When you are in a group, how likely are you to be the leader? Give reasons.

Grammar | *It's time, I'd rather, I'd better*

5 ● 2.19 Listen to the work appraisal interview and decide which sentence (1–3) best summarises the main points.

1 He's doing well in his role of team leader but he would like some more training.

2 He's finding his role of team leader difficult and he thinks he needs some training.

3 He's interested in becoming a team leader but he would like some training first.

6 a Complete the examples (1–4) from the interview in the Active grammar box.

b Complete the rules of form (A–D) by writing *past tense* or *infinitive*.

c Look at the examples (1–4) again and explain what each one means. Read the rules about meaning to help you.

d Look at audioscript 2.19 on page 171 and find one more example for each structure.

Active grammar

1 *I think it's _____ I had a bit more responsibility.*

2 *I think I _____ you did the first course.*

3 *I _____ not wait for two months.*

4 *I _____ get your name on the list immediately.*

A Form: *It's time* + subject + _____

Meaning: to talk about when you should have done something already, or at least started it.

B Form: subject + *would rather* + object + _____ (+ *than* ...).

Meaning: to talk about what you'd prefer someone else to do.

C Form: subject + *would rather* + _____ (+ *than* ...).

Meaning: to talk about what you'd prefer to do.

D Form: subject + *had better* + _____

Meaning: to talk about something when it is advisable to do it (in the present or future).

see Reference page 117

7 a Complete the dialogue with *It's time*, *'d rather*, or *'d better* and the correct form of the verb in brackets.

Anna: Hi, Will. How did your appraisal go?

Will: It went well, thanks. My boss thinks (1)_____ (have) more responsibility and maybe became a team leader.

Anna: Oh that's good. How do you feel about that?

Will: I'm pleased because I was thinking of looking for a better job in another company, but (2)_____ (stay) here if I can.

Anna: It would be great if you were our team leader. (3)_____ (be) in charge than someone we don't know.

Will: Thanks. Anyway, (4)_____ (go) because I've got a meeting in five minutes. See you later.

b ● 2.20 Listen and check your answers.

8 a Write three sentences about yourself starting with *It's time ...*

It's time I tidied up the living room.

It's time I got in touch with my brother.

It's time I changed my job.

b Work in pairs and compare your sentences. Give more details about your sentences. Try and include *I'd better* and *I'd rather*.

Vocabulary | describing personality

9 **a** Work in two groups. Group A, look at box A. Group B, look at box B. Make sure you understand the meaning of the words in your box.

A

> outgoing   open   proactive
> aggressive   opinionated
> single-minded

B

> easy-going   selfish   witty
> manipulative   introverted
> headstrong

b Work in pairs and take turns to tell each other about the meaning and pronunciation of the six words in your box.

10 Work in pairs and discuss the questions.

1   Which of the qualities from exercise 9a do you think successful people usually have, and which can stop you being successful? Give reasons.

I think that most successful people are very determined and single-minded but if you are too headstrong it could go against you because …

2   Can you think of three people who you can describe using some of the adjectives from exercise 9a? Give examples of how he/she behaves which show why you've chosen those adjectives.

My sister is a very headstrong person. She really wanted to travel around South America on her own. Everyone tried to persuade her not to because it was dangerous, but she decided to do it anyway and …

Speaking

11 **a** 2.21 Listen to two people discussing how they behave in different situations. Which situations do they talk about?

* talking about yourself in a job interview
* leading a discussion at work or school
* giving a presentation at work
* performing on stage
* being in a crowd of people at a party
* cooking for a small group of friends
* making a complaint in a shop or restaurant
* playing a team game (e.g. football)
* organising a group of children

b Do you think they are similar or very different from each other?

c Listen again and tick (✓) the phrases from the How to... box you hear.

How to... Introduce general and specific points

Introduce general points	*Most of the time, I'm quite a calm person.* *On the whole, I'm usually quite an easy-going type of person.* *Generally, at work I think that I'm fairly confident.* *As a rule, I'm a pretty confident person, I'd say.*
Introduce more specific points	*I actually became quite aggressive with the person.* *Suddenly, I changed into this aggressive person.* *Especially in social situations, I can get quite nervous.* *If I don't know people, then I find that I'm a lot less confident.*

---

12 **a** Prepare to talk about the different sides of people's personalities in different situations. You could talk about yourself, someone you know, or people in general. Make brief notes about what you're going to say using the situations from exercise 11a or your own ideas.

b Work in pairs and tell each other about the different sides of personalities in different situations. Do you have similar ideas or not?

Listening

1 Work in pairs and discuss the questions.

1 What do you think is happening/has happened in each photo?

2 Which photos match the feelings in the box below?

> completely ecstatic
> absolutely devastated
> totally single-minded

3 Can you remember any sporting moments that you've watched (or been involved in) when someone has felt in a similar way?

2 🔊 2.22 Listen to part of a radio programme and answer the questions.

1 What proportion of sportspeople use sports psychologists to help them with their mental attitude?

2 What are the main purposes of the Haka war dance used by the New Zealand All Blacks rugby team?

3 Listen again and write one sentence summarising the speaker's main points about each of the following.

1 self-belief
2 negative thoughts
3 personal lucky 'routines'

4 Work in small groups. Discuss the questions.

1 Do you think you have to be very good at the sport in order to be a good sports psychologist? Why/Why not?

2 Do you think you would be a good sports psychologist? Why/Why not?

Vocabulary | adjectives and intensifiers

5 **a** Look at the underlined adjectives from the table. What is the difference in meaning between gradable and non-gradable adjectives?

Gradable adjectives	Non-gradable adjectives
He missed an <u>important</u> goal. He missed a goal in a <u>big</u> match.	For some people, winning is <u>vital</u>. He had <u>huge</u> self-belief.

b Match the gradable adjectives (1–4) with the correct non-gradable adjectives (a–d). Use a dictionary if necessary.

1 happy   **a** starving
2 upset   **b** ecstatic
3 hungry   **c** exhausted
4 tired   **d** devastated

6 Read the rules (A–B). Then look at the sentences (1–6) and decide if one or both intensifiers are correct.

A We can use intensifiers *very*, *really* and *extremely* with gradable adjectives to make the meaning stronger.

B We can use intensifiers *really* and *absolutely* with non-gradable adjectives to make the meaning stronger.

1 Kelly Holmes must be *really/absolutely* ecstatic about her success.

2 A(n) *extremely/very* big sports centre near here has just opened.

3 If you want to get to the top in athletics, it's *really/extremely* vital to get yourself a professional trainer.

4 Whenever he plays football, he comes back *really/absolutely* starving.

5 She was *absolutely/extremely* exhausted at the end of the race.

6 I love running. I'd be *really/very* devastated if I had to give it up.

7 Think of a true story about you that relates to one of the phrases from the box in exercise 1. Tell your partner what happened.

I couldn't believe it when I won the prize for best actor. I was completely ecstatic!

Grammar | reported speech

8 **a** 🌐 2.23 Listen and complete each example with two words.

1 Today on *Sports Alive*, we _____ about success and achievement in sport.

2 Will he or she really _____ win?

3 _____ you help people to succeed?

4 My basic job _____ prepare the mind.

5 I _____ people change negative thoughts into positive ones.

6 His whole game _____ .

b Compare the reported speech in the Active grammar box with the direct speech from exercise 8a. Find examples of the changes (1–6) and write them in the box.

Active grammar

She said (that) **they were talking** *about success and achievement in sport* **that day.**

She asked him if he or she **would** *really help* **her** *win.*

She asked how **he helped** *people to succeed.*

He told her (that) **his** *basic job* **was** *to prepare the mind.*

He said (that) he **could** *help people change negative thoughts into positive ones.*

He told her (that) his whole game **had improved** *dramatically.*

Changes

1 Tense, e.g. *go → went*: <u>are talking → were talking</u>

2 Modal verbs, e.g. *will → would*: _____

3 Subject pronouns, e.g. *I → she*: _____

4 Object pronouns, e.g. *me → him*: _____

5 Time references, e.g. *now → then*: _____

6 Word order, e.g. *were they going → they were going*: _____

Rules

A We can use *that* after both *say* and *tell*, but it isn't necessary.

B We don't use an object after *say*.

C We must use an object after *tell*.

D We use a question word when reporting *Wh-* questions.

E We use *if* when reporting *Yes/No* questions.

F We can sometimes ignore the rule that changes the tense or modal verb back. This can happen if the situation is still true, or for dramatic effect when telling a story.

---

see Reference page 117

9 Read the rules (A–F) in the Active grammar box and decide if the sentences below are correct or not. Correct the ones which are wrong.

1 He said that he was totally devastated about the result.

2 She told me that she couldn't come to training this evening.

3 He told me he's training three times a week at the moment.

4 She said him she had taken up basketball the previous January.

5 I told them I was going to be late and that they should start without me.

6 I asked her she wanted to come round and watch the tennis.

7 He asked me why I went to a sports psychologist.

8 She told me she wants to move away from sport and further her career elsewhere now.

10 Rewrite the sentences and questions below as reported speech starting with the words given.

1 I really want to win the race tomorrow.
   He told _____

2 Are you going to watch the rugby final on TV this afternoon?
   She asked _____

3 I'll give you a lift to the football stadium.
   He said _____

4 What do you do to prepare yourself before an exam?
   He asked _____

5 I've been playing tennis for two hours.
   She told _____

6 I can concentrate much better when I listen to music.
   She said _____

7 Do you like watching athletics on TV?
   He asked _____

8 I'm going to pay a sports psychologist to help me.
   She told _____

Pronunciation | intonation: reporting

11 a 🔵 2.24 We use different intonation when we quote direct speech and when we report what people said. Listen to the pairs of sentences. Do we use higher intonation for the direct speech or the reported speech?

1. a The presenter asked him, 'How do you help people to succeed?'
   b The presenter asked him how he helped people to succeed.
2. a The sports psychologist said, 'My basic job is to prepare the mind.'
   b The sports psychologist said that his basic job was to prepare the mind.

b Listen again and repeat the sentences with a partner.

Speaking

12 Work in pairs and take turns to ask each other the questions in the quiz below. Make a note of your partner's answers.

Are you born to win?

1. When did you last win something? How did you feel?
2. Are you someone who is very motivated to win things? Why/Why not?
3. What's more important to you: winning or taking part? Why?
4. Do you know anyone who is more focused on winning than you? Give details.
5. Are you a good or a bad loser? Why do you think this is?
6. In which area(s) of your life do you think it might be useful to have a trainer/tutor? Why?
7. Do you have any lucky routines or superstitions for sports or exams? Give details.
8. How do you feel if the team you are supporting loses?

13 Work with a different student. Take turns to tell each other about the answers you made notes about and decide together if you think that your partner from exercise 12 was 'born to win' or not.

A: *I asked Marco if he was a good or a bad loser and he told me that he was a really bad loser. In fact, he said that there was nothing he hated more than losing …*

B: *And what did he say about winning and taking part?*

A: *He said that winning was far more important to him …*

14 a Work in pairs. Read the points in the Lifelong learning box. Which three points do you think are most important? Why?

b Discuss the questions.

1. Do you know anyone who is a very successful language learner? What kind of person is he/she?
2. Which of the characteristics in the box apply to you?
3. What other characteristics do you think are relevant?
4. How do you think you could be more successful as a language learner?

Successful language learning

❗ A successful language learner is generally someone who …

1. … is willing to make mistakes.
2. … wants/needs to communicate in the language.
3. … finds as many opportunities to practise as possible.
4. … doesn't worry about words he/she doesn't understand.
5. … sets aside specific times to practise the language.

Lifelong learning

Reading and listening

1 Work in pairs and discuss the questions.

1 At what age do you think children should learn how to use computers?

2 How do you feel about how much children use computers in your country?

2 Read the article. Which two ideas below are mentioned?

1 Using computers from a young age is good for children's speech development and concentration.

2 It's good to encourage young children to learn to use computers so they can spend time on other things later.

3 Young children who use computers a lot often develop problems with their eyesight.

4 Young children should be spending their time outside with friends, not using computers.

Technology for toddlers

A new school has opened recently where the pupils file into class to start their lessons, turn on their computers and obediently follow their teacher's instructions. For an hour, they are taught mouse techniques, keyboard skills and reading and writing, using the computer. Nothing unusual about that, you might think; except that these pupils are toddlers, aged just two or three. Next term, they will move up a class to begin instruction in computer science, still only four years old.

We asked two experts their opinions on the growing phenomenon of 'technology for toddlers': Do you think we should teach computer skills to very young children?

YES

Judy Clarke, director of technology, York College

At my college, we think that 'it's never too young to start'. Although the usual age for the national school exams is 16, we put our best pupils forward for exams aged seven if we think they are ready. Having had great success with these courses, the next logical step for us was to think about the 'Technology for Toddlers' classes. They are aimed at giving the pre-school pupils a head start not only in technology skills but also in writing, reading and communication using the computer. Apart from the actual lessons, we also encourage parents to get the children to practise their new skills at home. Parents say to me all the time, 'Sarah can count up to 30 and is way ahead of her peers' or, 'Jack has gained so much confidence from your classes.' Comments like these make it all worthwhile for me. Some people may be critical, but I would argue that it's a crime to hold children back. The only thing we are exploiting is their ability to learn. Most children love computers and they learn quickly. Starting young means they won't have to waste time in their secondary school years catching up with all the computer skills they need.

NO

Alan Jackson, educational psychologist, Cardiff

I've worked as an educational psychologist for many years and I must say that I'm very concerned about this trend for encouraging younger and younger children to use computers. The negative aspects of staring at a screen for a long time at a young age are well-documented. The lack of physical exercise, for example, can lead to obesity and the lack of interaction with real people can lead to problems with speech development. These are just two of the problems, but I could go on and on. It is bad enough for older children, but the idea of children as young as two being actively encouraged to go to computer lessons appals me. I feel sorry for these children who clearly need to be running around and climbing trees with their friends. To my mind, two parties are to blame: the colleges who run these courses and the parents of these children. They should be ashamed of their inability to think about the short and long-term effects on the child. As far as I can see, the former is just interested in publicity and profit, and the latter purely in satisfying their own egos.

3 Read the article again and write true (T) or false (F). Correct the false sentences.

1 Children can study computer science at the school from the age of two. ☐

2 Some children at the college take their national school exams seven years earlier than the usual age. ☐

3 Judy Clarke says children should start lessons as young as possible. ☐

4 She says parents shouldn't help their children with computer skills at home. ☐

5 She says children have the right to be taught things as young as they want/can. ☐

6 Alan Jackson says looking at a computer screen is harmless in itself. ☐

7 He says problems caused by computers are worse for younger children than older children. ☐

8 He says colleges often run these courses purely for financial benefit and don't think about the children. ☐

4 Work in pairs. Look again at statements 3–8 from exercise 3. Do you agree mostly with Judy's opinion (statements 3–5) or Alan's opinion (statements 6–8)? Give reasons.

5 **a** 🔊 2.25 Listen to two friends discussing the article. Is each person's opinion …

a similar to Judy Clarke's?

b similar to Alan Jackson's?

c not clear?

b Listen again and for each of the quotes (1–6) say who said it, and what he/she is referring to.

1 'I think that's ridiculous!'

2 'I mean, what's the point?!'

3 'She would say that I suppose.'

4 'I'm sure that comes into it.'

5 'He confirmed what I feel.'

6 'I think you should read it.'

6 Work in pairs and discuss the question. What other advantages and disadvantages do you think there are of encouraging children to study intensively and take exams early?

Grammar | reporting verbs

7 **a** Complete the examples (1–8) in the Active grammar box with the correct form of the verbs from the box below. Then look at audioscript 2.25 on page 172 to check your answers.

admit claim confirm deny explain remind suggest warn

b Complete the rules of form (A–C) in the Active grammar box with the verbs from the box above.

Active grammar

1 She _____ that some of their students sat the national school exams aged seven.

2 She _____ that the success of those exams led them to start children earlier and earlier.

3 She _____ having any problems.

4 She _____ feeling pleased that the parents gave her really positive feedback.

5 She _____ encouraging toddlers to do homework.

6 He _____ that studies show too much time on computers is bad for young children.

7 One study _____ people not to let their children on a computer for more than an hour a day.

8 Will you _____ me to get that article for you?

A verb + (*that*) + clause
(1) *claim* (2) _____ (3) _____

B verb + *-ing* OR verb + (*that*) + clause
(4) _____ (5) _____ (6) _____

C verb + object + infinitive OR verb + object + (*that*) clause
(7) _____ (8) _____

---

see Reference page 117

8 Rewrite the sentences as reported speech.

1 'I broke the laptop yesterday when I dropped it by mistake.'
He admitted …

2 'Please give your homework to me tomorrow.'
The teacher reminded …

3 'Why don't you look for a course you could do in the evenings?'
He suggested …

4 'My son took his exams a year earlier than all his classmates.'
She claimed …

5 'The school will be closed until next Monday.'
They confirmed …

6 'You really mustn't be late for your exam this afternoon.'
She warned …

7 'I didn't copy my essay from the internet.'
He denied …

8 'I'm doing the course because I need to improve my English.'
He explained …

Listening

9 **a** Work in pairs. Look at the survey below. What do you think the results of questions 1–4 were?

I think that most people admitted spending more than ten hours per week on the computer ...

b 🔵 2.26 Listen to someone reporting the results for the first four questions of the survey and see if your ideas were correct.

Information Technology Department
Queens College of Education

Number of students taking part: 20
Ages: 16–24

SURVEY

Computers

1 How many hours a day do you spend on the computer? What do you use it for mostly?
2 How many hours a day should children aged under 12 spend on a computer?
3 Should schools offer computer classes to children aged under five?
4 Do you think there is a link between obesity and computer use in children?
5 ...

School and exams

6 Should all school children receive a free computer to use at home?
7 Should parents push their children to take exams as early as they can?
8 Would you say that you've got pushy parents or that you are/would be one?
9 Which three subjects should children spend most time studying at school?
10 ...

10 Listen again and complete the How to... box.

How to... report the results of a survey

Report exact results	*Thirteen _____ of twenty people admitted spending three or more hours a day on the computer.*
	_____ of the group also said that they used the computer for fun.
	_____ suggested restricting the number of hours that children spend on the computer.
	_____ thought that children should never use a computer at home.
Report approximate results	*_____ people said that an hour a day was the maximum amount of time ...*
	A _____ people, however, disagreed, saying that obesity is a complex issue.
	The (vast) _____ confirmed my own feelings on this one.
	Only a (small) _____ were in favour of computer classes for toddlers.
	Nearly _____ the group admitted that it was quite difficult to enforce this.

Speaking

11 **a** Prepare to do the survey from exercise 9a. Work in groups and add one more question to each section of the survey.

b Do the survey in your groups. One person in the group should be the 'secretary' and make notes of each person's answers for every question.

c When your group has finished all the questions, collect the results and prepare to report them back to the class. Use your notes and the language in the How to... box to help you.

d Report the results of your survey to the class. How similar were the results from different groups? Were any of the results surprising?

1 **a** Match the <u>underlined</u> phrasal verbs with the correct meanings (a–j) below.

1 I'm <u>looking forward to</u> getting my exam results tomorrow.

2 They're <u>putting</u> her <u>in for</u> her Grade 8 piano exam and she's only nine.

3 I'd like you to <u>cut down on</u> the amount of time you spend on the computer.

4 I want to <u>make up for</u> all the time I wasted in my first year at secondary school.

5 How do you <u>put up with</u> all that noise while you're studying?

6 I'll never <u>catch up with</u> him – he's already way ahead of me.

7 He cheated in his last exam and <u>got away with</u> it.

8 Have you <u>come up with</u> any ideas for your next career move?

9 I've always <u>looked up to</u> my brother. He's a really single-minded person.

10 Please don't run so fast! I can't <u>keep up with</u> you.

a to think of, suggest

b to think you will enjoy

c to move at the same speed

d to formally apply to do something

e to tolerate

f to reduce

g to respect, admire

h to reach the same place

i to compensate for

j to escape punishment

b Work in pairs and test each other on the phrasal verbs from exercise 1a.

Student A: say the meaning.

Student B: say the phrasal verb.

A: *to think you will enjoy ...?*

B: *... to look forward to*

2 **a** Choose the correct phrasal verbs in *italics*.

1 Is there anything you are really *looking up to/looking forward to* doing over the next few weeks? If so, what?

2 Are you good at *coming up with/ keeping up with* good ideas for presents for people? Are you particularly pleased with any of them?

3 Do you think you need to *make up for/ cut down on* the amount of salt you eat? What else?

4 Is there anyone that you really *look up to/catch up with*? If so, who and why?

5 If you forgot someone's birthday, how would you *come up with/make up for* it? How do you feel if someone forgets your birthday?

6 Did you do anything naughty when you were a child that you *got away with/ put up with*? If so, what was it?

7 How good are you at *keeping up with/ cutting down on* your homework? What about other tasks or work?

8 Are you good at *catching up with/ putting up with* noise when you are trying to sleep? What else annoys you?

9 Were you ever *put in for/put up with* music exams when you were a child? Or any other exams?

10 When you were a child, was there anyone you wanted to *catch up with/ come up with*? What about now?

b 🔘 2.27 Listen and check your answers.

Pronunciation | stress on phrasal verbs

3 **a** 🔘 2.27 Phrasal verbs with three parts have two stresses. Listen to the questions from exercise 2a again. Which part of the phrasal verb has ...

• the main stress?

• the secondary stress?

b Listen again and repeat the questions.

4 Work in pairs and discuss the questions from exercise 2a.

8 Communication

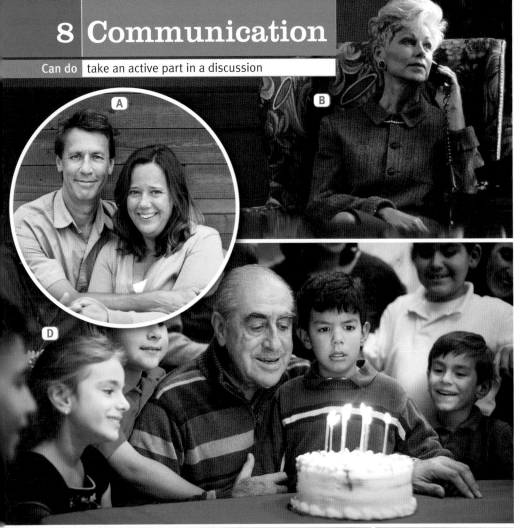

1 Work in pairs and look at the photos. How do you think each photo represents success? Think about the ideas below.
- successful career/high status job
- financial security/plenty of money
- good health/access to health care
- achieving your own specific goals
- strong marriage/personal relationship
- large close family around you
- lots of good, loyal friends

2 🔊 2.28 Listen to three people discussing the question 'What is success?'. Which ideas from exercise 1 does each person say best represents 'success'?

3 **a** Prepare to discuss this question.
- What is the most important factor in deciding how successful someone is?

First, look at audioscript 2.28 on page 173 and <u>underline</u> any useful phrases for getting your point across.

b Look again at the list from exercise 1 and decide which three factors you think are the most important. Make notes about your reasons.

4 **a** Work in groups of three and have your discussion. How far do you agree with each other?

b Work with another group and have another discussion. How far do people in your class agree/disagree about this question?

It's time/I'd rather/I'd better

It's time ...

Form: *It's time* + subject + past tense

Meaning: 'It's time I did something' is used to mean 'I should have done something already or at least started it'.

It's time you did your homework.

I'd rather ...

Form: subject + *would rather* + object + past tense (+ *than* ...)

'I'd rather you did/didn't do something' is used to talk about what you'd prefer someone else to do.

I'd rather you didn't smoke in here.

Form: subject + *would rather* + infinitive (+ *than* ...)

'I'd rather do/not do something' is used to talk about what you'd prefer to do.

I'd rather not spend all day lying on the beach.

I'd better ...

Form: subject + *had better* + infinitive

'I'd better do/not do something' is used to talk about something when it is advisable to do it (in the present or future).

I'd better mend that window as soon as I can.

Reported speech

We use 'reported' or 'indirect' speech to tell people what somebody said or thought.

Make the tense of the verb one 'step' further back into the past.

'*I want to go out.*'

→ She said (that) she **wanted** to go out.

Modal verbs also change.

'*Can you help me paint the kitchen?*'

→ She asked me if I **could** help her paint the kitchen.

Subject and object pronouns change.

'*I will give it to you soon.*'

→ He said **he** would give it to **me** soon.

References to particular times change.

'*The books will be delivered tomorrow.*'

→ She said the books would be delivered **the next day**.

Word order can also change.

'*What are you doing at the weekend?*'

→ He asked me what **we were doing** at the weekend.

We use *if* (or *whether*) when reporting *Yes/No* questions.

'*Did you enjoy the film?*'

→ He asked me **if** I had enjoyed the film.

Reporting verbs

We can use different verbs to report what people say. Different verbs are followed by particular structures. The following are some of the most common reporting verbs.

say, tell, ask, claim, explain, confirm, admit, suggest, deny, remind, warn

say + (*that*) + clause

*She **said that** John was ill and couldn't come.*

tell + object + (*that*) + clause

*He **told us that** we needed to show identification.*

ask + object + infinitive

*He **asked me to buy** some biscuits.*

claim/explain/confirm + (*that*) + clause

*She **claimed that** she hadn't seen him at all.*

admit/suggest/deny + verb + *-ing*

admit/suggest/deny + (*that*) + clause

*He **admitted eating** the last piece of cake.*

*He **admitted that** he ate the last piece of cake.*

remind/warn + object + infinitive

remind/warn + (*that*) + clause

*We **reminded him to post** the letter.*

*We **reminded him that** he should post the letter.*

> ### Key vocabulary
>
> **Success**
>
> succeed   manage   boast   have a go   give up
> proud   high-achiever   achievement
>
> **Describing personality**
>
> proactive   headstrong   opinionated   manipulative
> selfish   single-minded   open   easy-going   witty
> outgoing   introverted   aggressive
>
> **Adjectives/Intensifiers**
>
> important–vital   big–huge   happy–ecstatic
> upset–devastated   hungry–starving
> tired–exhausted
> very   really   extremely   absolutely   completely
>
> **Phrasal verbs with three parts**
>
> catch up with   get away with   keep up with
> put in for   come up with   cut down on   look up to
> look forward to   put up with   make up for

Listen to the explanations and vocabulary.

ACTIVEBOOK

see Writing bank page 157

8 Review and practice

1 Find the mistakes in six of the sentences and correct them.

I'd better wrote your phone number down before I forget it.

*I'd better **write** your phone number down before I forget it.*

1 I'd better went to the shops before they close.

2 Had you rather I didn't say anything to your boss?

3 Isn't it time you told him how you really feel?

4 I'd rather not working this weekend if at all possible.

5 Would you better take a raincoat in case it rains?

6 I'd rather you paid me back in cash than by cheque if that's OK.

7 What's that smell? I think it's time you get the cake out of the oven.

8 I'd rather took just hand luggage on the plane than a large suitcase.

2 Complete the sentences using past tenses.

Zoe/say/can't remember/where/leave/keys.

Zoe said she couldn't remember where she had left the keys.

1 Tony/ask/I like/play/tennis/this weekend.

2 They/tell/best time/visit Egypt/be/in January or February.

3 Helen/say/not know/what time/firework display/start.

4 He ask/me when/I want/go/see/the London Eye.

5 My boss/tell/I have to/make/presentation/at sales conference/in March.

6 The newspaper/say/one/our athletes/fail/drugs test.

7 She/ask/I watch/football match/last Saturday.

8 He/tell/he arrive/later/this evening.

3 Choose the correct words in *italics*.

1 My doctor suggested *taking/to take* a week off work.

2 They confirmed *being/he would be* about twenty minutes late.

3 They warned *not going/us not to go* climbing without proper equipment.

4 Will you remind me *to go/going* to the post office this afternoon?

5 She explained *not finishing/she hadn't finished* her essay because the computer had crashed.

6 He admitted *being/to be* wrong about the time of the train.

7 He claimed *that he hadn't heard/not hearing* about the flights being cancelled.

8 She denied *to tell/telling* anyone about my new job.

4 Complete the sentences using eight of the adjectives from the box. Two of the adjectives cannot be used.

> opinionated   starving   headstrong
> manipulative   out going   ecstatic
> exhausted   single-minded   aggressive
> proud   devastated   proactive

1 She's really _____ and always insists on doing exactly what she wants.

2 He's a very _____ person and never sits around waiting for things to happen.

3 She's absolutely _____ because she got all 'A' grades in her final school exams.

4 He's very _____ . He really thinks that his own opinions are the only ones worth listening to!

5 You should be very _____ of your achievement today. You worked hard and you deserve it.

6 I'm absolutely _____ today. We've been travelling for three days and I haven't slept at all.

7 My brother's very _____ . He really enjoys being with friends and meeting new people.

8 She will be _____ if she doesn't pass her driving test today. It's her fourth attempt.

9 He's a very _____ person. Nothing distracts him when he's decided to do something.

10 I'm absolutely _____ . I've been so busy today that I haven't had time to eat anything.

5 Find the mistake in each phrasal verb and correct it.

1 We're really looking forward with visiting my brother in Australia.

2 You really should come down on how many cakes and biscuits you eat.

3 I was ill for a week and found it very difficult to catch up for all the homework.

4 He's made up with several interesting ideas for the new advertising campaign.

5 I really look up with my grandmother – she's always been a real inspiration.

6 I'm finding it difficult to get up with you complaining all the time.

7 I can't believe he got down with not paying for the tickets.

8 He bought me some flowers to make up to being so late.

9 Wait for me! I can't keep up to you when you're walking so fast.

10 My instructor has put me on for my driving test.

Lead-in

1 **a** Look at the photos. Which aspects of crime/the law do they show?

Law court	Crime	Criminal	Evidence	Punishment
a judge	a robbery	a thief	fingerprints	a fine

b Look at the words in the table. Can you think of more words and expressions connected with crime and the law? Write them in the appropriate columns.

2 Work in pairs and check you know the meaning of the <u>underlined</u> words/phrases.

1 They say it helps the <u>victims</u> of crimes like burglary if the <u>criminals</u> apologise to them face to face.

2 People benefit much more from <u>punishments</u> like <u>community service</u> than from going to prison.

3 It is right that a <u>suspect</u> in a criminal case should be regarded as <u>innocent</u> until he/she is proved <u>guilty</u>.

4 <u>Witnesses</u> of crimes are right to feel nervous about giving <u>evidence</u> to the police.

5 People who commit <u>petty crimes</u> like traffic offences should get a <u>suspended sentence</u> but not go to <u>prison</u>.

6 <u>Graffiti</u> and <u>vandalism</u> are the main problems in my local area.

7 I'd like to be a <u>forensic scientist</u> and help solve serious crimes.

3 Work in pairs. How far do you agree/disagree with the statements from exercise 2? Give reasons.

9.1 Legal madness

Vocabulary | law and insurance

1 Work in pairs and discuss the questions.

1 Which TV crime dramas have you watched/heard about?

2 What types of crimes are usually involved in dramas of this kind?

3 Why do you think they are so popular?

2 Match the verb phrases from the box with the definitions (a–j) below.

> commit arson   commit fraud   be arrested
> convict someone of   sentence someone to
> get away with something   sue someone
> be insured/insure something   make a claim
> pay a premium

a to be taken to a police station because the police think you've done something illegal

b to commit the crime of deliberately making something burn, especially a building

c to officially decide in a court of law that someone is guilty of a crime

d when you pay money to a company and they pay the costs if you are ill, have a car accident, etc.

e to pay an amount of money for insurance

f to give a legal punishment to someone who is guilty of a crime

g to request that an insurance company pays you for something that has happened

h to commit the crime of deceiving people to get money

i to start a legal process to get money from someone who has harmed you in some way

j to not be caught or punished when you have done something wrong

3 Complete the sentences with the correct form of the verb phrases from exercise 2.

1 She plans to _____ the hospital after they gave her the wrong operation.

2 Bailey was _____ to three years in prison for his part in the robbery.

3 The cost of the annual _____ has gone up again because of the number of claims last year.

4 My neighbour has been _____ of shoplifting but luckily he doesn't have to go to prison.

5 I decided to _____ after my camera was stolen, and the insurance company paid for a new one.

6 I'd like to be _____ to cover things that are stolen from me while I'm on holiday.

7 They don't think the fire was an accident. They think someone _____ .

8 He tries to _____ not paying on buses whenever he can.

9 He was _____ and taken to the police station for playing loud music all night every night.

10 He _____ by pretending that an expensive painting had been stolen to get the insurance money.

4 Work in groups and discuss these questions.

1 Imagine someone buys a coffee in a fast food restaurant. They then spill the hot coffee on themselves and are burned. Should they sue the fast food company?

2 What different things do people insure? Have you ever heard about anyone insuring something strange?

3 Do you know any famous cases of fraud? If so, what happened?

Don't get mad...
Get evidence.

MIND OF THE CRIME

Listening

5 **a** You are going to listen to a story about a crime. Before you listen, work in pairs and predict what the story might be about using …

1 the words *cigar*, *lawyer* and *fraud*.
2 the verb phrases from exercise 2.

b 🔵 2.29 Listen to the story and compare your ideas.

6 **a** Put the sentences below in the order they happened in the story.

1 The lawyer was arrested and charged with arson.
2 The insurance company refused to pay.
3 He made a claim against the insurance company.
4 The lawyer was sentenced to prison.
5 He smoked the cigars.
6 The insurance company paid the lawyer.
7 Next, he insured the cigars against fire.
8 The lawyer sued the insurance company.
9 First, a lawyer bought some rare cigars.

b 🔵 2.29 Listen and check your ideas.

Pronunciation | consonant clusters (2)

7 **a** 🔵 2.30 Listen to the words ending with two or three consonant sounds and write them in the correct place in the table.

-st	-xt	-nce
first		*evidence*
-nst	-nts	-cts

b Listen again and repeat the words.

Grammar | participle clauses for sequencing

8 **a** Look at the participle clauses used as sequencing devices in examples 1 and 2 in the Active grammar box. Then complete examples 3 and 4 with *cashing* or *cashed*.

b Choose the correct options in the rules (A–E).

Active grammar

1 The lawyer made a claim, **having smoked all his cigars**.
2 The lawyer made a claim, **after smoking all his cigars**.
3 **Having _____ the cheque**, the lawyer was arrested.
4 **After _____ the cheque**, the lawyer was arrested.

We can use participle clauses to describe the order of events in a story.

A *Having* is followed by the *present participle/ past participle*.

B *After* is followed by the *present participle/ past participle*.

C The participle clause can come *before/after/ either before* or *after* the main clause.

D The event described in the participle clause happens *first/second*.

E In the main clause, we use the *Present Simple/Past Simple*.

see Reference page 131

9 Complete the sentences (1–6) by writing the correct form of a verb from the box below.

> stay   read   promise   do   go   win

1 After _____ to the bank a number of times, the robbers felt they understood all the security systems.
2 Having _____ to pick his friend up from the police station, Terry completely forgot.
3 After _____ extremely well in his first year law exams, we were surprised when he decided to leave the course.
4 Having _____ some excellent reviews of that new murder mystery, I wanted to get a copy to take on holiday with me.
5 Having successfully _____ her case against her old employer, she decided to go out and celebrate.
6 After _____ at the office until midnight to prepare her report for the judge, she took the next day off.

10 **a** Think about three things that happened to you last week and what you did after each one.

b Work in pairs and take turns to tell each other what happened, using a participle clause. See if your partner can guess what you did next.

A: *After doing my English homework …*

B: *… you watched a film on TV?*

A: *No. I collapsed on the sofa and fell asleep!*

Speaking

11 Work in two groups. Look at some pictures and work out the stories.

Student As: look at the pictures below.

Student Bs: look at the pictures on page 148.

12 Check your ideas by reading the story.

Student A: read story 1 on page 149.

Student B: read story 2 below.

Story 2

An ambitious burglar broke into a vast mansion on Millionaires' Row at Bel Air, Los Angeles. He went through the house room by room, putting anything of value that he could see and carry in the large bag he'd brought with him. Having completely filled his bag, he decided it was time to leave.

He started to realise that he wasn't sure of the way out but moved on quickly, through a large dining room, past an indoor gym and through another room filled with exotic parrots. By now, he was beginning to panic. Then, having run through a large library and a small room full of art, he began to get quite desperate.

He ran up a small circular staircase to what seemed to be a large bedroom. He knocked on the door and went in. The owners of the house had been asleep in bed, but sat up in fright only to find a traumatised burglar desperate to find his way out of the maze of rooms. After giving him detailed directions, they phoned the police, who arrived minutes later and escorted the relieved burglar to the safety of a nearby police station.

13 **a** Prepare to tell another student your story. Read the How to… box and make notes about the story you read in exercise 12.

How to... tell a short anecdote

Check you remember all the important information	*A lawyer bought some rare cigars.* *He insured them against fire.*
Check you know the key vocabulary	*cigar* *to make a claim*
Introduce the story	*Did I tell you about this really funny story … ?* *Have you heard the story about the robber who fell asleep?*
Involve the listener	*So, can you believe it? He was sentenced to 24 months in jail!* *You'll never believe what happened in the end … he was fined $24,000!*

b Work in pairs and take turns to tell each other your stories. Use your notes and the pictures. Include structures with participle clauses for sequencing, as appropriate.

Reading

1 Work in pairs. Look at the picture of some campers in a national park in the US and discuss the questions.

1 Have you ever been camping in a place like this? If so, did you like it? If not, would you like to?

2 What sort of petty crimes do you think are committed in parks like this?

2 Read about the mystery below and answer the questions.

1 What crime was committed?

2 How many possible suspects were there?

3 How confident is the park ranger that he knows who committed the crime?

Can you solve the mystery?

#235 The Yellow Park Campers

Reg Trimble had been the Park Ranger at Yellow Park, Ohio for nearly 20 years. In that time, he had seen many crimes committed by campers and other park users. Most of the crimes were petty, including dropping litter, parking illegally and picking wild flowers.

One day, however, Reg drove up to the ranger's cabin just in time to see two intruders walking out through the door and into the woods at the edge of the park. He saw them from a distance, and couldn't even see if they were men or women. They both had backpacks on their backs and one of them was carrying a tent. When he got inside the cabin, he saw that it had been completely trashed. The intruders had eaten the food, broken the furniture and left the place in a complete mess. Reg knew that he had to catch them, or he would lose his job.

Reg predicted that finding the intruders would be a difficult task. The park was huge and although it had been a dry and warm week, a cold wind had brought rain at around midday and it was getting chilly and wet. He set off through the park, hoping that he would be lucky and find the trespassing vandals quickly. He didn't, however, and it was early evening before he found any campers who even fitted a rough description of the two he had seen.

The first couple Reg spoke to were Jan Wysocki and his brother Marek who were camping in a tent by a small river. They were rather tongue-tied at first, but explained they had been hiking for two days and had spent the whole day fishing. Reg looked at the two fish they were cooking on their fire and asked if they had fished in the rain. The brothers admitted they had.

A while later, Reg came across a second pair of campers – a middle-aged, well-dressed couple called Adam and Jean Wiseman, who also fitted the description. He joined them for a quick chat, sitting on a backpack to avoid the wet ground inside the tent. They told Reg that they had set up camp the previous night. They said they had spent the day walking in the park and when it started raining, they had taken shelter in a small cave.

An hour later, Reg found Lara and Pia – a pair of friends in a campervan. He noticed them because their campervan was new and was parked in a place where vehicles were prohibited. Lara apologised for being there and explained that the van wasn't registered in her name because a friend had lent it to them. She offered to give Reg her friend's phone number so he could check.

But he didn't need to check. He already knew who was lying.

Who do you think is lying: Jan & Marek, Adam & Jean or Lara & Pia?

Click here for the solution

Listening

3 **a** Work in pairs and discuss this question. Who do you think committed the crime on page 123 and why?

b 🔵 2.31 Listen to the first part of a discussion between two friends about the story.

1 Who do you think is better at solving the crime? Why?

2 How close do you think they are to working out who did it?

4 Work in pairs and discuss the questions.

1 Do you think you are any closer to solving the crime?

2 Do you think you would be a good detective? Why/Why not?

Grammar | deduction: present and past

5 Look at the examples (1–7) in the Active grammar box and complete the rules (A–F).

Active grammar

1 He **must have** a good reason to be so sure.

2 It **might be** a big lie – don't just believe everything you hear.

3 They **can't be** guilty because they would never do something like that.

4 They **must have committed** the crime because now they are lying to cover their tracks!

5 They **might have done** it, but I'm not sure.

6 They had spent the whole day fishing so they **couldn't have committed** the crime.

7 The middle-aged couple **can't have stolen** the food.

When we are certain about something (based on some kind of evidence):

A in the present, we use <u>must</u> + infinitive without *to*

B in the past, we use _____ + _____ + past participle

When we think something is possible (based on some kind of evidence):

C in the present, we use _____ + infinitive without *to*

D in the past, we use _____ + _____ + past participle

When we think something is not possible (based on some kind of evidence):

E in the present, we use _____ + infinitive without *to*

F in the past, we use _____ / _____ + _____ + past participle

---

see Reference page 131

6 Choose the correct word in *italics*.

1 He *must/might/couldn't* have arrived yet because he promised to phone us the minute the plane landed.

2 He *must/might/can't* have told my parents I was caught shoplifting, but I hope he didn't.

3 That *must/might/can't* be Rob on the phone. Only he knows my new number.

4 The judge *must/might/can't* have liked you. It's unusual to only get a suspended sentence in this kind of case.

5 He *must/might/can't* be happy about losing his job. He really loved working in the police force.

6 She *must/might/can't* have left very quietly. I didn't hear her go.

7 Don't be negative. She *must/might/can't* pass her English test. We will only know when we get the results.

8 The burglar *must/might/couldn't* have got in through a window. They were all locked.

7 Complete the sentences using *must/might/can't/couldn't (have)* and the correct form of the verb in brackets.

1 Pete didn't turn up to do his community service. He _____ (forget) about it. I reminded him yesterday.

2 You knew it was illegal to park there. You _____ (see) the notice – it was very clear.

3 I'm not sure where Jo is. She _____ (go) round to Sally's. They're working on a school project together.

4 How did you know about the surprise party? Someone _____ (tell) you!

5 She's just run a marathon. She _____ (be) completely exhausted now!

6 You _____ (spend) all your birthday money already. You got nearly £100!

7 We don't know who took the money. There were lots of people in the office during the day and any of them _____ (be) the thief.

8 I _____ (leave) my keys at home. I remember feeling them in my jacket pocket when I got on the bus.

8 a Work in pairs. Think again about the crime story on page 123 and discuss the questions.

1 For what reasons might the crime have been committed by …
   a Jan and Marek?
   b Adam and Jean?
   c Lara and Pia?

2 Who do you think must have committed the crime? Why?

b Check your ideas with the solution on page 147.

Vocabulary | compound adjectives

9 Complete the sentences below with the correct compound adjective, combining a word from box A and a word from box B.

A

> middle-   well-   far-   tongue-
> colour-   pig-   gift-   red-   fire-

B

> fetched   proof   headed
> dressed   handed   wrapped
> aged   coded   tied

1 Adam and Jean were a _____ couple – probably in their 40s.

2 They were _____ in smart, clean clothes which looked new.

3 Jan and Marek were rather _____ and couldn't answer the ranger's questions clearly.

4 The explanation for the crime story is either something really simple or really _____ .

5 The thief was caught _____ as he walked out of the shop holding a laptop he hadn't paid for.

6 They were saved by the fact that the building has _____ doors.

7 A bag full of _____ presents were stolen from my car.

8 The thief was determined to do things his own way and was so _____ that he didn't listen to anyone's advice.

9 The books are _____ according to genre. Crime is red, science-fiction is blue, etc.

Pronunciation | stress: compound adjectives

10 🔊 2.32 Listen and write down six questions.

11 a Some compound adjectives have the main stress on the first part and some on the second part. Listen to the questions from exercise 10 again and underline which part of each compound adjective has the main stress.

b Choose the correct option to complete the rules below.

1 Compound adjectives which are 'noun + past participle' generally have the main stress on the *first/second* part.

2 Compound adjectives which are 'adjective + past participle' generally have the main stress on the *first/second* part.

c Listen to the questions again and repeat.

12 Work in pairs and choose five of the questions to ask and answer together. Give details in your answers.

Speaking

13 a Work in pairs. Look at the pictures and discuss the questions.

1 Who do you think the person might be?
2 Where do you think he might be?
3 What do you think he might be doing?

b 🔊 2.33 Listen to the conversation and check your answers.

14 a Work in pairs and discuss the questions.

1 How do you think they managed to take pictures of the burglar?
2 Do you think the burglar realised he was being caught on camera?
3 How do you think the police got the photos of him?

b 🔊 2.34 Listen and check your answers.

c Work in pairs and discuss the questions.

1 How do you think the burglar felt when he was caught?
2 Have you heard of any good ways of preventing crimes such as burglary, vandalism or graffiti?

9.3 The real Sherlock?

Grammar	relative clauses
Can do	take part in a discussion about crime and punishment

Reading

1 **a** Work in small groups and discuss the questions.

1 What do you know about Sherlock Holmes?

2 Was he a real person?

3 Why and when was he famous?

b Check your ideas with the article.

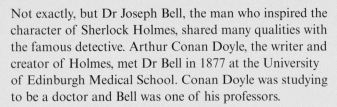

Was Sherlock Holmes a real person?

Not exactly, but Dr Joseph Bell, the man who inspired the character of Sherlock Holmes, shared many qualities with the famous detective. Arthur Conan Doyle, the writer and creator of Holmes, met Dr Bell in 1877 at the University of Edinburgh Medical School. Conan Doyle was studying to be a doctor and Bell was one of his professors.

Bell was 39 years old when Conan Doyle first attended one of his lectures. He is said to have walked with great energy. His nose and chin were angular and his eyes twinkled with intelligent humour. Bell, who was a brilliant doctor, liked writing poetry, playing sport and bird-watching.

By the end of Conan Doyle's second year, Bell had selected him to serve as his assistant. Being on a ward with Bell, where he had plenty of opportunity to observe, only increased Conan Doyle's admiration for the great doctor. Amongst other things he was able to witness Dr Bell's remarkable ability to quickly deduce a great deal about the patient.

Dr Bell observed the way a person moved. The walk of a sailor, who had spent many years at sea, varied greatly from that of a soldier. If he identified a person as a sailor, he would look for any tattoos that might assist him in knowing where their travels had taken them. He trained himself to listen for small differences in his patients' accents to help him identify where they were from. Bell studied the hands of his patients because calluses or other marks could help him determine their occupation.

Conan Doyle published the first Holmes story in 1887. His innovation in creating a character that would appear over and over in a series of self-contained stories meant that Holmes's popularity grew with each instalment. Perhaps the most famous story was *The Hound of the Baskervilles*, which has been made into several films. Soon the character was so beloved that people refused to believe he wasn't a real person; letters addressed to 'Sherlock Holmes, Consulting Detective' arrived daily at Baker Street and Scotland Yard, each begging him to take on a real case.

2 Complete the notes. Read the article again if necessary.

> Person who Sherlock Holmes was based on: *Dr Joseph Bell*
>
> Relationship to Conan Doyle:
> (1) _____
>
> Where/When met Conan Doyle:
> (2) _____ , (3) _____
>
> Dr Bell's hobbies: poetry, (4) _____ ,
> (5) _____
>
> Things Dr Bell observed about patients:
> the way they moved, (6) _____ , their
> accents, (7) _____
>
> Date first Holmes story published:
> (8) _____
>
> Letters for Sherlock Holmes sent to:
> (9) _____

3 Read the article again and find words that mean ...

1 good at understanding ideas and thinking clearly (adj – para. 2)

2 a feeling of great respect and liking for someone or something (noun – para. 3)

3 unusual or surprising and therefore deserving of attention or praise (adj – para. 3)

4 new idea, method, etc. that is used for the first time (noun – para. 5)

5 when a lot of people like someone or something (noun – para. 5)

4 Work in pairs and discuss the questions.

1 What new information have you learned about Sherlock Holmes?

2 Do you think you are observant like Dr Bell? Would you be a good witness in a crime situation?

Grammar | relative clauses

5 Read the Active grammar box and decide which examples (1–6) contain 'defining relative clauses' and which contain 'non-defining relative clauses'.

Active grammar

1 *Dr Joseph Bell was the man **who inspired the character of Sherlock Holmes**.*

2 *Bell, **who was a brilliant doctor**, liked writing poetry, playing sport and bird-watching.*

3 *Bell was 39 years old **when Conan Doyle first attended one of his lectures**.*

4 *Being on a ward with Bell, **where he had plenty of opportunity to observe**, only increased Conan Doyle's admiration for the great doctor.*

5 *Conan Doyle, **whose Sherlock Holmes novels were enormously popular**, died in 1930.*

6 *Perhaps the most famous story was* The Hound of the Baskervilles, ***which has been made into several films**.*

Defining relative clauses

The **bold** part of the sentence is essential to the meaning of the sentence.

Commas are not used to separate the clauses.

Who and *which* can both be replaced by *that*.

Non-defining relative clauses

The **bold** part of the sentence gives us extra information. This clause can be removed without affecting the central meaning of the sentence.

Use commas at the beginning and end of these clauses unless they end the sentence.

Who and *which* cannot be replaced by *that*.

see Reference page 131

6 Rewrite the pairs of sentences to make one sentence.

The police have found the man. He stole my bag.

The police have found the man who stole my bag.

1 John's been my best friend since school. He's helping me start a new business.

2 My current flat needs redecorating. I've been in it for a couple of years.

3 Tamsin's going to Australia for the winter. Her parents emigrated there last year.

4 My neighbour has given me his old computer. I've always liked him.

5 The family at the end of the road are thinking of moving. Their dog barks constantly.

6 Her car is for sale. She's had it for years.

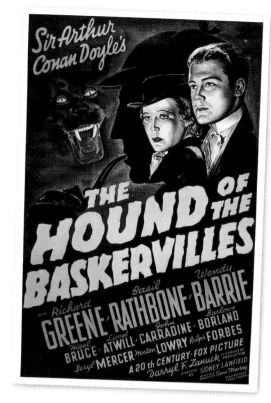

7 **a** Complete five of these sentences to make them true for you.

1 I'd like to live in a place where …

2 My best friend is someone who …

3 My favourite food is something which …

4 The person whose …

5 The busiest time in my life was when …

b Work in pairs and compare your sentences.

Listening

8 **a** You are going to listen to an interview with an ordinary American whose name is 'Sherlock Holmes'.

1 Why do you think he has this name?

2 What do you think are the possible consequences of having a name like this?

b 🔊 2.35 Listen and check your ideas.

9 Listen again and explain the significance of the following topics from the interview.

1 the name 'Holmes'

2 the Sherlock Holmes books

3 unusual and special

4 the question 'Where's Dr Watson?'

5 TV magicians

10 Work in small groups. Discuss the questions.

1 How do you feel about your name? Does it mean something?

2 What reasons do people have for changing their names? Do you know anyone who did this? If so, why?

3 Do you know anyone who has been a victim of identity theft? How and why do you think it usually happens?

Speaking

11 **a** Read the descriptions of the four people below and their crimes.

b Work in pairs and discuss the questions.

Who do you think is:

1 the person who committed the most serious crime?

2 the person who committed the least serious crime?

Paolo is 23 and unemployed. He has hacked into someone's bank account details online and stolen their identity. He has used their details to buy goods (e.g. a new TV and a holiday) worth thousands of euros.

Jenny is 35 and married with two children. She has been shoplifting from a supermarket over a period of a few months. She has stolen a few items on a regular basis, adding up to more than 1,000 euros' worth of food.

Akio is 19 and living with his parents. He has been going out late at night with his friends and spraying graffiti on public and private property (e.g. bridges, train stations and people's garden walls). His graffiti is well-done and quite artistic.

Teresa is 27 and a successful doctor. Recently, she has been speeding regularly. The speed limit is 30 mph and most days she drives at 40 or 45 mph. She says it's important that she gets around as quickly as possible for her job.

12 🔊 2.36 Listen to two friends discussing the same questions. Do you agree with them?

13 Listen again and complete the phrases in the How to... box.

How to... start, move on and finish a discussion

Start a discussion	*So, what do we have to decide?* *Why don't we _____ by talking about them individually perhaps, first?* *Shall we start with Paolo?* *Let's _____ for it. Any thoughts?*
Move on a discussion	*So, _____ on to Jenny …* *Shall we come back to this one?* *_____ come back to this one later.* *I'd like to go back to Jenny.* *What _____ do we have to decide?*
Finish a discussion	*I think we've agreed on everything.* *I think that's _____ .*

14 Work in pairs. Discuss the questions below and try to reach an agreement.

For each of the people described in exercise 11a, should he/she …

1 be let off with no punishment?

2 be fined? How much?

3 given community service? What and for how long?

4 go to prison? For how long?

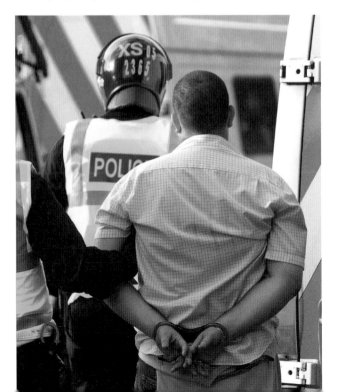

1 **a** Match the words which are often found in news headlines (1–12), with the meanings (a–l).

1	drama	a	strong request
2	quit	b	affect badly
3	back	c	explosion
4	bid	d	leave, resign
5	blast	e	essential, vital
6	blaze	f	cut, remove
7	axe	g	dispute, conflict
8	clash	h	attempt
9	aid	i	tense situation
10	hit	j	support
11	key	k	help
12	plea	l	serious fire

b Work in pairs and discuss what you think the headlines below might mean.

(A)

Hollywood star in bank drama

(B)

Top sports star to quit

(C)

MP spy drama

(D)

Prince and shop assistant to wed

2 Choose the most likely word in *italics*.

1 *Key/Plea* witness receives death threat
2 Toyota *axes/bids* top managers
3 Guests escape hotel *clash/blaze*
4 School governors *back/quit* teacher
5 Chat show host fight *drama/key*
6 Police and students *clash/hit*
7 Vodafone *bids/pleas* for US communications network
8 General *quits/aids* top job

3 Work in pairs. Would you be interested in reading articles with the following headlines? Why/Why not? What do you think each one might be about?

1 Man Utd crash to defeat in Cup match
2 Riddle of 2nd Van Gogh painting
3 Bomb blast in northern India
4 Votes scandal in California

4 Work in pairs. Look at the Lifelong learning box. Read the tip and discuss the questions.

Understanding the news

❗ Keeping up with the news is a very good way of improving your English.

1 How do you keep up with news in English: online, on TV, on the radio, by reading newspapers?
2 Which of those ways do you think you could do more? Why?
3 Which parts of the news are you most interested in?
4 How do you think you could use the news to improve your vocabulary in English?

Lifelong learning

Can do | solve problems with other people

1 A police officer was sitting on his motorcycle at a red traffic light when two teenagers in a sports car drove by him at 50 mph. He did not chase them or try to apprehend them. **Why not?**

2 A man was driving alone in his car when he came off the road at high speed. He crashed through a fence and went down a steep slope before the car plunged into a fast-flowing river. As the car slowly settled in the river, the man realised that his arm was broken and that he could not release his seat belt and get out of the car. He was trapped in the car. Rescuers arrived two hours later, yet they found him alive. **How come?**

3 A man rode into town on Friday. He stayed for three nights and then left on Friday. **How come?**

4 Bobby lives with his parents in London. Last week, while his parents were out, Bobby's neighbour Susie came round to spend the evening. At 8 o'clock precisely she went out to buy some cigarettes from the corner shop five minutes walk away. One minute after she left, two men burst into the house and, ignoring Bobby, took the TV set, the stereo and a computer. Bobby had never seen the men before and they had no legal right to remove the equipment – yet he did nothing to stop them. In fact, he didn't even act surprised by their behaviour. **How come?**

5 A man leaves hospital and begins to walk home. On his journey he passes a phone box which begins to ring. Instead of answering it he punches the air and runs all the way home cheering. **Why?**

6 When a fire broke out in an airplane, a panicking passenger opened the emergency hatch and threw himself out, even though he had no parachute. **How was it that when the rescue services found him, he was alive and well and without injury?**

1 Try and solve the lateral thinking problems above. Follow the instructions.

1 Read each problem and make a note of any vocabulary which stops you understanding them.

2 Ask other students and/or check in a dictionary to find out the meaning of the unknown vocabulary.

3 Work in pairs. Discuss ideas you have to explain each of the problems.

2 Work in six groups (1–6) and read the explanation for your story.
(group 1, look on page 147; group 2, page 149; group 3, page 148; group 4, page 147; group 5, page 149; group 6, page 149).

1 Make two *Yes/No* questions to ask about each of the other problems.

Was the policeman asleep? Were the teenagers invisible in some way?

2 Take turns to ask about and suggest explanations for the problems.

The teenagers might have been the policeman's children.

Participle clauses for sequencing

We can use *after* + present participle or *having* + past participle to show the order of events when telling a story or describing a series of events. We often use *having* + past participle in written form or in more formal situations.

After explaining to her boss why she needed a raise, she told him that she was thinking of leaving the company.

Having planned the robbery for months, the thieves entered the building unseen.

Other examples with a similar structure:

Before painting the room, she had to strip off the old wallpaper.

On entering the room, he noticed that all the windows were open.

While cleaning the room, she discovered a locked diary.

Deduction: present and past

We use *must* when we are certain about something (based on some kind of evidence).

We use *might* when we think something is possible (based on some kind of evidence).

We use *can't* when we think something is not possible (based on some kind of evidence).

In the present, we use *must/might/can't* + infinitive. We can also use *may/could* + infinitive.
This is the same for *I/you/he/we/they.*

Her plane didn't arrive until 1 a.m. last night. She must be exhausted.

John might know what to do. He's an experienced doctor.

That can't be Sally downstairs. She went to bed about two hours ago.

In the past, we use *must/might/can't/couldn't have* + past participle.
This is the same for *I/you/he/we/they.*

You must have enjoyed your holiday in Australia.

I think I might have left my wallet in that shop.

She hasn't phoned me so she couldn't have got my message.

We can use *may* instead of *might*.

She may have stopped to get some petrol

Relative clauses

Defining relative clauses

Defining relative clauses define or identify the person, thing, time, place or reason. They cannot be left out.

Tim is the teacher who I told you about.

That's the street where I grew up.

No commas are used before and after the defining relative clause.

That can be used instead of *who* or *which*.

The woman that/who I share an office with has been in the company for years.

The relative pronoun can be left out if it is the object of the verb in the relative clause.

Simon bought the jacket (that/which) we saw when we went shopping last weekend.

Non-defining relative clauses

Non-defining relative clauses give extra information which can be left out.

Commas are used before and after non-defining relative clauses unless they end a sentence.

Who and *which* cannot be replaced by *that*.

I've lent my new bike, which I really like, to my brother.

Joe, who I've known for years, is a great singer.

Key vocabulary

Crime

judge robbery thief fingerprints fine victim criminal punishment community service suspect innocent guilty witness evidence petty crime suspended sentence prison graffiti vandalism forensic scientist

Law and insurance

commit arson commit fraud be arrested convict someone of sentence someone to get away with something sue someone be insured/insure something make a claim pay a premium

Compound adjectives

middle-aged well-dressed far-fetched red-handed tongue-tied pig-headed gift-wrapped fire-proof

News headlines

aid axe back bid blast blaze clash drama hit key plea quit

Listen to the explanations and vocabulary.

ACTIVEBOOK

  see Writing bank page 158

9 Review and practice

1 Rewrite the pairs of sentences to make one sentence with *After* + present participle or *Having* + past participle.

She arrived at the office early. She worked hard and fast all morning.

Having arrived at the office early, she worked hard and fast all morning.

1 She travelled for hours to get to the village. She thought she should stay there for at least a couple of days.

2 He saw his neighbour struggling with a lot of heavy bags. He offered to help her.

3 She came first in her university exams. She was approached by a top firm of lawyers.

4 She took home an injured cat she had found by the side of the road. She felt she had to keep it.

5 He saw a young man take a CD without paying. He told the security staff.

6 He spoke to his father. He told his boss he wanted a raise.

7 They got a long letter from their cousin. They decided to go and see him.

2 Complete the second sentence so that it means the same as the first. Use *must/might/can't (have)* with the appropriate form of the verb in brackets.

I don't believe she got an 'A' in her exam. (get)

She can't have got an 'A' in her exam.

1 It is possible he stayed late at the office. (stay)
He ...

2 There's no chance that I left my gloves in the car. (leave)
I ...

3 It's possible that she is at the station already. (be)
She ...

4 I'm sure she's shown me her holiday photos at least ten times. (show)
She ...

5 It's not possible that she's finished all her homework already. (finish)
She ...

6 I have no doubt that they are really pleased to be the winners. (be)
They...

7 There's a chance my letter got lost in the post. (got)
My letter ...

8 There's no chance that he is serious about getting a dog. (be)
He ...

3 Add commas to the sentences as necessary.

Jakob Dylan who is Bob Dylan's son is performing in London this weekend.

Jakob Dylan, who is Bob Dylan's son, is performing in London this weekend.

1 I'm afraid I lost the book which she lent me.

2 I'm going to spend a few days in Seville where I first met Raquel.

3 These are the apples which I picked from the tree in my garden.

4 The young man who I spoke to has promised to give me a refund.

5 We decided to stay at the Regina Hotel which some friends had recommended to us.

6 Tim whose job involves a lot of travelling has offered to let us use his flat for a few weeks.

4 Find the mistakes in four of the sentences and correct them.

1 Steve works for a small company makes kitchen equipment.

2 I think the name of the film that I'd like to see is *Avatar*.

3 Did you hear exactly that he said?

4 The demonstration, had been going on for several days, is finally over.

5 Isn't that the place where you grew up?

6 My sister, that speaks French and Italian fluently, wants to be an interpreter.

5 Choose the correct words in *italics*.

1 There was one *victim/witness* to the crime and he saw everything that happened.

2 The fire wasn't an accident. They think someone committed *arson/fraud* and started it deliberately.

3 When he was caught shoplifting, he told the police a *far-fetched/red-handed* story which nobody believed.

4 It's sometimes difficult for courts to decide on an appropriate *punishment/evidence* for criminals.

5 After she had an accident at work, she *insured/ sued* the company and got £1 million.

6 He had to do 150 hours of *a suspended sentence/ community service* for vandalising thirty bus stops in the area.

7 I felt nervous and completely *tongue-tied/ pig-headed* when I had to give evidence in court.

8 He was *committed/convicted* after the forensic scientist found his fingerprints all over the stolen car.

Lead-in

1 Work in pairs and discuss the questions.

1   What can you see in each photo?
2   How do you think they are connected?

2 **a** Work in pairs. Match the quotes below with the photos. What do you think the <u>underlined</u> phrases mean?

'Great leaders use <u>the power of persuasion</u> to achieve their goals.'
'Walking on hot coals is a question of <u>mind over matter</u>.'
'I gave up eating all sweet things using nothing but <u>willpower</u>.'

b In what situations have you used: *mind over matter, the power of persuasion* and *willpower*?

3 **a** Check you understand the meaning of the <u>underlined</u> phrases below.

1   Do you ever <u>have premonitions</u>? Do you take them seriously?
2   Have you ever had <u>a feeling of déjà vu</u>? What happened?
3   Are you someone who is usually able to <u>trust your intuition</u>?
4   Do you know anyone who uses his/her <u>sixth sense</u> a lot?
5   Have you ever been <u>unconscious</u>? What happened?
6   Do you think you have any <u>subconscious fears</u>?

b Work in pairs. Ask and answer the questions in 3a.

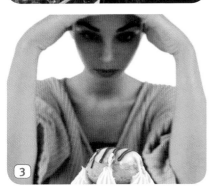

Reading

1 **a** Work in pairs and discuss the questions.

1 What do you think is happening in each photo?

2 What do you think is the difference between an illusionist, a magician and a hypnotist?

3 How do you feel about watching programmes or shows performed by these kinds of people?

b Read the article about Derren Brown quickly and answer the questions.

1 What does Derren Brown say he is interested in: tricks of the hands, tricks of the mind or both?

2 According to the writer, do most people want to know how magic tricks are done?

2 Read the article again and write true (T), false (F) or not given (NG).

1 According to the article, Britain is the only place that Brown is really famous. ☐

2 The writer doesn't care about analysing how Brown does his tricks. ☐

3 The most important thing for Brown is making sure the trick is performed perfectly. ☐

4 The article mentions five tricks that Brown has performed. ☐

5 Brown would like something strange and mysterious to happen to him. ☐

6 Brown is the most skilful illusionist the writer has seen. ☐

How does he do that?

Is he a mind-reader? Or is he playing games with people's heads? When I first heard about Derren Brown, I admit I was sceptical about his abilities but something has always fascinated me about this man. Brown describes himself as a psychological illusionist. His shows are full of seemingly-impossible feats, using different techniques – sleight of hand, hypnotism and suggestion. In Britain, he is now a media star, impressing audiences with his TV shows and stage performances. He says that he doesn't have any special magical or mind-reading powers. He is not psychic and he cannot read people's minds. Apparently, everything he does can be logically analysed. As I say, I myself am sceptical … but endlessly fascinated too. Every time I see one of his shows on TV, I'm drawn in. I don't want to care, but I can't help asking – every time – 'How does he do that?'

In the early days of his career, Brown taught himself standard forms of magic and hypnotism, and began performing in pubs and at parties. As he did more live shows, he realised that, although he loved doing the tricks perfectly, what really interested him was the relationship between the magician and the audience. He began working on a new kind of show, making more of the psychological aspect and combining the magic – tricks of the hands – with the psychology – tricks of the mind. Now his shows are full of his particular kind of illusion – sometimes simple and sometimes incredibly complex. In one episode of his TV show, for example, he tells people how many fingers they are holding up behind their backs. In another, he beats six world-class chess players in simultaneous games. I've seen him successfully predict the week's winning lottery numbers and state which of a number of salesmen are lying about their pasts. I've also seen him draw an almost exact copy of a picture that someone has drawn in secret and put in a sealed envelope. The tricks are diverse, but the effect is the same: the audience is always left staring in awe.

So, how does he do it? Perhaps more importantly, does it matter? Brown says he can explain everything he does. He himself admits, however, that it's sometimes disappointing that everything is explainable. It seems that everyone, including Brown, wants to be fascinated by unexplainable phenomena. And maybe that's the key to his success. People love to be amazed. Even when he tells the audience how something is done, they still look at each other in disbelief. They still don't really understand. Or, maybe it's that Brown is so clever and skilful at what he does, that the audience just don't want to understand. The combination of 'tricks of the hands' with 'tricks of the mind' works somehow. We ask the question 'How does he do that?' but we don't actually want to know the answer. We don't want anything to detract from our fascination and enjoyment of what is, essentially, 'magic'.

3 Work in small groups and discuss the questions.

1 Which of the tricks mentioned in the article do you think would be the most impressive to watch? Why?

2 Do you agree that it's sometimes disappointing that everything is explainable? Why/Why not?

3 Have you (or has anyone you know) had any experience of mind-reading, illusions or being hypnotised? Give details.

Grammar | reflexive pronouns

4 Read rules A and B in the Active grammar box and write the examples (1 and 2) in the correct place.

1 Brown describes <u>himself</u> as a psychological illusionist.

2 He <u>himself</u> admits that it's sometimes disappointing that everything is explainable.

Active grammar

Subject pronouns

I, you, he, she, it, we, you, they

Object pronouns

me, you, him, her, it, us, you, them

Reflexive pronouns

myself, yourself, himself, herself, itself, ourselves, yourselves, themselves

A We use reflexive pronouns to talk about actions where the subject and object is the same person. The reflexive pronoun is essential to the grammar of the sentence.
Example: _____

B We can also use reflexive pronouns for emphasis, when we mean 'that person or thing, and nobody or nothing else'. The reflexive pronoun is not essential to the grammar of the sentence, but is added for emphasis.
Example: _____

C Sometimes we need to use *each other* instead of a reflexive pronoun.

1 *We taught **each other** a magic trick.*

2 *We taught **ourselves** a magic trick.*

---

5 **a** Match the sentences below with the correct rule (A or B) from the Active grammar box.

1 I cut <u>myself</u> while I was cooking.

2 Emily <u>herself</u> said she's not very good at maths.

3 They blamed <u>themselves</u> for the accident.

4 I spoke to the boss <u>himself</u>.

5 You should put <u>yourself</u> in my position and try to understand.

6 She didn't go to the hairdresser. She cut her hair <u>herself</u>.

b What is the difference in meaning between sentences 1 and 2 in part C of the Active grammar box?

c Read the article again and find one more example for rules A, B and C.

see Reference on page 145

6 Complete the sentences with a reflexive pronoun (e.g. *myself, themselves*), an object pronoun (e.g. *him, us*) or *each other*. Sometimes more than one answer is possible.

1 I _____ have never been hypnotised but I know people who have.

2 My best friend and I often know what _____ is thinking.

3 A friend gave _____ a book about acupuncture for my birthday.

4 I'm so forgetful – I'm always locking _____ out of my house.

5 People in Britain usually give _____ presents at Christmas.

6 I'd like to speak to the doctor _____ , not the receptionist.

7 The teacher taught _____ to meditate by focusing us on our breathing.

8 The course _____ wasn't very good, but I loved the teacher.

Pronunciation | stress: reflexive pronouns

7 **a** ⊕ 2.37 When we use reflexive pronouns to add emphasis (to say 'that person or thing, and nobody or nothing else'), we also use stress to emphasise the meaning more. Listen to sentences 1, 6 and 8 from exercise 6 and <u>underline</u> the part of the reflexive pronoun which is stressed.

b Listen again and repeat the sentences.

8 **a** Complete the sentences in a way that you agree with or is true for you.

1 Magicians themselves should never …

2 It's easy to teach yourself …

3 Being with other students and teaching each other is …

b Work in small groups and compare your views. Do you agree? Why/Why not?

Listening

9 🔊 2.38 Listen to three people talking about Derren Brown and mind-reading. Which statement best summarises each person's opinion? One statement cannot be used.

1 He thinks some people are frightened by what Derren Brown does.

2 He admires Derren Brown for what he has achieved.

3 He thinks that going to shows by illusionists is often a waste of money.

4 He thinks it's good but doesn't understand how it works.

10 a Listen again and complete the verb phrases in the How to... box.

> ### How to... talk about beliefs and opinions
>
> *I _____ he's probably genuine, myself.*
>
> *I'm in _____ of just enjoying it as entertainment.*
>
> *I've always _____ that people like Derren Brown are just good showmen.*
>
> *I have my _____ about how much mind-reading he actually does.*
>
> *I'm _____ that any of it is real.*
>
> *I'm _____ people paying for a show which is really just a con.*
>
> *I _____ anything he does is real.*
>
> *I'm _____ that he really does have some kind of power.*
>
> *I _____ that a lot of people don't believe he's doing anything.*

b Work in pairs and answer the questions about the meaning of the verb phrases from exercise 10a.

1 Which two verb phrases mean: I feel almost certain that something is true?

2 Which three verb phrases mean: I think that something may not be true, or is unlikely to happen?

3 Which two verb phrases mean: I think something is true, or is likely to happen?

4 Which one verb phrase means: I agree with and support a plan, idea, or system?

5 Which one verb phrase means: I disagree with and am opposed to a plan, idea or system?

11 Rewrite the sentences below using the words in brackets.

1 My view has always been that there is life on other planets. (believed)

2 I think that ghosts don't really exist at all. (doubt)

3 I had a very strong feeling that I knew what she was thinking. (convinced)

4 I agree with people trying all sorts of different treatments. (favour)

5 I think that some people have supernatural powers. (reckon)

6 I am not sure about the existence of UFOs. (doubts)

7 I disagree with paying someone for a service I don't understand. (against)

8 I think it's unlikely that anyone can predict the future. (sceptical)

Speaking

12 a Choose a topic to talk about (either from the box below or your own idea).

> mind-reading   hypnosis
> vegetarianism   marriage
> military service   ghosts
> smoking in public places

b Prepare to talk about your views for one minute, using the notes below to help you.

1 What experience do you have of the topic and why does it interest you?

2 What are the arguments for and against the topic?

3 What are your personal views?

13 a Work in small groups and take turns to give your talks, using your notes and the How to... box to help you.

b Did anyone have similar views?

Listening

1 Work in pairs and discuss these questions.

1 What does each photo show?
2 What do you think is the aim in each case?
3 What different techniques are being used to achieve the aim?

2 🔵 2.39 Listen to an extract from a radio programme and decide which two things are being discussed.

a advertising
b politicians
c supermarkets.

3 Listen again and complete the notes with one or two words.

1 Most supermarkets have a transition zone at the _____ .
2 Many supermarkets also play music and have the smell of _____ .
3 When the price is £9.99, people are _____ into thinking the price is £9.
4 Working out the prices of fruit and vegetables is often difficult and _____ .
5 Customers like buying something when the price has been reduced and it's a _____ .
6 Adverts are either based on the thinking part or the _____ part of our brain.
7 Adverts for _____ often give us information about the product.
8 Adverts for clothes often work on our feelings of wanting to fit in with our _____ .
9 A fast and effective way of getting the message across is to use _____ .

4 Work In small groups. What do you think about the ways that supermarkets persuade you to buy more things or visit more frequently?

Vocabulary | advertising

5 Work in pairs and say what the difference in meaning is between each pair of words/phrases from the box.

> advertising/marketing   commercial break/target market
> brand/hype   slogan/logo   advertisement/trailer

6 Choose the correct words in *italics*.

1 Have you got any favourite *advertising/advertisements*?
2 What are three of the best-known *hypes/brands* of clothing in your country?
3 Would you like to work in *commercial break/marketing*?
4 Do you think you would be good at thinking up *commercial breaks/slogans*?
5 What do you usually do during *commercial breaks/marketing* on TV?
6 Do you like watching *trailers/slogans* for new films before the main film at the cinema?
7 Which film has had a lot of *brand/hype* recently?
8 What do you think the *advertisement/target market* is for eight-seater 'people-carrier' vehicles?
9 What do you think is the worst thing about the *commercial break/advertising* industry?
10 Do you prefer to buy clothes with or without a *logo/brand* showing?

7 a Work in pairs. Choose five of the questions from exercise 6 to ask and answer.

b How much do you think you are influenced by advertising?

Grammar | conditional structures (2): with conjunctions

8 a Complete sentences 1 and 2 in part A of the Active grammar box with the correct form of *stay* and *come*. Check your answers with audioscript 2.39 on page 176.

b Complete the rules (1–3) below with the phrases in **bold** in sentences 3–7 in the Active grammar box.

1 _____ means 'if not'

2 _____ is used to emphasise that something will still be true if something else happens

3 _____ , _____ and _____ have similar meanings. They are used to say that something is dependent on something else.
Supposing is often used to imagine a situation and suggest possible results.

Active grammar

A

1 *If there are large discounts on offer, customers _____ to the shops in huge numbers.*

2 *You certainly wouldn't have spent as much if you _____ at home and not bought anything!*

B

3 ***Unless*** *you're really good at doing maths in your head, you won't want to work out the price of each apple.*

4 ***Supposing*** *you're a customer, you might think that organic apples aren't so much more expensive.*

5 *People will buy something **as long as** it looks like a bargain.*

6 ***Provided that*** *you respond emotionally, you'll probably want to buy the product.*

7 *Shops know that people are tempted by lower prices **even if** you end up spending more in the end.*

---

see Reference page 145

9 Match the first parts of the sentences (1–6) with the second parts (a–f).

1 Even if you try to avoid adverts, …

2 Unless you look closely at prices, …

3 Provided that you don't let your children watch TV, …

4 If you go to the cinema, …

5 As long as the advert uses a celebrity, …

6 Supposing you only take cash to the shops, …

a … they won't see many adverts.

b … the product will be successful.

c … they are all around you.

d … you probably won't spend so much.

e … it's sometimes difficult to know which is cheaper.

f … you usually see lots of adverts before the main film.

10 Complete the sentences below with the correct form of the verb in brackets.

1 I'll buy this computer unless I _____ (find) anything cheaper online.

2 I _____ (not buy) those jeans even if my favourite celebrity was advertising them.

3 If I _____ (not go) to the sale, I wouldn't have wasted so much money on things I don't need.

4 If you weren't such a persuasive person, I _____ (not buy) any of these things.

5 I _____ (watch) that film as long as there aren't any adverts interrupting it.

6 She _____ (buy) the car provided that she has enough money.

7 If I _____ (not see) that advert yesterday, I wouldn't know about this new toothpaste.

8 Supposing you were watching TV and a really annoying advert came on, what _____ (you do)?

WHAT'S YOUR
M&S

11 a Choose the correct words in *italics*.

1 I like logos on clothes *unless/as long as* they are not too big.

2 I always get something on an offer for 'buy one get one free' *even if/provided that* I don't need two.

3 *Supposing/As long as* I could choose a celebrity to advertise a new car, I'd choose a film star.

4 I like going shopping during the sales, *supposing/ provided that* it's not too crowded.

5 *As long as/Unless* we understand the tricks that supermarkets use, we'll end up spending far too much money.

6 *If/Even if* I see a really good advert on TV, it definitely influences whether I buy the product.

7 *Even if/As long as* I spend time checking prices, I can usually get a good bargain.

8 *Unless/If* I really need some new clothes, I don't go into shops at all.

b Rewrite the sentences from exercise 11a to make them true for you.

c Work in pairs and discuss your sentences. How far do you agree?

Listening

12 a Work in pairs and discuss the questions.

1 Do you think you are someone who is easily persuaded to buy things? What do you think influences you most: persuasive adverts, discounts or something else?

2 Who do you think has the biggest influence on persuading you to do things: your family or your friends? Why?

b 🔊 2.40 Listen to two dialogues and answer the questions.

1 What do you think the relationship is between Anna and Zoë, and between Jamie and Alex?

2 What is Zoë persuading Anna to do, and what is Jamie persuading Alex to do?

3 In the end, are Anna and Alex persuaded or not?

13 Listen to the dialogues again and number the phrases in the How to... box in the order you hear them.

> ### How to... persuade someone to do something
>
> | Dialogue 1 | *Go for it then!* |
> |---|---|
> | | *You should just do it.* |
> | | *I'm sure you won't regret it.* |
> | | *You deserve it!* |
> | | *Go on ... treat yourself!* |
> | | *If I were you, I'd just do it!* |
> | | *Supposing you don't get it, how will you feel?* |
> | Dialogue 2 | *Come on!* |
> | | *It'll be fun.* |
> | | *What have you got to lose?* |
> | | *I'm sure you'll enjoy it.* |
> | | *There's nothing else, unless you want to get a DVD?* |

Pronunciation | intonation: sounding enthusiastic

14 a 🔊 2.41 When we are persuading someone to do something, we often want to sound enthusiastic and persuasive. We can do this by using particular intonation. Listen to the phrases in the How to... box and answer the questions.

1 Generally, is the intonation high or flat?

2 Which words are stressed in each sentence?

b Listen again and repeat the phrases.

Speaking

15 a Prepare to persuade someone else to do something. Choose one of the ideas from the box below or your own.

b Make notes on what you want to persuade your friend to do and why.

> buy something   see a film
> start a new hobby/sport   go on holiday
> get a pet   start cycling to work/school

c Work in pairs. Take turns to persuade each other to do something. Who was more persuasive?

Reading

1 **a** Read the sentences and decide which ones are true for you. Rewrite the others to make them true.

1 I take photos of the most important events in my life.

2 I store my photos on my computer.

3 I take a lot of video recordings of people who are important to me.

4 I love looking at old family photos.

5 I like sharing photos with lots of people by putting them online.

b Work in pairs and compare your sentences.

2 Work in pairs. Read the blog entry below and answer the questions.

1 What is 'lifelogging'?

2 What concerns does the writer have about making a 'lifelog'?

My life... a movie worth watching?

I've been wondering about this for a while and I've finally made up my mind – I've decided to become a lifelogger! I've just finished reading an interesting article about 'lifelogging' – recording your whole life digitally – and I must say, I'm inspired! Life just passes you by for so much of the time and if you're anything like me, you forget so much of what's happened. Things just slip my mind all the time – I forget everything: friends' birthdays, titles of books I want to read, names of business contacts … but more importantly, my memories of events just become a big blur to me and the details are all lost. I wish I had taken more photos of things when I was younger, because at least I would have those. I often think it's too late … I should've made video recordings of my school days and of holidays with my family when I was young. So, you can imagine how excited I was when I came across this article about creating a digital memory of your whole life! If I start now, maybe it won't be too late!

Apparently, a researcher at Microsoft has been experimenting with digital recording. He has spent several years recording every aspect of his life: all his communications with other people, as well as things like the images he sees, the sounds he hears and the websites he visits. The digital memory can do more than just store information you put in it, though. It can also record information that humans can't even see or hear, such as how much oxygen is in your blood, or the levels of carbon dioxide in the air around you. It can also log the three billion or so heartbeats in someone's lifetime, along with lots of other information about your body. It's interesting and they say it can give doctors an ongoing health record of a person and provide early warnings of many kinds of illnesses, including things like possible heart attacks.

Being able to record all this information is obviously a huge step forward in making lifelogging possible. Another essential factor is the staggering growth in digital storage capacity. Today, a $600 hard drive can hold one terabyte – that's one trillion bytes of data. That is enough to store everything you read (including emails, webpages, papers and books), all the music you buy, eight hours of speech and ten pictures a day for the next 60 years. They say that in 20 years, $600 will buy 250 terabytes of storage – enough to hold tens of thousands of hours of video and tens of millions of photographs. That kind of capacity should be enough for anyone's recording needs for more than 100 years!

So, improvements in the hardware for digital recording have improved dramatically – and more and more people have started to create electronic chronicles of their lives. As for me, I've been writing a blog for a while and uploading photos onto it. But right now, it doesn't feel like enough. I wish I could start recording everything … If only I had a proper digital recorder! If I had one now, I'd record myself doing this! I'm going to record everything about my life – I really am. I'm slightly concerned, however, that I might change my mind when I start recording everything. I might find that my life is really boring. A movie of my life might not be worth watching or remembering at all! I think I'll have to change my life a bit. In fact, I'm determined to make my life interesting from now on – though I'm not sure how I'll do that when I'm spending all my time recording it?!

Vocabulary | verb phrases with *mind*

5 Work in pairs and look at the <u>underlined</u> verb phrases. Look at the context of the whole sentence and say what you think each verb phrase means.

1 I've finally <u>made up my mind</u> – I've decided to become a lifelogger!

2 Things just <u>slip my mind</u> all the time – I forget everything.

3 I'm slightly concerned that I might <u>change my mind</u> when I start recording everything.

4 It has <u>crossed my mind</u> to make a lifelog, but I've never given it much real thought.

5 I'm wondering what to get for her birthday. Let me know if anything <u>springs to mind</u>.

6 A new camera is a really good idea for a present – I'll <u>keep it in mind</u>.

7 I've got an essay to do but I'm finding it hard to <u>keep my mind on it</u>.

8 If you asked him, he'd tell you what he thinks. He always <u>speaks his mind</u>.

6 **a** Choose the correct words in *italics*.

1 Has it ever *crossed/spoken* your mind to write a blog or make a lifelog?

2 Do you usually *keep/make* up your mind quickly or do you take a long time to decide things?

3 When was the last time something *slipped/changed* your mind and you forgot to do something important?

4 Have you got any good ideas that you're *springing/keeping* in mind for a present to give someone?

5 When you go shopping, do you often *cross/change* your mind about something when you get it home?

6 Do you know anyone who always *speaks/keeps* his/her mind and sometimes upsets people because of that?

7 Do you find it easier to *make/keep* your mind on your homework when you're listening to music or not?

8 When do good ideas usually *spring/slip* to mind for you – in the early morning or late at night?

b Work in pairs and discuss the questions from exercise 6a.

3 Read the blog entry again. Work in pairs and answer the questions.

What does Marco say about …

1 … his own memory?

2 … photos and videos of his childhood?

3 … the researcher?

4 … benefits for doctors?

5 … how much you can record?

6 … his blog?

4 Work in pairs and discuss the questions.

What do you think about 'lifelogging' in terms of …

1 health benefits?

2 recording family history?

3 your own life?

Grammar | futures (2)

7 Look at the examples (a–i) and write them in the correct place in the Active grammar box.

a I've decided to become a lifelogger.

b I wish I could start recording everything.

c I'm going to record everything about my life.

d If I start now, maybe it won't be too late.

e I think I'll have to change my life a bit.

f If only I had a proper digital recorder.

g I'm determined to make my life interesting from now on.

h If I had a digital recorder now, I'd record myself doing this.

i I'm meeting a friend to buy a digital recorder tomorrow.

Active grammar

Wishes and uncertain plans for the future

A Wishes in the present/future: *wish/if only* + past tense/*could*, e.g. (1) _____ (2) _____

B *will* for decisions (often with *I think/I don't think*), e.g. (3) _____

C Conditional structures:

First Conditional: *if* + Present Simple/ Continuous + *will/won't* to talk about future possibility, e.g. (4) _____

Second Conditional: *if* + Past Simple/ Continuous + *would/wouldn't* to talk about future unreal or imagined situations, e.g. (5) _____

Intentions and certain plans for the future

D *be going to* for intentions, e.g. (6) _____

E Present Continuous for arrangements, e.g. (7) _____

F Phrases to say you're certain about something in the future, e.g. *I'm intending to ...* , (8) _____ (9) _____

See Reference page 145

8 Find the mistakes in six of the sentences and correct them.

1 I wish I have a better camera so I could take good photos.

2 I'm determined to get a well-paid job when I've finished this course.

3 If I have time this weekend, I put my holiday photos on my blog.

4 I'm intending to having guitar lessons in the future.

5 If only I could do a course in computer graphics.

6 I study really hard if I took the exam this year.

7 I've decided buying a new laptop in the next couple of weeks.

8 If I'll save up enough money, I'll go skiing next year.

9 **a** Complete the sentences to make them true for you.

1 In the next six months, I've decided to ...

2 I wish I could ...

3 If I have time later this week, I'll ...

4 In the next month or so, I hope I'll ...

5 I'm determined to ...

b Work in pairs. Compare and discuss your sentences.

Speaking

10 Work in small groups. Read the web page extract below and discuss the questions.

1 How surprised are you by the percentage of people who achieve their wishes and intentions?

2 Can you think of any other ways of improving the success rate?

'He's full of good intentions but ...'

Many people start out with good intentions. Popular goals include: exercise more, eat better, save money, get a better job, get better grades, learn something new, become more organised, reduce stress, become less grumpy.

Research shows, however, that in a study about intentions and resolutions only 12 percent of people achieved their goals in the end. Their success was improved by: making measurable goals, making their goals public and getting support from friends.

---

11 **a** Read the web page extract again and make notes about three intentions/wishes you (or someone you know) could make.

b Work in small groups and compare your intentions/wishes, giving details. How likely do you think it is that you will achieve the intentions/wishes?

1 **a** Work in pairs and discuss the questions.

1 How many basic spelling rules do you think there are in English?

    a twenty-five

    b sixty

    c ninety

2 How many different ways do you think there are for spelling the sound /iː/?

    a at least five

    b at least eight

    c at least twelve

3 What do you think the Spelling Society in Britain wants to do?

    a simplify English spelling

    b encourage correct spelling

    c go back to old spelling rules

b Read the news article below and check your answers.

Should English be simpler?

There are 90 basic spelling rules in English and 84 of these have exceptions! For some sounds, there are no clear rules at all and identical sounds can be spelt in several different ways. For example, the sound /i/ can be spelt as in: *seem, team, theme, sardine, protein, thief, people, he, key, ski, debris, quay*.

The Spelling Society in Britain thinks that the English spelling system should be simplified. They say, for example, that we should spell the sound /i/ simply as 'ee', e.g. *peeple*, and save learners a lot of time and effort. Until then, however, it's just a question of lots of learning and testing!

2 Work in pairs and choose the correct spelling for each pair of words.

1 beleive/believe

2 intelligence/intelligance

3 subconscious/subconsious

4 psychologist/pyschologist

5 dout/doubt

6 existance/existence

7 successful/successfull

8 responsability/responsibility

3 **a** Find the eighteen common spelling mistakes in the blog entry below and correct them.

I'm having a grate time here in Scotland. All the people I've met have been very genrous. Of course, I'm still a foriener here and it felt wierd at first, but I'm begining to feel more at home now. The wether is definately very changable – and it rains a lot! So that feels like home!

I've now got my accomodation sorted out. I'm living in an intresting part of town with lots of restraunts and a good libarry round the corner. Everything is very close so it's not really nessasry to go to the university by bus. I usally walk, although I occasionly get a lift with some freinds in there car.

I'll write a seperate post about the course I'm studying later.

b Work in pairs and compare your answers.

4 Work in small groups. Read the Lifelong learning box and discuss the questions.

Spelling test

! Spelling correctly in English is an important, but sometimes difficult, skill.

1 Why do you think it is important to spell accurately?

2 Why is it difficult to spell accurately in English?

3 Are there any words that you particularly like or dislike the spelling of?

4 What are some of the ways you use to remember how to spell words?

5 What can you use to check your spelling?

Lifelong learning

10 Communication

1 Work in pairs and discuss the questions.

1 What jobs can you see in the photos?
2 What qualities do you think you need for each job?

2 Match the questions (1–6) with the appropriate answers in the boxes (A–F).

1 Which of these jobs would you like to do most?
2 Which one of these would you be most keen on doing as part of your work?
3 When you're in a group, which one of these are you most likely to do?
4 When you're learning a language, which of these appeals to you most?
5 What would you most like to spend your time doing when you're on holiday?
6 Do any of these statements describe you? If not, write one which does.

A

> playing sports   doing nothing
> reading a good book   doing a puzzle book
> talking to local people

B

> politician   artist   journalist   lawyer
> psychologist   teacher   astronaut   nurse

C

> I enjoy dancing   I like trying to figure people out
> I like telling stories   I'm interested in science
> I enjoy a good discussion

D

> wonder what other people are thinking
> be the 'entertainer' who keeps the mood high
> speak on behalf of the group
> take control of any money or number issues
> keep the group focused on reaching its goal

E

> working together in a team
> writing a story or poem
> doing scientific research
> doing something practical   being outdoors

F

> analysing grammatical rules
> speaking without worrying about mistakes
> immersing yourself totally in the country
>   where the language is spoken

3 **a** Work in pairs and answer the questions from exercise 2. Use the ideas from the boxes (A–F) and your own ideas.

b Read the descriptions on page 147.

1 Which description do you think you are most like?
2 Which description do you think your partner is most like?
3 Do you and your partner think/learn in a similar or a different way?

Reflexive pronouns

Singular: *myself/yourself/himself/herself/itself*

Plural: *ourselves/yourselves/themselves*

We use reflexive pronouns to talk about actions where the subject and object are the same person. The reflexive pronoun is essential to the grammar of the sentence – it would not make sense without it.

*I **cut myself** while I was cooking.*

We can also use reflexive pronouns for emphasis, when we mean 'that person or thing, and nobody or nothing else'. In this case, the reflexive pronoun is not essential to the grammar of the sentence, but is added for emphasis.

*They built that house **themselves**.*

We sometimes need to use *each other* instead of a reflexive pronoun. *Each other* means that each of two or more people does something to the other(s).

*We looked at **each other** and smiled.*

Compare: *We looked at **ourselves** in the mirror.*

Conditional structures (2): with conjunctions

Many conditional structures include the word *if*.

***If** it rains, we'll stay at home today.*

*I wouldn't have told her **if** she hadn't asked me.*

We can also use other conjunctions with conditional structures, e.g. *unless, provided that, as long as, supposing, even if.*

Unless means 'if not'

*The course won't run **unless** some more people sign up for it.*

Provided that and *as long as* are used to say that something is dependent on something else. We can also use *providing*.

*I'll come to the Karaoke bar **provided that** you don't make me sing.*

*I'll help you with the washing-up **as long as** you help me with my homework later.*

Supposing is used to imagine a situation and its possible result.

***Supposing** I won £1,000 ... I'd go on holiday immediately.*

Even if is used to emphasise that something will still be true if something else happens.

*I wouldn't buy that car **even if** I could afford it.*

Futures (2)

To talk about wishes in the present or future, we can use *wish/if only* + past tense/*could*.

*I **wish** I **could** speak better English.*

*I **wish** it **was** the summer holidays.*

*If only I **had** a car.*

To talk about decisions made at the time of speaking, we can use *will*. We often use *I think/I don't think* in this case.

I'll go shopping after work today.

I think I'll apply to an American university.

To talk about future possibility, we can use the First Conditional: *if* + Present Simple/Continuous + *will/won't*.

If I don't pass my driving test, I'll take it again next month.

To talk about future unreal or imagined situations, we can use the Second Conditional: *if* + Past Simple/Continuous + *would/wouldn't*.

If I was better at science, I'd study medicine at university.

To talk about intentions and plans for the future (when details haven't been decided), we can use *be going to*.

I'm going to see that new film this weekend.

To talk about arrangements in the future (when details, e.g. about time and place have been decided), we can use the Present Continuous.

I'm meeting my brother at the airport on Saturday morning.

To say we're certain about something in the future, we can use certain phrases, e.g. *I've decided to ... , I'm determined to ... , I'm intending to ...*

I've decided to take up football again.

I'm determined to finish my project this weekend.

I'm intending to visit my grandmother tomorrow.

Key vocabulary

The power of the mind

willpower   mind over matter   the power of persuasion
have a premonition   have a feeling of déjà vu
trust your intuition   sixth sense   unconscious
subconscious (fears)

Advertising

advertisement   trailer   advertising   marketing
commercial break   target market   brand   hype
slogan   logo

Verb phrases about *mind*

make up your mind   slip your mind
change your mind   cross your mind
spring to mind   keep your mind on something
speak your mind   keep it in mind

Commonly misspelt words

accommodation   beginning   believe   changeable
definitely   doubt   existence   friend   foreigner
great/grate   generous   intelligence   interesting
library   necessary   occasionally   psychologist
responsibility   restaurants   separate   subconscious
successful   there/their/they're   usually   weird
weather/whether

 Listen to the explanations and vocabulary.

ACTIVEBOOK

 see Writing bank page 159

1 Complete each sentence using the correct form of a verb from the box. Use a reflexive pronoun where necessary.

> relax   feel   ~~blame~~   enjoy   express   meet
> hurt   concentrate   burn

They are _blaming_ themselves for the accident, but it wasn't their fault.

1 Don't touch the iron. You'll _____ .

2 I _____ very disappointed when I found out I'd failed my driving test.

3 She's a good speaker. She _____ very clearly.

4 You've worked hard today. You should sit down and _____ now.

5 Jack's gone to the doctor because he _____ while he was playing football this morning.

6 My boss and I are going to _____ for lunch tomorrow.

7 Thank you for the party. We really _____ .

8 I _____ as hard as I could in the maths lesson, but I still couldn't understand it.

2 Choose the correct word in _italics_.

1 He'll miss the beginning of the film _unless/if_ he arrives soon.

2 You won't be tired tomorrow _provided that/unless_ you go to bed now.

3 _Supposing/Even if_ you trained your dog, you could put him in for a competition.

4 _As long as/Unless_ you pay me back by tomorrow, I won't lend you money ever again.

5 _Even if/provided that_ he gets a taxi, he's going to be late.

6 I'll tell you what she said _as long as/supposing_ you don't tell anyone else.

7 We can have a party _even if/provided that_ everyone helps clear up afterwards.

8 _Supposing/Unless_ I lived in the countryside, I could have a horse of my own.

3 Rewrite the sentences starting with the words given.

1 I'm sorry that I haven't got more willpower.
   I wish …

2 I'm definitely going to go for a run every morning.
   I'm determined …

3 I'm sad that I can't travel more this year.
   If only …

4 If I go to the beach or not, depends on good weather.
   If the weather …

5 It would be nice if I had enough money to pay for you.
   If only …

6 I'm sorry that I can't become a professional musician.
   I wish …

4 Complete the sentences with the correct form of a word from the box. Two of the words cannot be used.

> unconscious   spring   déjà vu   change
> premonition   subconscious   keep
> make   intuition   slip

1 I'm so sorry I forgot to phone you. It completely _____ my mind.

2 I was sure I'd seen her before. I had a strong feeling of _____ .

3 You need to _____ up your mind about what you want to do tomorrow.

4 I've been thinking about ideas for our project but nothing _____ to mind.

5 Don't worry about other people. Trust your _____ and do what you want.

6 I've decided to see a hypnotherapist to try to get over my _____ fear of spiders.

7 It's very difficult to _____ my mind on my work when there's so much noise in here.

8 I'm not going in a car today. I had a _____ about being in a car accident.

5 Choose the best word in _italics_.

1 Don't believe all the _brand/hype/logo_ about that new film. It's not much good.

2 I don't really care what _slogan/market/brand_ of jeans I wear as long as they're comfortable.

3 There are so many commercial _brands/breaks/slogans_ during this programme. It's really disruptive.

4 We are not allowed to wear any clothes with _logos/trailers/brands_ on them at my school.

5 'Just do it', for the company Nike, is one of the most famous _advertisements/trailers/slogans_.

6 I saw a _brand/trailer/hype_ of that film before it came out and it looked really good, but actually, it was really boring.

6 Find the misspelt words in six of the sentences and correct them.

1 I'll definately see you tomorrow evening.

2 Finding cheap accomodation in London is very difficult.

3 Having children is an enormous responsability.

4 We went to a great new restaurant yesterday.

5 Could you put the sandwiches in seperate bags, please?

6 Have you seen there new house?

7 I can't believe how rude the waiter was!

8 My sister is an extremely sucessful designer.

Communication activities

Communication 9 | Ex. 2, page 130

1 Explanation

The teenagers were travelling on the road that crossed the road that the police officer was on. They drove through a green light.

Communication 2 | Ex. 3a, page 32

You love your creature comforts
You love your holidays, but you prefer a touch of home wherever you go. Creature comforts mean a lot to you. Trekking through the desert with a camel is not your idea of a holiday. You prefer a complete rest and lots of sun.

You love a touch of adventure
You're a bit of an adventurer compared to some holidaymakers. You hate lying around sunbathing, but prefer something different, such as white-water rafting. However, you also prefer to sleep in a nice bed in a good hotel after a hard day's adventure.

You love to be independent
You're a true independent traveller who probably avoids package holidays and is rarely seen on a Greek island or the Costa del Sol. You love exploring far-flung countries and mixing with the locals. And you've probably got cupboards full of photos and interesting souvenirs.

You're a real explorer
You have the spirit of a Stanley or Livingstone – a real explorer who loves to get lost in places where no tourist has gone before. You love meeting the locals, hate bumping into anyone who speaks your language and don't mind sleeping in the open with the local wildlife for company.

Lesson 9.2 | Ex. 8b, page 125

The solution
The ranger joined the middle-aged couple, Adam and Jean, for a chat inside their tent. Inside the tent, he sat on a backpack to avoid the wet ground. The fact that there was wet ground inside the tent meant that they had put up the tent after it rained. They said, however, that they had put up the tent the previous night (before it rained), so they were definitely lying. They must have committed the crime because they were lying to cover their tracks.

Communication 9 | Ex. 2, page 130

4 Explanation

Because Bobby was only nine months old.

Lesson 2.2 | Ex. 13b, page 27

Group A

Bird watching in Mexico at
Yucatan Ecolodge

Price: $100 per person per night

Where? Yucatan Ecolodge is a 5-hour drive from Cancun airport and is surrounded by beautiful coconut trees with wonderful views of the Gulf of Mexico. The whole area is famous for its incredibly varied plant and animal life, especially birds.

Accommodation Stay in a comfortable bungalow with a veranda as well as bedroom, sitting room and bathroom. There are fans but no air conditioning. Meals are served in our main building – half board including tasty Mexican breakfast and 4-course candle-lit dinner. There is a lot of delicious fresh food and seafood available. There is also a bar, a games room and a swimming pool for you to enjoy.

Activities A variety of tours are available including bird-watching tours, trips to the famous caves in the area and moonlight safaris. There is also a small Natural History Museum, offering an overall view of the flora and fauna surrounding the hotel.

Lesson 5.3 | Ex. 13a, page 72

Up in the Air (2010)
Love story starring George Clooney.
109 minutes

Julie and Julia (2009)
Comedy drama based on a true story, starring Meryl Streep. 123 minutes

Communication 10 | Ex. 3b, page 144

Linguistic: They like to think in words and use complex ideas. They are sensitive to the different sounds and meanings of words and enjoy learning foreign languages.

Logical-mathematical: They like to understand patterns and the relationships between things. They are good at thinking critically and problem-solving. They like to analyse and understand the rules.

Interpersonal: They like to think about other people and are often peacemakers. They are aware that people have different views on life. They have lots of friends.

Existential: They like to spend time thinking about philosophical issues and don't like to be bothered with trivial questions. They are always asking questions provoking discussions and debates.

Kinaesthetic: They find it difficult to sit still for long. They are interested in fitness and health and learn best when physically involved.

Communication activities

Communication 4 | Ex. 5, page 60

London Centre for Business Studies

BSc Business Studies: Full-time, Part-time or Online Learning – a flexible mode of study which allows you to combine online learning with university-based study.

We offer excellent facilities and tuition to the candidate who is committed to taking initiative and studying to his/her full potential.

Nursing Diploma - Cambridge

Our programme is a full-time, 3-year course leading to an academic qualification and professional registration as a nurse. Half the course is classroom or private study and the remaining time is practice-based. Right from the start, students will be working with patients, with appropriate support, and this will involve working some evenings, nights and weekends. The training will be demanding. However, the potential rewards can be great.

You will need to have school-leaving qualifications and to be at least 17 years old at the start of the course.

Lesson 9.1 | Ex. 11, page 122

Communication 9 | Ex. 2, page 130

3 Explanation

He was riding a horse called 'Friday'.

Lesson 3.3 | Ex. 2a, page 42

Student A

Oliver – I read what you wrote about 'the good old days' with interest. Despite making some sensible points, to my mind your argument is wildly oversimplified in saying that the old days were better. All too often nowadays, we hear these black-and-white opinions about 'globalisation'. In my opinion, it's a grey area and there are important benefits as well as some inevitable downsides as we move away from the good old days.

I feel that thriving cultures are not fixed and many of the best things come from cultures mixing. For example, many British people didn't take to the very spicy food introduced by Indian people. As a result, Indian food in Britain is not the same as an authentic curry from India, but for some, it's even better. I took part in some market research recently and found out that even branded goods are often changed to suit local tastes. Did you know, for example, that McDonald's sell beer in France, lamb in India, and chilli in Mexico?

As far as I can see, the same is true of music. According to you, all we ever listen to now is bland American-influenced music. I know for a fact that the evidence does not back this up. Latin American salsa, Brazilian lambada and African music are all popular throughout the world, as well as a massive intermixing of musical types. And alongside this incredible diversity now available across the world, in most countries, local artists still top the charts. So, local tastes are alive and well, AND even more variety is being created.

I found it hard to take in what you said about language. Did you really mean that English is 'taking over the world', as you put it? I don't think so! I agree that huge numbers of people now speak English. At the start of the 21st century, about one and a half billion (1,500,000,000) people spoke English. That includes about 400 million speaking English as their first language and the rest speaking it as a second or third language. However, in many cases, a new type of English has been created. A kind of 'global English' has taken off across the world. I think this is good in that it facilitates communication in an ever-shrinking, ever-more commercial world. People certainly don't want a single world language, but a new common 'lingua franca' has major advantages for global business, scientific research and tourism.

Some people – like you – may be saddened by the passing of the 'old days' but it seems to me that most people are embracing the mixing of cultures and the new things that are being created all the time.

Posted by: Linda Mendes, Melbourne, Australia

1 Does Linda mostly agree or disagree with Oliver?
2 What is the main point she makes about food?
3 Does she agree with Oliver about music?
4 What does she mean by 'a new type of English has been created'?
5 What is the distinction she makes between a 'single' language and a 'common' language?

Communication 9 | Ex. 2, page 130

5 Explanation

The man had just been cured of deafness, and the ringing phone was final proof that it had been a success.

Lesson 2.2 | Ex. 13b, page 27

Group B

Camel trips at

 **DAKHLA OASIS** Egypt

Price: $160 per person per night

Where?

Dakhla Oasis is about 850km from Cairo. The hotel is situated at the top of pink cliffs which surround the oasis below. Within the oasis, there are beautiful fields and gardens full of grapes, olive trees, date palms, figs, apricots and citrus fruits. Beyond the oasis, there are the incredible sand dunes of the Sahara Desert.

Accommodation

Dakhla has 32 large rooms all with private bathrooms. The rooms are simply but tastefully furnished in the local style. They all have fans and also heaters for the cold winter nights. Some rooms have a terrace with spectacular views of the nearby mountain range. The restaurant serves delicious local food including the traditional 'falafel'.

Activities

There are camel trips and walking tours available from half a day to 3-plus days. These go across the sand dunes of the desert and also up into the mountains. The guides will help you set up the tents and prepare a delicious barbecue dinner on the campfire with homemade bread, baked in the sand.

Lesson 9.1 | Ex. 12, page 122

Story 1

At 5 a.m. one morning, two would-be robbers from Edmonton in Canada, raided a small petrol station in Vancouver. After locking the attendant in the toilets, they made their getaway with a few hundred dollars. Coming from Edmonton, they didn't know their way around Vancouver and 20 minutes later, they drove up at the same petrol station to ask directions.

The attendant, Mr Karnail Dhillon, having just escaped from the toilets, was alarmed to see the two robbers coming into the shop again. 'They wanted me to tell them the way to Port Moody,' he said. 'I guess they didn't recognise me or the petrol station.'

He was just calling the police when the pair came back again to say that they couldn't get their car to start. While they were waiting for a mechanic to help them, the police arrived and arrested them.

Communication 9 | Ex. 2, page 130

2 Explanation

The water in the river only came up to the man's chest.

Lesson 3.3 | Ex. 2a, page 42

Student B

So, Oliver, you are lamenting the passing of 'the good old days', are you? According to you, we now have identical high streets worldwide, local cultures have been eroded and national identities have all but disappeared. Personally, I couldn't believe how negative what you wrote was. I strongly disagree with almost everything you said. Far from the uniformity you described, I think we now live in a world of incredible diversity and that can only be good.

In the old days, we were far more stereotyped and more pigeon-holed by our nationality, or where we lived. You were an Italian in Italy, you were expected to be, like, and do things like 'an Italian'. The beauty of the new international view is that it can free people from the tyranny of geography. Just because someone lives in France does not mean they can only speak French, eat French food and listen to French music. We now take it for granted that a Frenchman, or an American, or a Japanese person can take holidays in Spain or Florida, eat sushi or spaghetti for dinner and have friends from around the world.

I see this diversity and availability as an extremely good thing. Look at things on a local level. Oliver, you may think that every high street is the same. I disagree. Yes, people from many different countries may recognise some of the shops but I can now go down my high street and I have choice! I can choose to eat many different types of food. I can also buy clothes from shops originally from many different places: we've got shops like Zara from Spain and Muji from Japan, and countless other brands from all over the world. Far from having limited choice; the choice is almost endless.

There is no doubt that in some ways the world is becoming more uniform but the significance of this uniformity is often exaggerated. Different cultures remain and we can choose to be the same or different. The truth is that we increasingly define ourselves rather than let others define us. Being Italian or American or Polish does not define who you are: it is part of who you are. It seems to me that most people want the best of both worlds – old and new. Admit it, Oliver! Most of us want to have our cake AND eat it, don't we? And maybe we can!

Posted by: Paul Hodges, Florida, US

1 Does Paul mostly agree or disagree with Oliver?
2 What does he mean by 'the tyranny of geography'?
3 What is the main point he makes about his own high street?
4 Why does he mention brands like Zara and Muji?
5 What does he mean by 'we increasingly define ourselves'?

Communication 9 | Ex. 2, page 130

6 Explanation

The airplane was on the ground when he leapt.

1 An informal email to a friend

Can do write personally, highlighting the significance of experiences

1 Read the email and answer the questions.

1 What is the relationship between Martha and Fernanda?
- friends who are in close contact
- friends who haven't seen each other for a long time
- family members who haven't seen each other for a long time
- colleagues who see each other at work

2 Who else does Martha mention?

Hi Fernanda!!

It's so great to find you after all this time. I can't believe it – Facebook is so fab – I've tried to think about how to get in touch with you so much and I couldn't think what to do. I looked on Facebook loads of times and there were so many people with your name. I couldn't see your picture anywhere so I sent a couple of emails to some of them without pix but nobody got back to me. :-(Then the other day, I decided to look again and your face was there!!! :-D

So, some of my news. When I left Portugal – all those years ago!! – I came back to England and got a job teaching at a secondary school. I didn't stay long cos it was really awful. You know, just really difficult kids and long hours and stuff like that. Well, after that I messed around for ages, sort of looking for another job, but not doing much really. After a bit, I got into helping at my friend's café and things went from there. She had to go abroad for a while so she left me in charge and I became the sort of manager. Love it! So, at the moment that's what I'm doing – though I think I might go back to college and do some training. I'd like to learn how to cook properly – maybe get into that side of things. You know, a professional chef or something.

Anyway, enough about me – what about you?! How's it going? Are you still living in Lisbon? What are you doing? I want to hear about your brother Paulo, too. What's he up to? Email me back straight away!! Can't believe I lost touch with a great friend like you!

Lots of love,

Martha

---

2 Read the email again and answer the questions.

1 Which of these things does Martha include in her email?
- how she made contact with her friend
- news about her personal life
- news about her work
- news about other people
- questions about her friend's life

2 Is the language in the email more informal or more formal?

3 a Complete the How to... box with the underlined examples from the email.

How to... use informal language appropriately

Sentence structure	Miss out the subject: **Can't believe I lost touch ...**/ (1) _____
	A clause without a verb: **You know, a professional chef or something.**/(2) _____
Fillers, vague phrases and colloquial language	Fillers: **so**/**well**/(3) _____
	Vague phrases: **loads of**/**a couple of**/**stuff like that**/**sort of**/(4) _____
	Colloquial language: **kids**/**mess around**/**How's it going?**/(5) _____
Colloquial expressions and symbols	Colloquial expressions: **fab (fabulous)**/**pix (pictures)**/ (6) _____
	Symbols: **:- (**/(7) _____ (Generally only used in emails/texts)
Unconventional punctuation	Overuse of exclamation marks: **... and your face was there!!!**/(8) _____
	Asides: **Facebook is so fab**/ (9) _____

b What kinds of people do you think would choose to write in this way? When would it not be appropriate to write like this?

4 a Prepare to write an email to a friend you haven't seen for a long time. Choose who you are writing to, and what you want to write about. Make brief notes.

b Now write your email. Make sure you write in an appropriate style for you and your friend.

150

2 | Blog/diary entry

Can do | write clear, detailed descriptions of recent news in a blog or diary

1 Read the blog and answer the questions.

1 Where is the writer? Why is he there?

2 What other people does he mention?

3 Who is he writing to?

19th August – Day 1

I'm finally here in India! I've come to do some voluntary work with elephants for four weeks. It goes without saying that it's exciting here – but it's a bit daunting too as I don't know anybody. But I'm staying with a family in the village and they seem very friendly. I know that some things are going to be challenging because everything is different here. The weather was really scorching today, and it's all a bit of a culture shock at the moment! I think the work will be fun but also quite exhausting – we have to work long hours and it's quite demanding physically. The elephants work giving rides to tourists – then they come here and our job is to look after them. They said that we have to do things like feed them, clean out their living areas and even give them massages! Sounds difficult to me!

24th August – Day 6

Sorry to all my blog readers that I haven't written anything for a few days. By far the hardest work I've done for a long time! I've been working an early shift which means setting off for work at 5 a.m. It's tough getting up so early but I love looking after the elephants. Giving them massages is quite tricky because they're so big! But it's really rewarding. They are really amazing animals. I finish the shift at about 11 a.m. so then I've got plenty of time to go and explore the local area. Yesterday, I went to the city of Jaipur with Alex (another volunteer on the project). Fascinating place – we spent hours there and didn't get back to the village until about 7 p.m. I was exhausted but it's hard to go to bed early because there are so many fantastic things to do.

2 Read the blog again and write true (T) or false (F).

When writing a blog, generally you:

1 write about what you've been doing. ☐

2 write about how you feel. ☐

3 use mostly formal language. ☐

4 sometimes address the reader directly. ☐

5 always use full, grammatically correct sentences. ☐

3 **a** To make our writing clearer and more interesting, we choose vocabulary according to the precise meaning the words/phrases convey. Read the blog again and complete the How to... box with six other adjectives which are related to the word *nice* and six other adjectives which are connected with the word *difficult*.

How to... choose vocabulary according to precise meaning

difficult	:	*daunting*	(1) _____	(2) _____
	:	(3) _____	(4) _____	
	:	(5) _____	(6) _____	
nice	:	*exciting*	(1) _____	(2) _____
	:	(3) _____	(4) _____	
	:	(5) _____	(6) _____	

b Rewrite the blog entry below using more precise vocabulary instead of repeating the words *difficult* and *nice*. Change the word order of sentences if necessary.

So, here I am in a small village somewhere in Mexico! At first, the idea of travelling all the way from the US on my own was difficult. I spent about three days travelling on buses, which was nice but difficult. Then, trying to find my way to the village was difficult, but I managed in the end. I've met a lot of local people already, which has been a nice experience. Everyone I've met has been so nice and really made me feel welcome. I haven't explored the area a lot yet because it's been quite a difficult day. It seems like a nice place here – tomorrow I'll have a good look around. Off to bed now!

c Work in pairs and compare your paragraphs. Which different words have you chosen? How do your different choices affect the meaning you convey?

4 **a** Prepare to write a blog or diary entry. Write about: real events in your life, one of the situations from exercise 13a on page 24, or one of the holidays from exercise 13a on page 27.

b Now write your blog or diary entry. Try to use a range of vocabulary and to express yourself as clearly and precisely as possible.

Can do write a clear, engaging narrative

1 Read the competition entry and answer the questions.

1 What is the purpose of the text?
2 Is the writer describing somewhere he:
   (a) had been on holiday, (b) had worked,
   (c) had lived, or (d) had visited before?
3 In the end, is the writer: (a) disappointed or (b) more pleased than he expected?

2 Look at the competition entry again and complete the sentences in the How to... box.

How to... engage your reader

Introduce what you are going to write about in a general way.	*I had been looking forward _____ to the village where I was born for a long time.*
Use a range of tenses and time expressions.	*My family _____ away from the village 15 years ago and I _____ back _____ then.*
Use a range of vocabulary to include details and interest (e.g. adjectives, adverbs, verb phrases).	*I _____ walked along the _____ road. As I got nearer, what I saw _____ .*
Include your personal response.	*Immediately, _____ and from that point on, I found that _____ the worst.*

3 Read the competition entry and the How to... box again. Work in pairs and discuss the questions.

1 What other way do you think you could start the story?
2 What tenses are there in the text? Why is each one used?
3 What time expressions and linkers are there? What effect do these create?
4 What adjectives, adverbs and verb phrases are used to create interest?
5 How many paragraphs are there? What is the purpose of each one?

4 **a** Prepare to write a short story called 'Going back' for an international English magazine competition. Choose one of the ideas from exercise 1 question 2. Decide how many paragraphs you need and use the How to... box to help you make your writing engaging.

b Now write your short story.

International English Magazine
Short story competition

Topic: *Going back*

Name: *Giacomo Alessi*

I had been looking forward to going back to the village where I was born for a long time. My family moved away from the village 15 years ago and I hadn't been back since then. In the days before I went, I was excited. The village is special to me as I was born there and my family had lived there for years before that. I also felt slightly worried, however. I remembered a peaceful place with small shops along the main street, traditional houses and people sitting under the trees, chatting to each other. I don't know why it mattered to me so much, but I didn't want to find that the village had changed beyond recognition.

On the day I went, the sun was shining. I had decided to arrive on foot so I got off the bus at the edge of the village and I slowly walked along the rough road. As I got nearer, what I saw took my breath away. Right in front of my eyes was a large, modern building, which I quickly realised was a huge shopping centre. Immediately, I felt disappointed and from that point on, I found that I was expecting the worst.

I walked along the main street, however, and felt better and better. I saw trendy, new shops but old, traditional ones as well. There were new blocks of flats alongside the beautiful old houses. The roads were busier than I had remembered, but there were still people sitting under the trees in the main square. I realised that my village had changed, but that it wasn't the disaster that I had imagined. In fact, it was a good thing that the village had moved with the times and remained a thriving place.

4 CV

1 Read the CV (Curriculum Vitae) and write the headings (a–e) below in the correct place (1–5).

a Skills
b Education
c Interests
d Work experience
e Personal statement

2 **a** Read the CV again and answer the questions.

1 What kind of job is Alexandra looking for?
2 What skills and qualities does she mention?

b Match each piece of advice (1–5) below with the headings (a–e) from exercise 1.

1 Write a sentence or two about the skills you used/developed in each job.
2 Write a sentence or two about the skills you use/develop in the sports or hobbies you do.
3 Include the level of your language ability and whether you have a driving licence.
4 Start with the most recent course/place, and include specific modules/areas of study and specific grades (in your higher level exams).
5 Write a sentence or two about the type of job/course you want and briefly state any relevant skills, experience or special interests.

3 Complete the sentences in the How to... box.

How to... write a successful CV

Promote yourself in a positive way	*I have _____ problem-solving skills.* *I provided a _____ service to customers.*
Include appropriate details	*I am looking for a _____ trainee position.* *I worked in a _____ team sometimes under pressure.*
Write concisely and clearly	*I enjoy the dedication and _____ of karate.* *Spanish (_____) and French (good).*

4 **a** Prepare to write your CV. Make some notes for each heading from exercise 1, using the advice from exercise 2b. You can invent details if you want.

b Now write your CV. Use the How to... box to help.

Alexandra Brown
23, Monkton Road, Coventry, CV3 9QT
Mobile: 07789 345222
abrown3@yahoo.co.uk

1 _____

I am a Business Administration graduate from the University of Manchester. I have the skills and knowledge for managing key areas of an organisation and I have excellent problem-solving skills. I am looking for a graduate trainee position in marketing where I can use my strong influencing skills.

2 _____

2007–2010 University of Manchester – BA (Hons) Business Administration 2:1

Modules included:
Human Resources Management
Marketing
Strategic Management
Business Mathematics
Accounting and Finance
E-commerce

Heartlands High School, Coventry

2007 A levels: Mathematics (A), History (A), Geography (B)

2005 GCSEs: 9 GCSE passes including Maths and English

3 _____

June–Sept 2009: Wayfield Supermarket, Store Assistant: I worked in a busy team, sometimes under pressure, and provided a quality service to customers.

June–Sept 2008: NewsShop, Cashier: I worked in a small team in a busy newsagent shop. I often had responsibility for the whole shop, including cashing up at the end of the day.

4 _____

Sport: I believe a healthy body is the key to a focused mind in today's hectic society. I enjoy the dedication and discipline of karate, and the team-playing involved in basketball.

5 _____

Languages: Spanish (fluent) and French (good)

Driving: Full, clean driving licence

1 Read the report and answer the questions.

1 Who do you think wrote the report and who is the intended reader?
2 What does the writer recommend and why?

2 Read the report again and write true (T) or false (F).

1 In the first paragraph, recommend your preferred option. ☐
2 The purpose of the second paragraph is to describe the disadvantages of the first idea. ☐
3 The purpose of the third paragraph is to describe the disadvantages of the second idea. ☐
4 The purpose of the last paragraph is to state the purpose of the report. ☐
5 In a report, you can use sub-headings and bullet points. ☐
6 In a report, you can only express your opinion in the last paragraph. ☐

3 Complete the How to... box with examples from the report.

How to... outline arguments and make recommendations

Outline arguments	*Installing solar panels **would offer many** _____ .* *There are a number of good _____ **about** providing bicycles.* *Cycling to school **would make a big** _____ **to** the health and fitness of the students.* *Reducing car use **would have a large** _____ **on** local pollution.* ***It would** _____ **other people by** setting a good example to other family members.* *Providing bicycles **would be extremely** _____ .*
Make recommendations	*I **would strongly** _____ this option.* ***I have no hesitation in recommending that** providing bicycles is the best option.* ***Considering all the options, it would seem that** providing bicycles is the best option.* ***On balance, we have decided that** the best option would be to provide bicycles.*

---

4 **a** Prepare to write a report for the task below. Make notes for each sub-heading.

- Introduction
- Advantages of a white-water rafting trip
- Advantages of a Health Spa weekend
- Recommendations.

Your school/company has been given some money to spend on a team-building trip for the members of your class/department. The director would like to spend the money on either a white-water rafting trip or a weekend at a health spa. You have been asked to write a report for the director, describing the advantages of each idea. Say which one you think should be chosen and why.

b Now write your report.

Introduction

The aim of this report is to compare the benefits to our school environment of installing solar panels and of providing bicycles to all students, and to suggest which of these would be preferable. I interviewed several students in the school in order to find out their opinions.

Installing solar panels

Some students thought that installing solar panels would offer many benefits, for the following reasons:

1 the school could earn money by creating more energy than it uses;
2 the school would be sending out a good ecological message.

However, the costs of installation may be very high, especially when offset against the relatively small reduction in electricity bills.

Providing bicycles

There are a number of good points about providing bicycles, and the majority of students preferred this option, because:

- cycling to school would make a big difference to the health and fitness of the students;
- reducing car use would have a large impact on local pollution;
- it would benefit other people by setting a good example to other family members.

Recommendations

Both ideas have advantages, but it would seem that most students felt that providing bicycles would be extremely beneficial in terms of improving the school environment. Therefore, I would strongly recommend this option.

Can do | write a review, describing your personal reaction to a book or film

1 **a** When you write a review of a book or film, in which order would you put the paragraphs (a–c)?

a Give your overall recommendation to other people

b Give your opinion, including positive and negative points

c Give some information on what the book/film is about and why you chose it

b Read the review below and check your ideas.

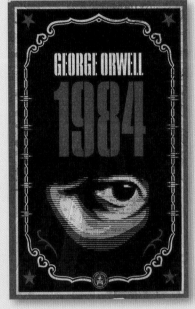

It was when I saw the TV series *Big Brother* that I first became interested in reading the book *1984* by George Orwell since the idea of 'Big Brother is watching you' is central to the plot. The book is set in the future (in the year 1984) and focuses on the main character Winston Smith and his struggle to live in a world completely controlled by the government.

I must admit that before I read it, I was sceptical about whether I'd enjoy it. However, one of the strengths of the book is the way the author uses very detailed descriptions of the feelings of the main characters. It is also an extremely gripping story. Once I started reading it, I couldn't put it down, as I really wanted to know what happened in the end. It is not only the story which is totally fascinating, but also the fact that the ideas about government and freedom are still very relevant today, even though it was written over 60 years ago. The only negative thing I would say about the book is that sometimes it is very frightening, especially when you think about the similarities with some aspects of our society. At times, I was shocked by how similar the fantasy world in the book was to our real world.

I would highly recommend this book. It is obvious to me now that everyone should read it. Even if you're not really interested in government and politics, don't be put off. It is a very well-written book, with very believable characters and an exciting plot.

2 Read the review again and write true (T) or false (F).

1 The story takes place in the past. ☐

2 Before reading the book, the writer thought he would definitely enjoy it. ☐

3 The writer thinks the plot is very good. ☐

4 The writer thinks there are no negative points about the book. ☐

5 The writer thinks the book is only interesting if you like politics. ☐

6 The writer writes in a personal way, giving his own opinion. ☐

3 In a book or film review, you need to convey your opinions clearly. Complete the sentences in the How to... box.

How to... convey your opinions clearly

positive opinions	*One of the _____ of the book is the way the author uses very detailed descriptions.* *My favourite part of the book is the incredibly sad ending.* *Once I started reading it, I couldn't put it _____ .* *I would highly _____ this book.*
negative opinions	*The only _____ thing I would say about the book is that sometimes it is frightening.* *The main weakness of the book is sometimes it is a bit slow.*
Using precise vocabulary	*It is also a very _____ story.* *It is a very **well-written** book, with very _____ characters and an **exciting** plot.* *It is written by an incredibly **talented** writer.*

4 **a** Prepare to write a review of a book you've read or a film you've seen. Make notes using the paragraph plan from exercise 1a and the language from the How to... box.

b Now write your review.

Can do explain a problem and request action

1 Read the email and answer the questions.

1 What is the problem the customer is writing about?

2 What action does she request?

3 What is each paragraph about? Write a brief description starting with the words given.

Paragraph 1: *state ...*

Paragraph 2: *give ...*

Paragraph 3: *request ...*

2 Work in pairs and discuss the questions.

1 How would you feel in the same situation as Diana? Why?

2 What action do you think you'd request? How would you do it?

3 Complete the sentences in the How to... box.

How to... explain a problem and request action

Introduce the problem	*I am writing with reference to my recent purchase.* *I am writing to complain about the service I received.* *I am writing in order to _____ I have recently experienced with your airline.*
Give details about the problem	*The DVD player which was delivered yesterday was **faulty**.* *The food was **below the standard** that I usually expect from your restaurant.* *I _____, however, that **I couldn't** change the flights I'd booked.*
Request some action	***I'd like you to** send a replacement immediately.* ***Please refund me** the full amount.* ***I'd be grateful if you could** _____ as soon as possible.*

Dear Sir/Madam

(1) I am writing in order to explain a problem I have recently experienced with your airline and to request that you provide me with adequate compensation.

(2) Details of the issue are as follows. I recently went on holiday to Spain using your airline. While I was there, members of your company went on strike and many flights were subsequently cancelled, including my return flight from Malaga to London Stansted. When I phoned to talk to your representative in Malaga about this, I wasn't offered any food or accommodation costs, or any information about rebooking my flight once the strike had finished. In fact, I was given misleading information and eventually rebooked a flight for four days later, at double the standard price. Having done this, cheaper flights then appeared for sale, departing the next day. I was told, however, that I couldn't change the flights I'd booked.

(3) I am very disappointed at the misleading information, the lack of immediate compensation and the way I have been treated in general. I would be grateful if you could compensate me as soon as possible for the price of the return flights I had to book, and also for the extra food and accommodation costs that I incurred. I'm sending details of these costs in an attachment to this email. As I'm sure you are aware, compensation of this kind is a legal requirement in circumstances such as this. Thank you for your help with this matter.

Yours,

Diana Jones

4 a Prepare to write an email explaining a problem and requesting some action. Choose one of the situations in the list below or use your own idea. Make brief notes using the paragraph plan from exercise 1.

- Your holiday was ruined because the hotel was very poor quality.
- The engineer who came to fix your heating system failed to do his job properly.
- You injured yourself in a supermarket on a broken shelf.

b Now write your email. Use the language from the How to... box to help you.

Can do write a positive description of someone's personality and skills

1 Read the reference letter and answer the questions.

1 What is the relationship between Rebecca and Melanie?

2 Why is Melanie writing the reference letter?

3 How would you summarise her description of Rebecca?:
a totally positive
b mostly positive
c partly positive and partly negative

2 Read the reference again. Which of the tips (1–6) do you think the writer has followed?

1 say how you know the person and for how long

2 give positive details about the person

3 summarise the main points

4 give your details (position, company, contact details)

5 don't overdo the praise as it can sound insincere

6 don't refer to nationality, age or marital status

3 **a** Look at parts A, B and C of the How to... box and complete each phrase with two words.

b Look at part D of the How to... box. Look at the reference again and <u>underline</u> as many positive words and phrases as you can find in the second paragraph.

How to... use appropriate language

A Opening the reference	*To whom it _____* *For the attention of Ms L. Deacon*
B Recommending	*I am pleased to be able to _____ her for the position of Team Leader.* *I have _____ in recommending her for the position.*
C Offering further contact	*Please do not hesitate to contact me for any _____ you wish to know about her.* *For more information, please contact me at the email address below.*
D Positive words and phrases	*... a very **hard-working** person* *Her ability to work **efficiently** ...*

---

4 **a** Prepare to write a reference for someone you know well (or you could invent someone). Refer to a job you think that person would like (or already does). Make notes for the four parts of the reference, using the tips from exercise 2.

b Now write your reference.

To whom it may concern,

Rebecca Jennings has worked as an accountant in my department for six years, both as a trainee and as a qualified accountant. As we are also close personal friends, I feel I know Rebecca very well and I have seen her working and relating to people in a variety of settings. I am pleased to be able to strongly recommend her for the position of Team Leader.

Rebecca is a very hard-working person who takes her responsibilities seriously. Her ability to work efficiently under stressful conditions and to meet difficult deadlines speaks volumes about her determination and calm personality. She is used to managing her own time which she does professionally and without fuss. She is an outgoing person who shows good leadership qualities and excellent team spirit, demonstrating sensitivity and awareness of other people. She also has an eye for detail and is good at using her initiative appropriately. Rebecca is a high-achiever and single-minded in her attitude to professional development and I consider that this promotion would be an excellent career move for her.

I am sure that Rebecca would be an asset to your company as Team Leader and I have no hesitation in recommending her for the position. Please do not hesitate to contact me for any further details you wish to know about her.

Yours faithfully,

Melanie Katzen

Supervisor, Accountancy Department, Lucas Williams and Co. Ltd.
m.katzen@lucaswilliams.com

1 Read the factual account of a news story and answer the questions.

1 How well had the burglar thought about his plan?

2 How successful was it in the end?

2 Answer the questions. Read the account again if necessary.

1 Who do you think the intended reader is?

2 Why do you think the writer wrote a factual account?

3 Which of the ideas (a–e) does a factual account of a story contain?

a the main facts and events of the story

b the writer's opinion

c extra information (e.g. about the burglar's age, the time of year ...)

d logical paragraphs (e.g. introduction, main events, possible difficulties, how the story ends)

e precise vocabulary

3 Read the information in the How to... box and write the headings in the correct place (A–C).

• Be objective

• Be concise and precise

• Think about the purpose of your writing

How to... summarise clearly and concisely

A _____

Decide who your intended reader is.

Decide why you are writing the account.

B _____

Include the main facts of the story.

Don't include your opinion.

C _____

Use precise vocabulary.

Divide your account into clear paragraphs.

Don't include a lot of unnecessary, background facts.

---

4 **a** Prepare to write a factual account of a news story. Think of a news story that you've heard recently or use the cigar story from page 121, the Yellow Park Campers story from page 123 or the security camera burglar story from page 125. Use the How to... box to plan what you're going to write.

b Now write your factual account.

First-class thief

Burglar Stanisław Muchy nearly got away with a potentially brilliant plan for robbing large companies. His imaginative but complicated idea meant sealing himself up inside a large parcel. Luckily, he is a fairly small, lightweight person because his accomplice then had the task of taking the parcel to the post office and mailing Stanislaw to the company he had written on the address label.

Stanisław had thought his plan through and he knew that timing was crucial. Firstly, he had to decide when to arrive at the company. Someone had to be there to let him in, but he didn't want anyone to open the parcel. Ideally, he wanted the unwrapped parcel, with himself inside, to be left alone in the building all night. When he was sure he was alone, he would climb out and steal whatever he could find. He would then seal himself up in the parcel again, having put his own address on the address label, ready to be mailed back.

Although he had thought about things carefully, there were a number of difficulties that he hadn't worked out. There was the obvious possible problem of the parcel being opened by someone in the company, revealing himself as an intruder. Another problem could have been that nobody would mail him back to his home address.

In the end, however, Stanisław didn't foresee what would ultimately lead to his downfall. His plan and his career as a criminal came to an abrupt end after falling out with his accomplice, who was so angry with Stanislaw that he betrayed him. Instead of mailing him to a company, his accomplice mailed him to the local police station. He also included a note on how the whole process worked – or didn't work.

1 Read the essay. Does the writer agree or disagree with the title of the essay?

2 **a** Read the essay again and put the paragraph headings (a–d) in the correct order.

a Arguments in favour of the statement

b Arguments against the statement

c Introduction: general statement about the issue

d Conclusion: briefly summarise your opinion

b Answer the questions.

1 What are the two arguments against the statement? What phrases introduce each point?

2 What are the two arguments in favour of the statement? What phrases introduce each point?

3 Look at the phrases in the How to... box and tick the ones which are used in the essay.

How to... introduce the topic and state your conclusion

Introducing the topic	*In this essay, I will consider the question of* whether companies should be allowed to advertise to children on television.
	This essay is concerned with the issue of advertising aimed at children.
	It is an important issue and there are strong feelings on both sides of the argument.
Stating your conclusion	*In conclusion, I am convinced that* companies should be banned from advertising to children.
	To summarise, I feel that advertising on TV during children's programmes is wrong.
	On balance, I think it is wrong that children are exposed to so many adverts.

---

3 **a** Prepare to write an essay using one of the statements below. Make notes of the arguments in favour of and against your statement.

1 Teenagers should not be allowed to wear designer clothes or shoes at school.

2 Shows which include mind reading and hypnosis should be banned.

3 Background music and TV screens should be banned in public places, e.g. shops, cafés, etc.

b Now write your essay using the paragraph plan from exercise 2a.

Advertising on TV during children's programmes should not be allowed

In this essay, I will consider the question of whether companies should be allowed to advertise to children on television. Advertising for young people and children is a huge industry. It is an important issue and there are strong feelings on both sides of the argument.

Firstly, companies know that children can be persuaded to want things very easily. They know that if children want things, they will use 'pester power' to persuade their parents to buy things; and it is not right that companies use children in this way. Another reason against advertising during children's programmes is that children are exposed to too much commercialism and too many products which may encourage them to grow up too quickly. Children should be allowed to watch programmes which are appropriate for them and not be continually shown products.

On the other hand, it is not only the companies who have responsibility for what children watch. Parents need to be aware of what kind of things their children are watching on TV. They also need to stand up to pester power and not give in to what their children ask for all the time. Finally, it is important to remember that many children enjoy watching advertisements and finding out what is available in the shops. Some adverts are entertaining and informative and children can be made aware of the purpose of advertising.

In conclusion, I am convinced that companies should be banned from advertising to children, especially on television. Parents do have a responsibility to control how much television their children watch. However, on balance, I think it is wrong that children are exposed to so many adverts: they should be able to watch TV without the intrusion of advertising.

Pronunciation bank

English phonemes

Consonants

p	b	t	d	k	g	tʃ	dʒ
park	bath	tie	die	cat	give	church	judge
f	**v**	**θ**	**ð**	**s**	**z**	**ʃ**	**ʒ**
few	visit	throw	they	sell	zoo	fresh	measure
h	**m**	**n**	**ŋ**	**l**	**r**	**j**	**w**
hot	mine	not	sing	lot	road	yellow	warm

Vowels and diphthongs

iː	ɪ	e	æ	ɑː	ɒ	ɔː	ʊ	uː	ʌ
feet	fit	bed	bad	bath	bottle	bought	book	boot	but
ɜː	**ə**	**eɪ**	**əʊ**	**aɪ**	**aʊ**	**ɔɪ**	**ɪə**	**eə**	**ʊə**
bird	brother	grey	gold	by	brown	boy	here	hair	tour

Sound–spelling correspondences

Sound	Spelling	Examples
/ɪ/	i	this listen
	y	gym typical
	ui	build guitar
	e	pretty
/iː/	ee	green sleep
	ie	niece believe
	ea	read teacher
	e	these complete
	ey	key money
	ei	receipt receive
	i	police
/æ/	a	can pasta
/ɑː/	a	can't dance*
	ar	scarf bargain
	al	half
	au	aunt laugh
	ea	heart
/ʌ/	u	fun husband
	o	some mother
	ou	cousin double
/ɒ/	o	hot pocket
	a	watch want

Sound	Spelling	Examples
/ɔː/	or	short sport
	ou	your bought
	au	daughter taught
	al	small always
	aw	draw jigsaw
	ar	warden warm
	oo	floor indoor
/aɪ/	i	like time
	y	dry cycle
	ie	fries tie
	igh	light high
	ei	height
	ey	eyes
	uy	buy
/eɪ/	a	lake hate
	ai	wait train
	ay	play say
	ey	they grey
	ei	eight weight
	ea	break
/əʊ/	o	home open
	ow	show own
	oa	coat road
	ol	cold told

Weak forms

Word	Strong form	Weak form
a, an	/æ/, /æn/	/ə/, /ən/
at	/æt/	/ət/
and	/ænd/	/ən/
are	/ɑː/	/ə/ (or /ər/ before vowels)
been	/biːn/	/bɪn/
can	/kæn/	/kən/
do	/duː/	/də/
does	/dʌz/	/dəz/
has	/hæz/	/həz/, /əz/
have	/hæv/	/həv/, /əv/
than	/ðæn/	/ðən/
them	/ðem/	/ðəm/
to	/tuː/	/tə/ (before consonants)
was	/wɒz/	/wəz/

* In American English the sound in words like *can't* and *dance* is the shorter /æ/ sound, like *can* and *man*.

Sounds and Spelling

Consonant clusters (units 6 and 9)

Some words start or finish with 'consonant clusters' (two or three consonants together).

Two consonants: <u>sk</u>inny, <u>sw</u>im, fi<u>rst</u>, conte<u>xt</u>

Three consonants: <u>scr</u>uffy, <u>spl</u>ash, evide<u>nce</u>, agai<u>nst</u>

Stress

Emphasis and sounding sure (units 4, 5, 7 and 10)

When we want to sound sure or to emphasise what we're saying, we often put more stress on certain words and say certain phrases more slowly.

That's so kind of you.

Believe me, I know what I'm talking about.

It was the director himself who spoke to me.

Phrasal verbs (unit 8)

Phrasal verbs with three parts have two stresses. The main stress is on the second word (first particle) and the secondary stress on the first word (the main verb).

I've cut down on the amount of sugar I eat.

Compound adjectives (unit 9)

Compound adjectives which are 'noun + past participle' generally have the main stress on the first part.

tongue-tied, poverty-stricken

Compound adjectives which are 'adjective/adverb + past participle' generally have the main stress on the second part.

well-dressed, far-fetched

Connected speech

Weak forms (units 1, 2 and 5)

Auxiliary verbs, modal verbs, prepositions and articles are often pronounced with weak forms.

You must buy a ticket for the show as soon as you can.
   /məs/   /ə/   /fə/ /ə/   /əz/   /əz/

Consonant to vowel (units 1, 2 and 5)

When a word ends with a consonant sound and the following word starts with a vowel sound, we often run the two sounds together.

I got in touch with him as soon as I arrived.

Consonant to consonant (units 1, 2 and 5)

When a word ends with a consonant sound and the following word starts with a consonant sound, we often run the two sounds together.

Could you tell me what they're planning to do?

Linking sounds /w/, /j/, /r/ (units 2 and 5)

When a word ends with a vowel sound and the following word starts with a vowel sound, we sometimes add sounds to link the words together. Common linking sounds are: /w/, /j/ and /r/.

You are welcome.
   /w/

My mother is a teacher.
      /r/

He earns a lot of money.
   /j/

Elision (unit 3)

Some sounds almost disappear so we can't hear them. These may be sounds at the start or end of words, or some complete small words, e.g. articles (e.g. *a, an, the*), prepositions (e.g. *for, of*), conjunctions (e.g. *and, that*).

I've got a book ~~for~~ you th~~at~~ I though~~t~~ you migh~~t~~ like.

Speech units (unit 3)

When we read from a written text, we usually divide our speech into logical parts. Between each part, we pause slightly to make it easier for the listener to follow what we're saying. The pauses have a similar function to punctuation and often occur at the end of a sentence, between clauses linked by *and, but* or *because*, and before and after a phrase which adds extra information.

My best friend, // who I've known for years, // is called Maria. // I'd like to see her more often // but she lives in America now.

Intonation

Effect on the listener (units 1, 6 and 10)

Generally, when we want to have a particular effect on the listener (e.g. to sound interesting, enthusiastic, tentative, persuasive, nostalgic), our intonation has a wider range and we pause more between groups of words. If our intonation is flatter, we usually sound more bored and boring.

Questions (unit 7)

When we ask a question, our intonation is different depending on the type of question. If we are asking for information we don't know, our voice goes down at the end.

Where do you live?

If we are checking information we think we already know, our voice goes up at the end.

Are you going to the party tonight?

Reporting (unit 8)

We use different intonation when we quote direct speech and when we report what they say. We use higher intonation for the part of the sentence in direct speech quotes, as if it was real speech.

She said, 'I'm going to the cinema tonight.'

She said she was going to the cinema that night.

Audioscripts

Track 1.2

S=Sarah, F=Fiona

S: Hello. My name's Sarah. Pleased to meet you.

F: Oh, hello. A pleasure to meet you, too. My name's Fiona. It's really nice to see a friendly face actually. I'm feeling a bit nervous.

S: Oh, don't worry. There's no need to be nervous. I've been to this class before and everyone is really nice. The teacher really makes you feel at ease. Have you done any Spanish classes before?

F: Just a bit, but not for ages. I feel like I've forgotten everything!

S I know what you mean. So, do you live near here?

F: Erm, not too far. I live in Wood End …

S: Oh really? That's not far from where I live … I live in Whitefields, you know, just at the top of the hill.

F: Oh yes, that's really near me actually!

S: So, how did you get here today? Did you come by bus?

F: Yes, I did. I got the 17 all the way. It took me ages though because there was so much traffic. What about you?

S: Yes, I got the 17 too. The traffic was awful, wasn't it?

F: Yeah, really bad. I was a bit late leaving the house as well, 'cos I didn't get back from work till after six …

S: What's your job?

F: I'm a teacher.

S: Are you?

F: Yes, I teach children. Primary school age, you know, mostly aged between 7 and 11. I love it, but it's really hard work! And you? What do you do?

S: Oh, well, I'm certainly not a teacher. I wouldn't have the patience for that! I work in advertising.

F: That sounds fun!

S: Yeah, it's OK. But I'd like to do something different now I think. Oh, here's the teacher. Well, it's been really nice talking to you. Maybe we could meet up after the class and … well, if you're going straight home, perhaps we could go together?

F: Yes, that would be great.

Track 1.3

And now a story about another large family. Being in a large family usually means learning to juggle several tasks at once – shopping, cleaning, making dinner, helping with homework, bandaging a knee and keeping an eye on the children playing outside. However, in addition to a normal family life, the Boehmer family juggle clubs, rings, torches, balls and anything else they can get their hands on. It all started while Larry Boehmer was working as a pipeline worker for Shell Oil. His job took him away from his wife Judy and the four children they had at that time. He had spent the first few weeks sitting in his motel room between shifts, when one day, while he was feeling bored, he decided to take up a new hobby. Using a book, he taught himself to juggle. When he had mastered the basics, he went home and showed his children what he could do. Immediately, they wanted to learn too. Larry is a big family man, so he was only too happy about that, and soon the whole family was juggling. Larry and three of the children gave their first family performance at an amusement park, and from there it all went from strength to strength. Now, there are four sons and seven daughters in the family, and they are the largest family of jugglers in

the world, working together and performing regularly as a family. As Judy puts it, they didn't plan on this happening. When the kids saw each other, they picked up on different things. One would do rings, another would do clubs, acrobatics or the unicycle. Before they knew it, they had everybody doing something. Even Casey, the second son, who was born with only one arm, is a champion juggler in his own right, as well as part of the family troupe.

Larry insists the children's talents aren't inherited, it's simply a matter of practice and persistence. This is a skill that basically anybody can do – you just have to put your mind to it. It's just that most people who try to learn juggling give up too soon. Each member of the family has a speciality but they all have to practise … a lot! Each member of the family not only takes part in the show, they also help with preparing the costumes, transporting everything and setting up the show. In the end, though, performing in the show makes all the practise and hard work worth it. It's great fun and they all love it.

Track 1.4

J=Julia, A=Andrew, M=Maria

J: So Andrew, how many people are there in your family?

A: Erm, there are … well there are three really. I have … I have an older brother, he's about two years older than me, and I have a younger brother, he's about a year and a half younger than me.

J: Mm, so you're the middle child then?

A: Yeah I'm the middle child …

J: A lot of people say that middle children have the worst time. What do you think about that?

A: It's, ah, it depends, erm, I think, erm, there's, ah – you end up, I suppose, looking up to your older brother, ah, as a kind of a leader, you look to him for guidance …

J: That's quite interesting. I've got an older brother and I definitely don't look up to him …

M: I have an older sister and I don't look for gui … to her for guidance for sure, no.

A: I think, erm, when I was young I did, yeah. Definitely to my older brother, yeah. And your older brother does certain things first – first to ride a bike, pass a driving test, first to university. Ah – so maybe they get more attention than the middle child.

J: Yeah, I suppose. And I suppose parents kind of spoil the younger children because they've had the toughest with the older children and then by the time they get to – for me, there's five children in my family – so by the time my parents got to the fifth child they were kind of ready for her to just let herself go.

M: That's not the experience that … that I had, my parents were quite liberal with … I have one sister who's only a, a year and a bit older than me, and, ah, my parents were quite liberal with both of us and we grew up …

J: Oh right, you were lucky.

M: … kind of as friends, yeah, it was great.

J: Mm, I don't know, and did you have lots of, do you think everyone in your family has a lot of friends, or is it different depending on which, which, erm …

M: No, I think it's, it's quite similar. I suppose my sister maybe has a, a wider network and perhaps I have a slightly smaller

network but, of very close friends maybe … But I don't think it's connected to position in the family at all.

J: Mm. What about only children, I mean none of us are only children but …

M: No, well …

J: Do you think they need more friends or less friends?

M: I don't know about needing friends but I do think that sometimes they … they can need a lot of attention. I think maybe if they've been the sole … yeah.

A: But they … they're used to the attention.

M: Exactly.

J: I mean, I guess though, it depends on how much attention they get. Do all parents give, you know, if they have one child, do they all give them loads of attention or just only children? Are they quite lonely and do they want more attention? I don't know.

M: I suppose it must, must be the case for some but I, I … I don't know anybody like that.

Track 1.6

Before I had my mobile, my parents worried about me all the time because they couldn't contact me when I was out. You know, I wasn't able to tell them where I was or what time I was coming back. There was one particular time when I lost track of time … I know I should've been more careful but I ended up missing the bus. I wanted to let my parents know that I was going to be late, but I couldn't phone them. In the end, I got to a friend's house and I was able to phone from there … but they had been very worried because I was already 45 minutes late. I felt really bad – I knew I shouldn't have put them in that situation. After that, they bought me a mobile phone, which was good – except, at first, I had to phone them every half an hour to tell them where I was – which was a real pain. After a while, they changed their minds and I didn't have to phone them so much, but I had to have it turned on all the time. I don't find it too annoying – in fact, I like having a phone and it makes me feel safe, knowing that I can phone my parents at any time.

Track 1.9

M=Morgan, F=Friend

M: Look – have you seen this great website? It's about genealogy, you know, family history …

F: Family history? What … your family?

M: Yes, well, any family. It basically helps you to find old relatives and build a family tree. Actually, there are loads of websites like this now. It's quite popular now – lots of people are doing it.

F: Oh really? I've always thought I'd like to know a bit more about my family in the past.

M: Well, this is just the thing. It's great. Even before I found this website, I had started putting together my own family tree – but the website really helps.

F: So, how far back can you go?

M: Well, I'm pretty confident about as far back as my great-grandparents, Cicely and John.

F: You didn't actually know them, did you?

M: No, unfortunately, they died in the 1970s. By all accounts they were an amazing couple, devoted to each other … and of course they'd lived through two World Wars.

F: Yes … that generation went through such a lot … Do you know when they were actually born?

M: Well, yes, I do. My great-grandfather, John, was born right on the turn of the century in 1900. And my great-grandmother, Cicely just a year before that in 1899.

F: Wow … So did they have children?

M: Yeah, they had two children, Laura and Ben, both were born around 1930 I think.

F: So, Laura's your grandmother, isn't she? I've heard you talk about her.

M: Yeah, that's right. I get on really well with her. My mum says I take after her in lots of ways. I even look quite like her … same nose!

F: Really?

M: Yeah. I usually go and visit her about once a month, up in Leeds. I'm going up there this weekend, actually …

F: Is her husband still alive?

M: Julian? No, he died a couple of years ago. So, she's on her own now.

F: So, obviously Laura is your …

M: … my mum's mother. Laura and Julian had three children: my mum, Alison, and my aunts, Sue and Deborah.

F: Three girls!

M: Yeah … but all very different in character!

F: Really?

M: Oh yes … have I never told you about Aunt Sue?

F: I don't think so.

M: Well she was … is … an anthropologist, a kind of adventurer really. She's spent most of her life in and around Borneo, studying the culture, religion and so on. She's quite an expert apparently.

F: And have you got any cousins?

M: Yes, my aunt Deborah had a son and a daughter, Leon and Esther. Esther's a year or so older than me … and I'm a few years older than Leon. We all got on really well with each other. We saw each other a lot when we were growing up, you know – we'd see them at weekends, and we also used to go on holiday quite a lot together.

F: And do you see them now?

M: Well, I try to keep in touch as much as possible, but it's not as easy as it was … I mean, Esther lives in New Zealand now …

F: Oh!

M: … and Leon divides his time between being a diving instructor in the summer mainly around Egypt and Turkey … and a skiing instructor in the winter.

F: Hard life!

M: Yeah, I know …

Track 1.10

I was about 25 and I'd been with the same company for five years. A friend showed me his photos of an amazing holiday he'd had in Central America. One photo in particular really struck me. It was when he went diving and saw the most beautiful fish you've ever seen! I began to have itchy feet and wanted to leave work and do something exciting. I'd never been out of Europe before then and I was a bit worried about going straight into uncharted territory! I mean, I didn't know anything about countries so different and far away from mine. So, I decided to go to Spain first, to learn a bit of Spanish and get used to being away from home. I went as an independent traveller on my own, because I really wanted to do it all by myself. I spent a month wandering around the town where I was living, learning Spanish and loving every minute! I was bitten by the travel bug then and wanted to explore lots of other places. About six months later, after saving up some money, I went off to Guatemala, feeling very confident and pleased with myself. The first two months were difficult and I experienced real culture shock, I think. It seemed that everything was different. Lots of things went wrong too, like I was robbed twice, I couldn't find anywhere to live and I was really homesick and missed my family like mad! So I had a bit of a bumpy ride to start with, but after a while, I found a job teaching English, made some friends and started to really enjoy myself. In fact, I grew to love it so much I stayed there for three years!

Track 1.12

I=Interviewer, O=Oliver

I: So, Oliver, just to remind the listeners, let me ask, what have you been doing here?

O: Erm … yes, OK … well, basically I've been living with a family in a small village. I've been here for about a month and a half now.

I: Mmm … a month and a half …

O: Yes, since about the beginning of July. And … erm … I've been teaching in the village school … I've been teaching maths mostly … but other things as well. It's all part of a bigger project … a lot of university students from the UK come for a couple of months at a time. It's voluntary work, you know … in the university holidays … to help people here and get some work experience.

I: So, it's all coming to an end now … how do you feel about leaving?

O: Oh, well, mixed feelings I suppose. I mean, I'll be really sad about leaving everyone here. I've had such a good time. You know, it's been challenging at times … especially the heat. It's so hot here! But I've had a great time … really fantastic. Kenya is a really inspiring place.

I: Mixed feelings though?

O: Well, yes, I mean, I'm looking forward to seeing my family. I've missed them while I've been here. Everyone in the village has been really friendly though and really looked after me.

I: And what will you miss about this place when you leave?

O: I'll definitely miss the children in my class … all the children in the village actually. They're great.

Track 1.13

1 The summer is generally hot and very <u>humid</u> and you are often quite uncomfortable. It's often <u>overcast</u> too and there is no <u>breeze</u> to cool things down. It's very different in the winter, when it's <u>cool</u> and the sky is <u>clear</u>.

2 I'm not so keen on <u>mild</u> weather – when it's not really hot or cold. I much prefer it when the weather is quite dramatic. Like when you are somewhere with <u>scorching</u> days and then it suddenly <u>pours</u> for hours. Or when it's hot in the day and you get <u>sub-zero temperatures</u> at night.

3 The weather is very <u>changeable</u>. In the summer, the days are often <u>bright</u> but can be <u>showery</u> and the nights are sometimes <u>chilly</u> but not very cold. In the winter, it seems to <u>drizzle</u> a lot and the sky is often grey.

Track 1.15

P=Presenter, J=Jamie, W=Woman, M=Man

P: Hello everyone. I think we'll make a start as it's 7.30 already. Let me introduce Jamie. He's our 'Bhutan expert' … He's spent a substantial amount of time in this amazing country and I'm sure he'll be able to help you with whatever queries you may have.

J: Hello. Thank you. Well, I'll do my best … Please feel free to ask whatever you want and if I can't answer anything, well, I'll say so! So, fire away …

W: Erm … yes … when is the best time to go?

J: Well, in the winter it can be up to about 15°C in the daytime, but you often get sub-zero temperatures at night. There is a lot of snow in winter, which can make travelling difficult. It's hot in the summer, sometimes really scorching, but it's often very wet too. In my experience, the best seasons to visit are spring and autumn. Spring is beautiful with wonderful flowers and lovely sunny days. And autumn is fantastic too with mild weather and clear views of the Himalayas … Yes?

M: What activities do you recommend?

J: One of the most popular activities for visitors to Bhutan is to go trekking in the Himalayas. The high mountains and deep valleys are truly spectacular and you can sometimes walk for several days before coming to the next village. You'll see a huge variety of plant life ranging from dense forest to tiny mountain flowers. I've been many times … You won't be disappointed, I can assure you!

M: Thank you.

W: Excuse me … I'd like to know whether we need to take anything special.

J: Ah yes, good question. The changeable climate means that you will need an assortment of clothes, including rain gear and good walking boots. The sun can be very strong especially up in the mountains, so you'll need a hat and sunglasses. I'd also recommend warm clothes for the evenings … it can get pretty chilly, even in summer.

M: Would we need to carry all our equipment on a trek?

J: No. Trekking is done in organised trips and they provide yaks to carry your luggage. They also carry the food and camping equipment, which is all provided. I've always found them very well-equipped and helpful.

M: And who goes with the trekking group? I mean do they provide a guide?

J: Oh yes … There's always a guide who speaks English and a cook and other assistants to help make the trek run smoothly. They're all very friendly … you really don't need to worry about getting lost or anything …

W: Could I ask you what the food is like?

J: Mmm … interesting, yes. The Bhutanese eat a lot of meat, dairy foods, vegetables and rice. The national dish is a fabulous chilli-pepper and cheese stew called Emadatse. In fact, chillis are very common in Bhutan and you'll find that a lot of their dishes are flavoured with spicy chilli peppers. I love the food, I must say.

M: I'm thinking of going in the autumn. Do you know if there are any interesting festivals at that time?

J: Well, yes, this year there are, although the dates of festivals vary according to the moon. The most popular one for tourists is held in Thimphu, the capital, and this year it's in October. People dress in their colourful, traditional clothes and there is a lot of music and dancing, including the masked sword dances. All the festivals are important religious events for the people to offer thanks to their gods.

M: I've seen pictures of strings of flags in the mountains. Can you tell me what they are?

J: Yes, they are prayer flags. As I said, the Bhutanese people are very religious and they use the flags as a way of communicating with the heavens ...

Track 1.16

N=Natalie, M=Man

M: Natalie, you've lived abroad, right?

N: Yeah, yeah, I've lived in Italy.

M: And when you went to Italy, how did you find it? Was it easy to integrate or more difficult than you thought it was gonna be?

N: Oh it was easy actually. Erm, I think once you learn the language then, erm, things just come naturally. And it took me a long time to learn the language but, erm, I don't think it's such a big issue that many people think it is.

M: Do you think that many people think it's a big issue?

N: Yeah I think it's a lot easier than ... than people, than most people think. Because it's maybe the fear of the unknown, people haven't tried it, they think it will be more difficult.

M: I think you're right, I think the more time you spend abroad, the easier you'll find integrating in to new places. But it's that first, first step the first time you go and do it, it seems quite daunting.

N: Definitely, but then you have ... I don't know ... less fun if you stay in your own country or you, erm ... I think it's quite safe to stay in your own country, too.

M: Yeah I completely agree, I mean, we only get one life right, so might as well see as much as you can.

N: Exactly, and there's nothing more interesting than getting to know other cultures and finding out about another language or ... I mean, how did you find moving here?

M: Erm, for me moving here was a lot easier than, for example when I moved to South Korea but, erm, obviously I needed to learn the ... a new language in Korea, but al ... but also I think Canadian and British culture are a lot closer than Canadian and Korean culture are to each other.

N: Do you find that you're more adventurous, erm, in Britain than in Canada?

M: Yes I think once I'm at home I'm much more in a routine. Erm, but then again I'm only home for brief periods of time so I just go home and spend it with my family.

N: See the family, yeah.

M: Whereas, if I was living there, maybe I would venture out and travel more in Canada.

N: Mm, but I think the more you, erm, explore a country, the more you find out about it and the more you learn ... I mean, for me it's, you can learn so much more living abroad from different people, and maybe you're more open too, I don't know.

Track 1.17

Well, I'm sure that many people have different definitions of what a hero is, and in most cases we see it in the context of war. Erm, if I had to think of the people who I consider heroic in my life, I would think of people who do things, erm, that we can learn from and things that give us inspiration for how we can react in times of pressure and times of crisis. Erm, and in that sense my father is probably one of my big heroes. Erm, he wasn't famous, erm, although he travelled internationally and, erm, he achieved a fair high degree of success in his job. He was actually born, erm, not in poverty, but he was born in a mud brick house in the Kalahari, erm, in a family of farmers, sheep farmers, erm, living in the desert. And when I was a young man he told me – and he didn't tell me this as a lesson really – he was just telling me about something that mattered to him – he told me that his father had once explained to him that a person, a man or a woman, should want no more in life than the satisfaction of being able to rest with their head on a stone. And it sounds perhaps a bit clichéd but I do think, erm, my father actually believed in that, erm, and lived by that. Now what did he do? Well, he was a human rights activist. Erm, his job was mainly to help people who were confronted, erm, by social injustice in one form or another. So, in a way he – he did fight wars, but he didn't fight his wars with weapons, he fought his wars with words and public opinion, information and at times, erm, the legal system.

Track 1.18

P=Presenter, M=Mei

P: Hello, welcome to *Then and Now*. Today we're talking about an incredible country, with a fascinating culture and a long history going back over 3,000 years. China is hugely rich in art and culture, and its food and traditions are well-known around the world. But two aspects of China are perhaps lesser known. Firstly, this vast country has a long history of inventing things and secondly, it is now the third-biggest economy in the world, with ultra-modern cities and many booming industries. Today we've got China expert Mei Zhang here to tell us all about this flourishing 'Land of invention'. Hello Mei.

M: Hello.

P: Well, this programme is called *Then and Now*, so let's start with 'Then' – China's history, and this idea of a 'land of invention'. I knew that the Chinese invented paper, but I must admit I didn't know that they invented so many other important things. Before we talk about those, can you remind us about the story of paper?

M: Yes. It was in 105 AD that paper-making was perfected in China. The first paper was made of silk. Well, it was really the waste from silk-making, which they pulped up to make paper.

P: Of course, paper had an enormous impact on China, didn't it?

M: Yes, with paper and then printing, it meant people could get information much more easily.

P: Mm. So, what else did the Chinese invent?

M: Well, quite a few simple but important things. I think one of the simplest inventions was the wheelbarrow, invented around 220 AD, which meant that enormous loads could be carried by just one person – as well as other things that we take for granted today like silk, porcelain, the kite and even the umbrella!

P: And we have the Chinese to thank for fireworks, don't we?

M: Yes, that's right! In the 8th century, the Chinese discovered gunpowder. And by the 10th century, it was being used to make fireworks, the gun, the rocket and the bomb – so, it eventually had a huge influence on the whole world of course. Another major invention was a machine for making cast iron, which they first developed in the 6th century BC.

P: Wow! That really is a long time ago! That must have made a big difference to people's lives too.

M: That's right. A lot of iron was used for agricultural tools, so production was increased hugely, which brings me quite nicely to the present really – to the 'Now' – to present-day China.

P: Mm. Is agricultural production big in China now?

M: Well, yes, there's a lot of agriculture – about 15 percent of the economy is based on agriculture. You know, things like rice, tea, cotton and fish. But, it's certainly not just countryside and agriculture. There are some massive cities in China, like Shanghai, whose population is around 20 million. And, as I said, China is now the third-biggest economy globally. Industry is huge and expanding all the time. Production of iron, for example, is growing at a rate of about 22 percent a year at the moment.

P: That's certainly a booming industry. So, what other industries are important now?

M: Well, so many of the things we buy are made in China, aren't they? Industrial production accounts for over half of China's economic wealth, including such consumer items as toys, clothes, shoes, cars and electronic goods, as well as the heavier industrial products like iron.

Track 1.20

C=Carla, J=James

C: So James what do you think, what's the most important invention?

J: Well, perhaps gunpowder.

C: Why do you think that?

J: Because it's ... even though it's had quite a negative influence on world history it has had a significant in ... influence on world history. It changed, um, the power in ... in global communities ...

C: But it only changed, erm, in some countries. I don't think you can really say that that has had the biggest effect in every single nation or every single country. And also, I mean if you take into account what a negative influence it's had too, I don't think it is the most important, because the most important is more influential and ... and therefore positive.

J: Right OK, so we could argue that importance ... or that we want to look at importance from a positive perspective, yeah.

C: I think so, yeah.

J: So what would you say?

C: Well I would actually say paper. I think paper really changed, ah, changed the world. Changed how the fact that we, ah ... you can document history, can communicate, that was really the first way of ... of communicating something, ah, in a concrete way rather than just word of mouth.

J: Communication, yes ... and communication which you can hold on to rather than ... yes, as you say, rather than just anecdotal.

C: And we ... and we would never have had computers if we hadn't had paper I think. And it's a knock on effect.

J: Although, ironically we possibly don't need paper now that we have computers.

C: I still write letters.

J: Yes we're sat here with paper in front of us, both of us, yeah.

C: Exactly, I don't think ...

J: You write letters?

C: Of course. Do you not?

J: I don't, no, I only write emails now.

C: I send birthday cards and ...

J: Birthday cards yeah, yeah you're right.

C: What about the computer, then? Was that really as fundamental as the others?

J: It's changed our lives, hasn't it … our generation?

C: Unfortunately, yes.

J: Erm, for work it's something that we use all day every day.

C: Mm … But then again, so is the light bulb.

J: Yes the light bulb is something, the light bulb … and what's the other one and the wheel, and paper to an extent, you don't even notice them any more, whereas a computer, a telephone you would … you would notice.

C: Yeah, because they were all invented before we came along.

J: Yeah, they've become normalised.

C: Exactly.

J: So, what would you say, what would you say is the most important, pa … would you stick with paper, or the computer?

C: I … No, I think paper.

J: Yes I like the communication idea. It has, it has, erm, changed the way that communication happens throughout the world yeah OK, paper it is.

Track 1.22

There's a saying that your school days are the best days of your life. Well, I definitely wouldn't agree with that. My life since leaving school has been much more interesting and rewarding and I definitely wouldn't want to live my school days again. But that said, my memories of school were pretty good, and I've still got really good friends that I went to school with, you know, 30 years ago. When … when I was at school, there was some idea that if you studied hard and you passed your exams and maybe went to university and got a degree that somehow you were, you know, guaranteed to get a good job and a good salary. But with the benefit of hindsight I've realised that while that's true to an extent, success in life is really about what you can do, not what you know. And I think that in schools these days with … with teaching these days across all subjects, they have a much greater emphasis on vocational skills where school children learn to think and they learn to apply their knowledge, which I think can only be a good thing. When I was at school the most important subjects were English and maths, and I don't really think that's changed. Of course it's essential to have, you know, good language and communication skills, and a good grasp of, you know, at least basic mathematics, whatever you end up doing in life. But, erm, in addition to English and maths, I think it's become more and more important to learn a foreign language. I think it really opens up opportunities for work and travel, and I really regret not studying harder in French class at school. I left school without any foreign language qualifications which, erm, which is a real shame. But you know I shouldn't complain, I ended up with a career in marketing which is stable and yes, you know, I find it interesting and enjoyable, and you know I'm … I'm quite good at it. But looking back, I wish I'd followed my heart a bit more and not just my head. When I was at school, I was really passionate about drama and the arts, but I never studied it or pursued it. My parents always encouraged me to be, you know, sensible and study maths and sciences, which I did, and you know I … I was quite good at those subjects … but now, now I'm, you know, I'm a bit older and wiser, one of the biggest lessons I've learned in life is that you can … if you can find your passion in life, you should follow it whether it's art or science or sport or economics, whatever, it will inspire you and it will energise you and you're more likely to be happier and fulfilled in life, and you're more likely to be good at it too.

Track 1.23

1 Recently, I've realised that investigating and writing about important issues is what I really want to do, so I'm now considering a change of career. I'd like to get a job with a newspaper or perhaps a specialist magazine.

2 You could call my job a labour of love, I suppose. I don't get paid much and it's very hard work, but I really love working with children and I really wouldn't want to do anything else.

3 There's a pretty strict career path for my field of work. After the basic five-year training, you have to work in various different hospital departments to build up experience. That's what I'm doing now, but eventually I'd like to specialise in heart operations.

4 I used to work in an office but it was really boring, so I left and took a year out to retrain. The training I did was hard but I like the fact that this job is physically challenging and that we're providing a really vital emergency service for people.

5 What I really like about my job is being able to help people. I mean, I get a great deal of job satisfaction from knowing that I've helped individuals and families with some pretty serious problems – like having nowhere to live.

Track 1.24
Dialogue 1
M=Mark, J=Julia

M: Hi Julia. What's the matter? You look a bit upset.

J: Oh I don't know. I'm so fed up with work at the moment. It's so stressful here … I'm supposed to do a nine-to-five day, but I'm working longer and longer hours. I'm not being paid to do all this extra admin. Basically, I'm totally overworked and underpaid – and I'm on the verge of collapsing with sheer exhaustion!

M: I know. It's been awful for ages, hasn't it?

J: I'm thinking about leaving … Actually, I'm on the point of leaving really. You know, I'd like to have a complete break … really soon.

M: That's a good idea. That would be great. Have you got any plans?

J: I'm not sure yet but as I say, I think I'll leave … in the next month or so, even. I can use the time to think about what to do next … perhaps I'll do some voluntary work or something. One idea is to do some voluntary work abroad. I've seen an ad recently and I'm going to get some more information about it …

M: You could research some stuff on the Internet …

J: Yes. That's a good idea! I think I'll go to the library now and do it there. It's my lunch break and I've got at least half an hour.

M: Good idea! Let me know how you get on …

Track 1.25
Dialogue 2
J=Jane, A=Andreas

J: How are you, Andreas? What have you been doing?

A: Oh I'm fine. I've been making plans! I'm really excited.

J: Oh? Really? What's going on?

A: I've decided I'm going to leave work and go back to college. I'm planning to retrain and do something completely different.

J: Retrain? Really? What are you going to do?

A: Well, I've always wanted to be a vet … And life's too short … you know, I want to get on and do it now! I know it's going to be tough. You know, it's sure to be really hard work, but I've decided I'm just going to do it.

J: Wow, that's great. When are you going to start?

A: Well, it depends on being accepted on the course this year. I have to take an exam first. I'm doing that in about three weeks' time … and then, if it all goes to plan, if I pass … , I'll probably start the course this coming September.

Track 1.26
Dialogue 3
H=Helen, C=Cassia

H: Hi, Cassia. Do you fancy coming out for a meal tonight?

C: Well, I'd love to, but I can't I'm afraid. I'm having an interview tomorrow, so I'm about to have dinner and then have an early night.

H: An interview? What for? I thought you liked working for yourself from home.

C: Well, it's been OK, and I suppose I like the flexible hours and not having to commute and stuff, but to be honest, I'm feeling a bit isolated.

H: Yes, I know what you mean.

C: I really miss having colleagues, you know – not going to a sociable workplace every day. So I've applied for this job – it's to work for a small firm of architects. It's a small open-plan office and they seem really friendly on the phone. I'm meeting them at 10 o'clock tomorrow morning and then having the interview in the afternoon.

H: Oh, well. Good luck. I hope you get it.

Track 1.27
Dialogue 4
T=Tom, J=John

T: I think I'm going to try and look for another job.

J: Why? Don't you like where you are?

T: Yes, it's OK. But I want to be promoted and take on more responsibility. I really want a more senior position now and there are lots of other people who I work with who are certain to get those jobs before me.

J: Oh, you don't know that.

T: Well, I do. I think they'll offer Ania the job of departmental manager. She's really good and she's been there ages.

J: OK … but what about assistant manager?

T: No, Dominic's going to be assistant manager. He's a workaholic and a bit of a rising star, isn't he? He's bound to get the job. It's obvious. He's being fast-tracked for it … you can tell … I heard him talking to Miguel about it.

J: That's just because he wants the job … you don't know if he'll get it.

Track 1.29

I'm standing in the extraordinary Rock Gardens of Chandigarh in India. And I've spent the morning talking to Nek Chand, India's most visionary artist and creator of these gardens. He is a small, elderly man with a wrinkled face and silvery hair, and is extremely modest about his work. I've been trying to find out what has driven him to create these gardens, but he told me, simply, one day I started, and then I continued. His modest manner, however, hides an incredible story.

Audioscripts

Nek Chand was the son of a poor farmer and in 1958 he started work as a government road inspector. At that time, his city, Chandigarh was being designed and built by a famous Swiss architect. Chand was fascinated by the process of design and construction using concrete, and decided to build his own 'kingdom'. He started to collect rocks and other bits of 'rubbish' from the building sites. Secretly, he took these things to a forest area outside the city and began to build his garden. It had to be done in secret because he was building on land which belonged to the government. At first, he spent time making walls and paths and buildings. And then he moved on to the second phase, creating over 5,000 sculptures. These sculptures provide an incredible array of different figures: people, animals, birds and many other strange and wonderful creatures. Each one is different and they are all made of material that had been thrown away. Chand recycles anything he can find – old bicycles, bricks, lumps of concrete, broken plates, old sinks, electric plugs, pebbles ... the list goes on.

Many people find that they waste a lot of time, but it's amazing what you can do when you really want to. For 18 years, Chand worked on his secret garden. He made time to do a bit more every day after work and every weekend. In fact, whenever he had time to spare he worked on this huge project that nobody else knew about. Then after 18 years, the garden was discovered by accident. At first, Chand was afraid that it would be destroyed as he had built it illegally on government-owned land. But quickly, people became interested in it and the government realised that the garden could become a tourist attraction. They paid Chand a small salary to work full-time on the project and one year later the Rock Garden was officially opened. Now it is one of India's most popular tourist attractions with 5,000 visitors every day. His huge achievement doesn't seem to have changed Chand at all, however. He told me, 'I am just doing my work. Everyone has work they do. This is mine.' He says his life is utterly regular. 'I eat. I sleep. I work.' Tomorrow morning, he will be doing the same as he's doing today. And the day after, he will be doing the same. He says it makes him happy, just doing it. Which is a good thing, because soon, he will have spent half a century just doing it.

Track 1.30
M=Man, W=Woman
M: Well, what's interesting about the whole work-life balance thing is that most of us only spend more or less a third of our day in work. So, actually, there's plenty of time for other things ... and if you're organised, you can have a very good work-life balance. I mean, I'm not the best organiser in the world, but I think I can organise my time pretty well ... and divide my time between work and other things.
W: Mmm ... yes, I know what you mean, but although in theory, people spend about a third of their day at work ... eight hours or something... in reality, it's often much longer. Your time gets swallowed up by having to work longer hours. The fact is, I have a really busy work schedule. I really do. You know, there are pressures of deadlines and things, and I end up coming to work earlier and staying later ... so the work-life balance gets a bit lost.

M: Yes, true. Believe me, I know, it's not easy, but I do think it's possible to improve it. It's something that people need to work at, in a sense. You know, it might not just happen, if you don't work at it – you need to be quite disciplined, in a way. My non-work life is really important to me, so I make sure that I prioritise it. Without a doubt, I'd say that I 'work to live' and not the other way round. I want to be able to have spare time, you know, leisure time, and not be too tired to do anything with it!
W: Yeah. What do you like doing in your spare time?
M: Well, I think it's important to make time for the fundamental things in life: family and friends, and relaxing on your own too, sort of recharging your batteries.
W: Yes, I agree. Family and friends are the most important, for sure. What do you do then, you know, to recharge your batteries?
M: Well, I go to the gym a lot. I find it a really good way of relaxing, and keeping fit, of course. If I don't have time to fit in at least three trips to the gym every week, I begin to feel a bit anxious, I must say.

Track 1.32
M=Marc
M: I started learning English when I was about 15 and my main goal was to have a chance to study in the UK. I wanted to do a course in London and I had to get to a good level of English so I studied really hard to get the right grades. Then when I first arrived in the UK, and I was around a lot of native speakers, I became quite self-conscious of my accent. So, although I had a good level of English in general, my aim became to sound like a native speaker. I think that I really wanted to fit in and sound like one of them ... I didn't want to sound different. However, I found it very difficult to change my accent, and more importantly, maybe, I found that it didn't really matter. Nobody seemed to have a problem understanding me. And anyway, at the school there were lots of native speakers, but there were also lots of non-native speakers from lots of different countries. It was a multi-cultural community and people had different accents and sounding like a native speaker didn't matter. We tried to communicate with each other and we could all understand each other – I'm happy with my English and my accent ... it isn't a problem.

Track 1.33
Dialogue 1
I=Interviewer, S=Susanna
I: It's Susanna, isn't it?
S: Erm ... yes ...
I: Hello Susanna. Pleased to meet you. My name's Michael Harrison. Come and sit down.
S: Thank you.
I: So, thank you for applying for the job and coming to the interview today. First, I'd like to ask you about your experience. In your letter, you say you've worked in an office before. Tell me about that.
S: Oh well, it was ages ago actually.
I: OK, well, what did you do there?
S: Nothing much really ... I was just an assistant. You know, answering the phone and stuff ...

Track 1.34
Dialogue 2
I=Interviewer, J=Joana
I: Ah, here you are ...
J: Oh dear. I'm so sorry ...
I: Let's see ... You're Joana, aren't you? Joana Mendes?
J: Yes, that's right.
I: Well, come in Joana. I'm Peter Manning, head of the economics department and I'll be interviewing you today. Very nice to see you. Thank you for coming.
J: I'm really very sorry. I thought it would be a much quicker journey. The traffic was terrible and then I couldn't find the building.
I: OK. Can I start by asking you about your reasons for applying for the course? What do you think you'd get from studying economics in this particular university, Joana?

Track 1.35
Dialogue 3
I=Interviewer, K=Karema
I: Well, thank you very much for talking to me today, Karema. We're coming to the end of the interview now. Is there anything that you'd like to ask me?
K: Yes, I do have a question, if that's OK.
I: Of course. Fire away.
K: Well, I was wondering about promotion prospects. Obviously I'm keen on staying in the journalism business and I'd like to know what kind of opportunities there might be.
I: That's a good question. We are very interested in the professional development of our staff and offer many opportunities for further training and promotion within the company. The right person can be promoted to a position such as senior editor and we are always looking for people to manage completely new magazines. Anything else?
K: Could you tell me when you're going to make your decision?
I: I've got some other candidates who I'll be interviewing this afternoon, but we'll let you know by tomorrow afternoon.
K: Thank you very much.

Track 1.37
I guess I am what you call an adrenaline junkie ... a bit of a risk taker. I love to challenge myself but more in the outside world away from work. Erm, I like to try and give myself things that I wouldn't normally do that might be a bit scary at the start, erm, to try and see whether I can do them or not. This has included jumping out of an aeroplane, erm, doing rap jumping in Aus ... in New Zealand, which is like running down the front of a building face first, kind of like abseiling but in reverse. Erm, swimming with sharks, all of those kind of things. I think it's just the thrill of doing something that you're so scared of in the beginning, to accomplish it and do it is quite an achievement. And in that sense, erm, I definitely think it's good to take risks. Erm, I try and do some things at weekends as well, erm, like sea kayaking, abseiling, just to give myself a bit of excitement, and to be in an environment that isn't as controlled as, ah, working life, which has so many rules and regulations it gets a bit boring.

Track 1.38

M=Man, W=Woman

M: I've decided to leave my job soon … maybe, even, this coming summer. I'm fed up of working for a big company and I think I'd like to be my own boss.

W: Really?

M: Yes, I'm thinking about starting my own business.

W: That's brave, I mean, it's a bit of risk, don't you think? What would happen, for example, if things got difficult? You would have nobody to fall back on.

M: Well, I suppose it's brave, but actually it feels like totally the right thing to do. To be honest, I really like working on my own, well, in fact, I like being on my own, generally. You know, I'm somebody who enjoys my own company, in a way.

W: Do you? I'm not like that. I like being with other people. I get really lonely, I mean, if I had to be alone for a long period of time, I would get really miserable. I need people to talk to, I think. And if I had to work on my own, I'd hate it! It would be so boring.

M: I don't mind. I like it. I find that I can concentrate on my goals more easily, and I'm in control of everything. Also, with my own business, if things go well, I think I'll feel really good about it. You know, it'll be my own achievement and nobody else's.

W: True, but it's still a big risk, leaving a secure job and the salary that goes with it. Are you really prepared for that?

M: Yes, I think I am. I've got the experience and the motivation, and I really want to go for it.

W: Well, I'm impressed! Your confidence is inspiring me! Maybe I should be braver with things and take a few more risks. I've always thought that if I were a different person, the characteristic I'd like to have would be to be more of a risk-taker – to have more confidence in my own abilities and just go for things more.

M: Well, you could. Just think about what you really want to do, and really get yourself well-prepared. You know, don't rush into things, but get prepared and do your research – and I'm sure you can do anything you want, if you want it enough.

Track 1.39

M=Man, W=Woman

W: Hey, Daniel, I'm dying to hear about your hang-gliding. How did it go?

M: Oh yeah, it was fantastic, really amazing actually.

W: Oh really? I think it looks really scary … !

M: Well, the place I went was very organised and the instructors were really good, and I just felt very safe. I got there quite early. You could arrive anytime after 8.00 in the morning – and I got there soon after that, you know, I wanted to do as much hang-gliding as I could.

W: Did you have to do a lot of training before you could go up? Or were you allowed to just start without doing any training?

M: Well, I couldn't go straight up without any training at all. But there wasn't much – just information really. The amount of training you have depends on what kind of hang-gliding you're doing. I mean, I didn't go up alone, you know, I went up with an instructor – so he was doing all the flying and the technical stuff, like steering, and knowing how and where to land. Basically, you can't go up alone on your first time. I'm not sure how many times it is, I think you can go alone after doing a few flights with an instructor and some longer training.

W: Oh, I see.

M: Anyway, I wasn't allowed to go up before having some brief general instructions. But that's all it was really – no training as such. Then I got into the harness, they attached me to the hang-glider. I was literally hanging in a lying-down position from the frame of the glider. It felt quite strange! Then a small plane pulled the glider – and me – to the taking off position, and then up into the sky. It's really simple.

W: But really scary!

M: Well, strangely, it didn't feel too scary at that point – just exhilarating. We climbed higher and higher, until the gauge said we were at 2,000 feet – that's about 600 metres! Then the plane let us loose and went back towards the field below. Once the plane had gone, everything was silent – you just hear the sound of wind rushing around your ears. It was amazing!

W: Did you look down? I mean, what could you see on the ground?

M: It looks incredible from up there – you can see beautiful fields and mountains, and lots of tiny specks which are houses and things! Anyway, at one point, my instructor explained how to steer. You just move your weight to one side in order to change direction.

W: Did you do it?

M: Yes, but, well yes I did, but it didn't just gently change direction. The hang-glider suddenly went veering over to the left.

W: Oh, maybe you should've moved a bit more gently.

M: Yes. I think so, I mean, I did what he said. I leaned to the left.

W: Mmm, maybe you shouldn't have leaned so far then.

M: Yes, anyway, it was fine. I just scared myself a bit! I was quite happy to give the controls back to the instructor!

W: Yes!

M: After that we circled around the valley for about 15 or 20 minutes. It was so beautiful and calm up there.

W: What about the landing?

M: Well, that was another bit that I was a bit scared about. As we got closer to the ground, I got a bit less calm! Suddenly the ground seemed to be rushing up towards me really quickly! But the instructor was really good and he landed the glider really smoothly. And once the glider has stopped, you just stand up and take off the harness.

W: Wow, great.

M: Yeah, it was really good. I loved it. I did two more flights that day. I can see how sports like this are addictive. I'd definitely like to do it again. Next time, I think I'd like to do some training and go up alone. You should come with me next time …

W: Erm, well, sounds a bit too scary for me.

M: It's not really. If I were you, I'd just go for it. It's not scary once you're up there – being a spectator is probably worse!

W: Could you do a really low flight? I mean, are you allowed to go up just a little way above the ground – not go up so high?

M: Erm no! I don't think so. I think that would be much more dangerous. I mean, think of all the things in your way – buildings, trees …

W: I suppose so, yes. I hadn't thought of that.

Track 1.41

P=Paul, L=Lidia

P: So, did you go and see it?

L: See what?

P: *Million Dollar Baby* … you remember, you said you were going to get the DVD …

L: Oh, yes, *Million Dollar Baby* … you were right … it was quite good.

P: Quite good!? Come on, it was really good. I think it's a brilliant film.

L: Do you? I do like Clint Eastwood but I suppose I've never really been that into films about boxing.

P: OK, but it's not really about boxing is it?

L: Isn't it? But one of the main characters runs a boxing gym, and the other wants to be a boxing champion.

P: That's all true, but there's a lot more to it than that. There are so many different themes running through the film. I mean, I thought the whole theme of risk was so interesting.

L: Risk?

P: Well, you know at the beginning of the film, one of Clint Eastwood's most promising boxers leaves him just as he has a chance to make the big time.

L: Oh yes, that's right. Doesn't he go off with another promoter or something?

P: Yeah, after years of training in the gym with the Clint Eastwood character. And actually, it's because Clint won't take a risk with him.

L: He won't put him up for a big championship fight – and the other promoter will.

P: Exactly. The Clint character plays it safe. He's just too cautious. And then this young woman turns up and she turns out to be a really good boxer – and then he faces another risk.

L: You mean, he'll train her up and then she'll leave him.

P: Exactly – and that nearly does happen, doesn't it?

L: Oh yes, that's right, but she does stay with him in the end thank goodness!

P: Then there's a kind of emotional risk he takes too. You remember how he keeps writing to his daughter and never getting any replies? He's upset about something, which we never really find out about.

L: Mmm. I couldn't work out what all that was about.

P: No, it's not really clear. Anyway, I think there's a growing emotional connection between him and the woman boxer, and because of whatever's happened with his daughter it feels like there's a big emotional risk too.

L: I see what you mean. I hadn't really looked at it like that before, but now you say it. Actually, it reminds me of another Clint Eastwood film, *Gran Torino*. Have you seen that?

P: Oh no, I haven't. Why, is that about risk too?

L: Well, it's very different, but yes, I think there's quite a lot about risk. Basically, it's about an old guy called Walt – played by Clint Eastwood – who is an old war veteran. He's quite bad-tempered and bitter about the world. His wife has just died, he's fallen out with his family and doesn't get on with his neighbours or anything. The only thing he likes is his car – a beautiful *Gran Torino* – which he mostly keeps in his garage. You know, he likes his car, but he doesn't like, or trust, people.

P: So, where's the risk?

L: Well, he gets to know his neighbour – a teenager originally from South-east Asia. He gets to know him by chance, really, when the boy tries to steal his beloved car. The risk then comes – the emotional risk, as you say – when Walt decides to become friends with him and help him in various ways.

P: Help him?

L: Yes, he gradually takes the boy under his wing in a way. He teaches him a few things about life and helps him get a job. It's a risk, partly because of the violent gangs around, but I think mostly it's a risk because the old man has to confront his own prejudice and racist ideas and get close emotionally to someone who previously, he had felt angry towards.

P: Mmm. It sounds interesting.

L: It's a really, really good film. I'd definitely recommend it. In fact, I think it's the film I've enjoyed most this year. I think Clint Eastwood is an amazing actor – and he's also an incredible director. He directed and acted in both *Million Dollar Baby* and *Gran Torino*, didn't he? They're such great films.

P: Yes, well, I definitely want to see *Gran Torino*. It sounds like such an interesting film. I think I'll try and get the DVD of it tomorrow.

Track 1.43

H=Heather, E=Eben

H: OK, so which movie do you wanna see?

E: Well, looks good, you … you've taken two Clint Eastwood ones, I love Clint Eastwood as a director. He's brilliant.

H: I do too … he's so good.

E: Yeah. Did you see *Bird* by the way?

H: No I haven't seen that one.

E: Really, really good about Charlie Parker jazz musician.

H: OK.

E: Incredible music, incredible acting, erm …

H: Really? I'll have to try that one out some time.

E: So which one do you … do you wanna go for?

H: Mmm. I don't know, I mean I think I like the look of *Mystic River*, just because it's a bit mysterious and …

E: Yeah.

H: You know, I really like Tim Robbins.

E: Yeah so do I. Sean Penn as well, and …

H: Mm, they're both so … such good actors.

E: Yeah, and Madison … *The Bridges of Madison County*.

H: Yeah.

E: Judging by the cover, it looks like a romance.

H: Yeah, I think so.

E: And it's got Clint Eastwood in it as an actor.

H: Yeah, I mean Meryl Streep's really good. She … she is really, really … and so is … obviously so is Clint Eastwood.

E: But, I have a hard time seeing him as a romantic lead.

H: Yeah …

E: I wonder what he plays?

H: I have to agree with you there.

E: Also, *Madison County*, OK *Madison County*, that's not necessarily Wisconsin but it makes me think of Wisconsin.

H: Mm.

E: I don't know, to- … today that sounds a bit tame to me, rated 12 years old, *Mystic River*, 15. Two Academy awards.

H: Yeah.

E: Sean Penn, Tim Robbins.

H: Oh, and Kevin Bacon's in it too.

E: Oh yes.

H: Oh he's rea- … oh, and Laurence Fishburne, OK, definitely *Mystic River*.

E: I think that's the one. I think that one sounds really good.

H: Yeah, I agree.

E: I wonder what it's about?

H: Mm …

E: Have you seen any … you haven't seen any reviews or trailers?

H: I heard something about, that it's based on a book and it's about three brothers.

E: OK.

H: So … but I don't know much else about it.

E: OK. But you, like you say, you know, great actors.

H: Mm.

E: Good title.

H: Yeah.

E: Sounds like it could be intense.

H: Yeah definitely not boring, the other one has potential to be boring.

E: Yeah it does, I think maybe not today, the other one looks kind of tame. Another day.

H: Alright then, well let's get *Mystic River* then.

E: OK, *Mystic River* it is.

H: Yeah? Alright.

E: Good.

Track 1.45

M=Man, W=Woman

M: Thank you very much for coming to the meeting today. My name is Liam Davidson and I am here to represent the views of the local government on the proposal to build a nuclear power station on the edge of our town. So, I'd like to introduce the other people here today. We have Mr Daniel Hawke, representing the local businesses, Ms Sarah Holmes, representing a local group of environmental campaigners and Mrs Laura Franks, representing local people living in the area. Welcome to everybody. I will outline some of the issues, then everybody will get a chance to put their ideas and concerns forward. We will then have time for further debate and questions. OK, so, first of all, I'd like to say that I'm very pleased that this area has been chosen as a possible site for the development of a new nuclear power station. It is a fantastic opportunity not only to produce cheaper, more efficient energy, but also for us to regenerate the area, by creating a lot of job opportunities for local people.

W: Excuse me, if I could make a point here. My name is Laura Franks and I'm representing the local people, as you said, and yes, we need jobs in the area, but the last thing we need is a nuclear power station in order to create jobs … I mean …

M: Sorry, I'd just like to interrupt you for a minute. As I said, everyone will get a chance to put their point of view …

W: OK, but if you could let me finish my point.

M: Erm … everyone will get a chance …

W: I'm sorry but I haven't quite finished … because already what you're saying is wrong. What I mean is, you're introducing this by saying local people want this project. We don't! You are here representing the local government. In other words, you are obviously FOR the whole project and you will say anything you can think of to make it sound like everyone is with you on this. I want to say, right from the outset, that's wrong. Most people are against the idea. I mean, the health implications are huge. Local

people are rightly concerned about the health of our children. And what about the effect on the environment and local wildlife?

Track 2.4

W=Woman, M=Man

W: Oh … look at these photos of Brad Pitt … He used to look so different – I'd forgotten that he used to have a beard!

M: A beard? Did he?

W: Yeah, look. In this photo, he's got a really long, scruffy beard … and long, scruffy hair too. I think he looks awful! What was he thinking of? Do you think it was for a film or something?

M: No, I don't think it was. I mean, I don't remember him looking like that in any films.

W: No … nor do I … Hmm. I mean, he's so good-looking in this picture. I think he looks great when he's clean-shaven and with short hair … He looks great. I really can't understand why he grew that beard. I mean, I don't mind the long hair so much … although I do think he looks better with short hair …

Track 2.5

E=Eben, I=Interviewer

E: Well, I'm sure you've all heard that Switzerland is … is as beautiful as a postcard or one of those famous Swiss chocolate boxes with all the postcard pictures on it. Well, I actually grew up in Geneva, Switzerland. I lived there for all of my teen years starting at the age of 11. And like most teenagers, I wasn't terribly happy. The other reputation, of course, that Switzerland does have is, you know, that it's, it … it's like clockwork. It's the perfect place, natural beauty and lots of things to do. And as an adult, I suppose I sometimes regret that I didn't appreciate it when I was a teenager, when I was younger. I had all the opportunity to live there. I could've stayed there and finished my university there, erm, but I chose not to. I'd … I was more interested in going to North America. But as a parent, and going there, and that's what this picture's about. This picture was actually only taken a few years ago, of my family, standing, not at one of my favourite spots, but certainly a spot that repre- … represents Geneva to me. It's the lake, it's the boats in the background, and the Salève, that's the mountain. Well, in many ways I feel that if I'd settled there, you know, as an adult, as a parent, that would've been the ideal place, and … to raise my children. All the things that I took for granted, that I couldn't quite appreciate as a young person, I appreciate as a parent, and would've wanted, in a way, to give my kids the opportunity to … to experience life there. I suppose what it comes down to is, you know, although I'm not Swiss, having lived there for so many years, there is so much that I'm attached to, including things, that you know, are part of the community, the people. And those are the things that I would've wanted to share with my kids and my wife, I guess.

Track 2.6

J=Jeanette, I=Interviewer

I: Well Jeanette, these photographs on your wall are really interesting. Can you tell me where they're from?

J: Ah, they're from, ah, Kyoto actually. I used to live, erm, very close to Kyoto and I'd often go at the weekends and visit the temples and the shrines and the gardens, and they were absolutely exquisite. They were so beautiful, I loved them so much. In fact I was going to create, ah, a Japanese garden when I came back to the UK, ah, but unfortunately, erm, we didn't and I, I ... When I was there I would ... would, ah, often take photographs, and to remind me of different features and, erm, I often, erm, bought ... looked for and bought, erm, bamboo ornaments and, erm, things that I would put in the garden. And in fact I ... I always knew that my parents were going to, erm, design and create a Japanese garden, and they have, so I ... I also bought those things for them. Erm, yes, erm, I would have liked to, ah, create a pool with carp in and have, erm, bamboo and azalea and Japanese pines and, erm, but unfortunately, it never really happened because when we came back, erm, we had the children very quickly and somehow the garden just became filled with things for the children to play on, trampolines and play houses and so on, and there was never any room for a Japanese garden. I do have some, I did buy some bamboo and azaleas and so on but, erm, yeah unfortunately ... well, maybe in the future some time.

I: Yeah maybe yeah, well the ... the water is very calming as well isn't it, it's very serene looking.

J: Yeah. It's, it's beautiful, really relaxing.

Track 2.7

1 Some of my happiest memories are from when I used to go on holiday. We often went to the same place ... I went with my parents, my grandparents and my brother. I can remember that place so clearly ... it was such a lovely beach, and in my mind, it was sunny all the time. I don't know if it was, really! It makes me feel really nostalgic about my childhood ... I can picture it so well. I tell you, in a way, it feels like last week ... even though I was about six ... I can still smell the sea and ... oh, I would've liked to live there all the time ...

2 Well, if we're talking about great memories ... well some of my best memories are of playing football with our team. Just thinking about it ... well, it brings back so many memories. We'd get together every Sunday and play down at the park. And we'd also play matches against other local teams. We had such a good time ... I mean, we weren't very good ... we didn't win much, but that wasn't really the point. We were all friends at university together ... it was about five years ago, I suppose ... Those were the days! I wish I hadn't lost touch with so many of them ... We just had such a laugh together ...

3 I found a photo the other day of when I was living in Italy and my friend Siena and I used to have breakfast at the weekends in this lovely little café on the main square ... It was so nice. It reminds me of one of the best times of my life ... I regret leaving that place in a way. I loved living in Italy. The people were so friendly and the town where I lived was so beautiful. It doesn't feel that long ago really, although I suppose it must be about, what ... nine or ten years ago now ... yes, about ten years ago.

Track 2.9

1 This year hasn't been great but I'm sure things will be better next year.

2 A: I saw this great film last night.
B: Oh yeah ...

3 ... but I don't really understand what you're saying. Do you mean that ...

4 Kate ... Kate ... thank goodness you're home ... I've been so worried ...

5 Listen ... I think we're lost ... and we shouldn't be walking round here late at night ... I'm not sure that it's safe, you know ...

6 So, go on, why exactly did you agree to go out on a date with him?

7 Well, of course, he said that was why he was late home but you don't believe him, do you?

8 I can't believe it. We're flying off to Australia for a month on Monday to see my twin sister. I can't wait ...

9 You're always late ... why can't you be on time for once in your life?

10 Can you see that young guy ... standing ... looking into that car? What on earth do you think he's doing?

11 She said what?! I can't believe it. That's terrible ...

Track 2.10

Well ... where shall I start? Well ... the basic story is that a girl, Catherine, is left a box by her mother, who died when she was a baby. Catherine discovers the box when she's 31, the same age as when her mother died. Inside the box are 11 objects, like a red hat, a map of part of England and so on ... all of them meaningless at first, but when Catherine begins to examine each object, she finds new truths not only about her mother but also about herself. Through these objects Catherine finds that her mother was not the sweet and innocent woman that everyone likes to remember her as.

So, what did I think of it? Well ... overall ... I really enjoyed it – it's a really interesting idea for a story – and I thought it was very well-written. Not only that but there are lots of aspects of Catherine's life that I can totally relate to – different events, feelings and thoughts which so accurately mirror my own life that I found myself constantly underlining parts of the text.

However, sometimes I found it a bit slow. I wanted to know about the objects and it seemed to take ages to work out what they were all about. Still ... apart from that one small thing ... it was very easy to read and I'd certainly recommend it.

Track 2.11

M=Man, W=Woman

M: Hi ... what are you reading?

W: Oh, it's *1984* by George Orwell. It's really good. Have you read it?

M: No I haven't. I've heard of it ... but I haven't read it. I would like to read more books in English though ... My teacher is always saying that it's a really good way of improving your English.

W: Yes, that's true... Obviously, you can improve your reading skills by reading a lot, but you can also learn a lot of vocabulary ... and improve your writing.

M: The problem for me is that I find extended reading in English very difficult – there's always so much I don't understand that I get frustrated and then give up.

W: Yes, me too ... I think a lot of students feel like that ... It's really frustrating when you want to look everything up in a dictionary all the time! But there are some techniques you can use ... some ways of improving your reading so you won't find it so difficult ...

M: Mmm? Like what?

W: I used to try to read and concentrate on every single word ... but it makes it so slow and boring. Now, I've really increased the speed of my reading by reading in chunks.

M: Reading in chunks?

W: Yes ... try to look at about four or five words at once before you move your eyes to the next group of words. You'll find it much easier to understand because you're looking at words more in context. If you only look at one word at a time, it often doesn't really have any meaning on its own.

M: Oh, I see what you mean. Yes, that makes sense.

W: I think the other thing you can do is time yourself. You, know, you can test yourself by seeing how fast you can read something ... a newspaper article, let's say. Give yourself five minutes or something to see how much you can understand.

M: Yes, I suppose you get more aware of your level then ... and you can focus on how much you do understand instead of all the words you don't understand!

W: Yes, that's right.

Track 2.12

M=Man, W=Woman

M: OK, well, this is fun, it's quite exciting to think that someone might open this up in 100 years' time.

W: Yes, and see what kinds of things we had. I wonder if they would be able to work out what the things were ...

M: Mmm ... well, what things shall we put in? I mean, five things ... that's not many. We have to try to decide on five really good things to try and show our world as it is now.

W: Yes. OK, well, I think we should include a globe so that they can see what the world looked like. I mean, whoever opens this thing up can see how the world was divided up. I mean, because in 100 or 1,000 years' time, the world might look very different.

M: OK, yes, good idea. And in my opinion, we should also include a sort of everyday thing. You know, like, maybe some typical clothes in order to show something about daily life.

W: Like a pair of jeans, or something?

M: Yes, jeans would be good, since most people nowadays own at least one pair of jeans, don't they?

W: Yes, true. OK, well, what else then?

Track 2.13

C=Carol, S=Sarah

C: Do you have any plans for today?

S: Erm, yeah I'm going to make a special meal for some friends tonight.

C: Oh that sounds good. What ... what are you going to make?

S: Erm, it's my grandma's, ah, pancake recipe, it's quite unusual.

C: Oh. How is it different from normal pancakes?

S: Erm, well what you do is, first, you, erm, make a pancake mix, erm, you must make sure it's not too thick, the pancake mix ... and then you fry lots of pancakes. When you've done that, you put one pancake in the pan ... And then in the other pan,

Audioscripts

you cook, erm, onions and spinach and tomatoes and herbs and …
C: Oh, so, it's a savoury pancake?
S: Yeah.
C: OK.
S: Yeah, so it's savoury … And then you put a layer of, erm, the … the spinach mix on top of a pancake. You know, to make another flat layer … You should be careful not to put too much spinach mix in one layer.
C: Right. Is that because there are lots of layers?
S: Yes, you put another pancake on top flat, and then you put more spinach mix on top. Then you put another pancake on top, and you keep doing this, layering spinach mix and pancakes … and then on the top you put lots of cheese and a sort of white sauce.
C: Mmm. So, you mean you pour the sauce over the whole thing?
S: Yes, that's right.
C: And, erm, what's the white sauce made of?
S: Erm, I think it's just, ah, usually I use it from a jar, but I think it's just flour and eggs and butter and that sort of thing.
C: OK, OK.
S: And cheese sometimes.
C: So, it sounds like there are quite a lot of layers?
S: Yeah, it's a bit, it looks like lasagne but it's not.
C: Do you put it in the oven?
S: Yeah. Finally, you bake it in the oven, erm, for a little while and the top goes sort of crispy … the important thing is not to overcook it at this point. And …
C: OK.
S: … you cut it into slices.
C: Interesting. And so did your grandma make this for you a lot when you were young?
S: Yeah she did.
C: OK. OK, so it's quite a traditional thing in your family?
S: Yeah … I still cook it quite a lot … I love it….
C: Yeah, it sounds really delicious …

Track 2.15

P=Presenter, E=Expert
P: Today, on *It's a Buyer's World*, we're talking about buying things at the top end of the market … Julia Taylor is with us, from *Everyone's Auction Magazine* and we'll be looking at some of the incredible prices people pay for celebrity items, pop and film memorabilia, as well as fine art. Hello, Julia.
E: Hello.
P: So, first, one story to hit the headlines recently was the record sale of the Giacometti sculpture … Tell us about that.
E: Yes, well, a life-sized bronze sculpture, called *Walking Man I*, by the Swiss artist Giacometti was sold at auction for a record $104.3 million, making it the most expensive piece of art ever to sell at auction.
P: Wow, 104.3 million, that seems incredible. Who has that kind of money?
E: I know, it's amazing. We don't actually know who bought it, as the winning bid was made by an anonymous telephone buyer after just eight minutes of bidding!
P: It's not just fine art, though, is it? Some people spend huge amounts of money on quite ordinary things.
E: Yes. There was another record set recently, when an original comic book was bought for one and a half million dollars. It was issue number 1 of *Action Comics* which came out in June 1938, and it was the first time Superman had appeared in a comic,

and you know, comic books like these are extremely popular at the moment.
P: Mm. If you're lucky and you happen to have something like that, you can make a lot of money.
E: Mm. That's right. One of the six storm trooper helmets used in the original *Star Wars* films was found by chance at a second-hand sale and bought for just $75. The owner then sold it at an auction and ended up getting around $25,000 for it!
P: Amazing! What about celebrities, too? They can make a lot of money, can't they? You know, selling their clothes or other items. Huge sums of money have been paid for all sorts of things.
E: Absolutely, yes. Some huge numbers which spring to mind are: something in the region of $1,200,000 was paid for one of Marilyn Monroe's dresses, and erm, oh, one of Michael Jackson's gloves, covered in jewels, was bought for $350,000 by 36-year-old Hong Kong businessman Hoffman Ma. Apparently, it will now be displayed in a hotel in China.
P: Sometimes, things really do get a bit ridiculous, though, too. I mean, you hear about people paying huge prices for, well, crazy items,
E: Well, that's right. When it comes to being a superfan, people want everything and anything. Erm, for example, a clump of Elvis Presley's hair, which they say was cut from his head when he joined the Army in 1958, well, it was sold for $15,000!
P: Really? 15,000?
E: And apparently, this is amazing. When Justin Timberlake finished a breakfast interview at a New York radio station, the interviewer put the left-over toast on the Internet auction site, eBay. Lots of people bid for it, and in the end it was bought by a fan for $3,154!
P: That's just mad!
E: Yes, although I think the worst one I've ever heard of is a used tissue, yes, a used tissue, which the actress Scarlett Johansson used to blow her nose on was sold on eBay for $5,300!!
P: Wow, yes, I think that is the worst. That's really ridiculous and quite disgusting!! What on earth would you do with that?!

Track 2.16

M=Man, W=Woman
M: Hello, Electrical Solutions?
W: Hello my name's Ella Fernandez and I recently bought a TV from your website.
M: Mmm?
W: It was the Panasonic 32-inch widescreen, and it was delivered yesterday.
M: Oh, yes, I hope there are no problems?
W: Well, first of all, I'd just like to complain about how long it took to deliver … I mean, you promised on the site that delivery would be within three days… but in the end, I waited two weeks … and to be honest, I don't think that's acceptable.
M: Oh, I'm terribly sorry about that … we did have some problems with the stock and so it took a little longer than usual … I can only offer my apologies for that.
W: Well, it would've been better if you'd let me know beforehand about any possible delays.
M: Yes, I do apologise for that.
W: Well, anyway, I would've been OK with the delayed delivery if the TV had been in perfect condition when it arrived, but I'm afraid to say that it is far from perfect.
M: Oh?

W: Yes, the top left corner of the TV is slightly damaged and the on/off switch is loose.
M: Is the TV itself working? I mean, can you turn it on and is the picture clear?
W: Yes, it is. It's fine in that respect … but given that this is a brand new TV and cost a lot of money, I'm not prepared to accept damaged goods, and I'd be grateful if you could send a replacement as soon as possible please.
M: Well, we'll send someone to pick up the faulty TV as soon as possible and then when we've got that back in the warehouse, I'll send out a replacement.
W: Well, OK, but when could you pick this TV up?
M: Erm, let me look, erm, next Thursday … we could do it next Thursday …
W: Next Thursday? That's over a week from now! Can't you do it any earlier than that? I mean, I've already waited nearly two weeks … And how can I be sure that you'll come on Thursday? I don't want to be waiting around and then nobody turns up.
M: I can assure you that we'll definitely stick to the appointment … and I'll send you an email to confirm it.
W: Oh, well. OK. If that's all you've got, yes, next Thursday, and yes, could you send me an email, please, confirming that?
M: Yes, of course. So, next Thursday between 8 and 6 … someone will come and collect the faulty TV … That's all booked for you. And then, as I say, we'll contact you to arrange a time to deliver the replacement TV …
W: OK, fine. Well, thank you for your help.
M: And thank you. And once again, I can only apologise for the problems you've had.
W: OK. Thank you. Goodbye.
M: Bye …

Track 2.18

1 I can't believe the trouble I've had over this jacket I bought on the Internet. It was unusual because I've ordered stuff from the same company before and never had one single problem. But this time, I ordered a waterproof rain jacket and when it came it was an extra-large, even though I'd ordered medium. When I sent it back, the same thing happened. I sent it back about three or four times. So, eventually I phoned the customer services department, but the man I spoke to was so rude I couldn't believe it. Throughout the whole conversation, he spoke to me in a sort of bored, monotonous voice and clearly wasn't interested in my problem at all. He didn't even apologise!

2 I'd forgotten to set the alarm clock that day, so I overslept and woke up three hours later than I was supposed to … Then, I'd seriously underestimated the time it would take me to get there. On the way, it started pouring with rain and I got completely soaked to the skin. In the end, it took me nearly two hours which meant that I was really, really late. When I did finally arrive – wet through – I walked into the interview room and who was sitting there, waiting to interview me, but my ex-boss from my previous job! I felt so awful because I know for a fact that he hates me and I'd made such a fool of myself.

3 A couple of years ago, I decided to have a change of career. Having been a Spanish teacher for nearly 20 years, I decided to retrain as a translator and interpreter. It's a really difficult job and I found the training very hard work, but I'm really pleased with myself for having done it. I was brought up bilingual so the language

itself wasn't difficult for me, but you have to learn completely different skills. I now work for a huge multinational holiday company specialising in organised trips around South America and I really love it! It's the best job I've ever had.

Track 2.19

B=Boss, E=Employee

B: So, Will … generally, it seems that things are going fine. We've talked about your attitude to work, which is very good … And, over the three years that you've worked here, you've shown a consistently professional approach to your work.

E: Thank you … I must say that I've enjoyed it very much. My colleagues are very helpful and supportive … and testing computer games is great fun. I must say, it's great doing something you love in a job.

B: So, well … the next part of this appraisal is to think about the future. What do you see yourself doing next?

E: Well, as I say, I've really enjoyed the games testing work that I've been doing, but I feel that it's time I moved on now … I mean I think it's time I had a bit more responsibility, perhaps.

B: Yes, I think we need to think about that. You've shown some good leadership skills and I wonder how you would feel about becoming a team leader. You know, then you'd be supervising a team of games testers and making sure everything gets done properly. Or maybe you'd be interested in the marketing side of things?

E: Oh, well … Marketing is interesting, but I think I'd rather stay in the same department and become a team leader. Yes … I'd be very interested in that … though I'm not sure that I've got all the necessary skills to be honest. I mean, I'd like the responsibility, but erm … would there be any management training?

B: Yes, of course. We run some excellent in-house courses which I think would give you confidence. There's one coming up next week and then another in two months' time. And I think I'd rather you did the first course. You know, I'd rather we didn't waste any more time than we have to. What do you think?

E: Well, yes. I'd be very interested. It would be great to get some training underway as soon as possible. I mean, I'd rather not wait for two months, if that's OK with you. I'd like to be as prepared as I can.

B: OK. Great. In that case, I'd better get your name on the list for the one next week immediately. I hope it's not full up already. I don't think it will be but I'd better not promise anything before checking with my secretary … Erm … Perhaps I'll do that right now. Excuse me just one minute … Oh, hello Jeannie. I just wanted to check if you've still got places on the Management Skills course for next week … ah, you have … great … Could I put Will Scott's name down please? … Yes, S-C-O-double T …

Track 2.21

M=Martin, E=Evan

E: You know, Martin, I was reading this interesting article the other day, and it said that people had different personalities in different situations. So the way you behave in one given situation would be different than how you would behave in another situation. Do you think that's true?

M: Yeah I really do think it's true because, erm, I mean most of the time I'm quite a calm person but, erm, yesterday I had to make a complaint in a shop, I had to take something back.

E: Right.

M: And, erm, I actually became quite aggressive with the person because I wanted my money back and they wouldn't give it and I, suddenly, I just changed into this aggressive person and I think most of the time I'm … I'm pretty calm. What about you?

E: Yeah I think there's definitely some truth in that, erm, for example, generally at work I think that I'm fairly confident in that I don't have trouble speaking to people or leading discussion … or a presentation, or something like that, but if I don't know people or it's a social event then I find that I'm a lot, a lot less confident, erm, and more introverted, I … if I had to speak to a crowd of people at a party then I would say I'd be very nervous and would find it difficult to speak to people I didn't know.

M: Oh right. What are you like with the presen- … at giving a presentation because I'm s- … quite calm when I have to give a presentation, is it the same for you or do you … ?

E: Yeah, I think it's because I know exactly what has to be done. Erm, whereas in a social situation, it's maybe, you have to improvise a little bit more and feel it out, whereas at work you have to get a task done, so you do what you have to do.

M: I can understand, if I have to give some kind of presentation I find you've got, you've got, ah, ah, something to follow, so you know what you're going to say.

E: Right.

M: So it's better.

E: Absolutely.

Track 2.22

P=Presenter, T=Tony

P: Today on *Sports Alive*, we are talking about success and achievement in sport. Who are the most successful sportspeople in the world and just how do they achieve their success? There is a huge sports psychology industry working with almost all athletes these days. But does it work? Is it all really necessary? We've got sports psychologist, Tony Greenwood here to help us answer these questions. Hello, Tony. Welcome to the programme.

T: Hello …

P: So, first of all, Tony, let's think about that question. Is sports psychology really necessary? I mean, if I pay for a sports psychologist, will he or she really help me win? Some people would say that you've either got the determination to succeed or you haven't. What do you think?

T: Well, I suppose that's sometimes true. There are examples of sports people who are extremely successful and have never needed any help with their mental determination. You know, for some people, winning is vital. Mohamed Ali was probably the most famous of all those people. He had huge self-belief … he totally believed that he was the best and absolutely unbeatable.

P: That's right. Nobody needed to remind him to focus on his goal!

T: No … and then there are other examples of sportspeople who seem to be really committed to their own success: tennis player Roger Federer, racing driver Michael Schumacher and basketball player Michael Jordan to name but a few. But these people are actually quite rare … most sportspeople do a lot of work on mental preparation and get a lot of help with staying focused on winning.

P: OK, so what do the sports psychologists do? How do you help people to succeed?

T: Well, my basic job is to prepare the mind … and, well, I can do this in different ways depending on who we're working with. One of the most important things I do is that I can help people change negative thoughts into positive ones. I did some work with a footballer recently. He missed an important goal. You know, he missed a goal in a big match and he was devastated … and he started thinking that he couldn't do it anymore. I told him he could do it by thinking about something different, not on missing the goal. After practising thinking about the way the ball was turning instead, his whole game improved dramatically.

P: The British runner Kelly Holmes is a good example of that too, isn't she?

T: Yes, that's right. For much of her career, she was constantly getting injured and then worrying that it would happen again. I remember that she admitted feeling really out of control when she got injured all the time. But the fact is, athletes have to get over that and start to take control mentally. That's exactly what she did – and then of course won two gold medals at the Athens Olympics … and she was absolutely ecstatic … I mean it was obviously a fantastic achievement!

P: Yes, she was really brilliant!

T: There are other things we can do to help with mental preparation too. Things like routines to get the players focused and working as a team can really help.

P: Routines? What do you mean?

T: Well, the New Zealand All Blacks rugby team do their Haka war dance to focus themselves and to try and worry the other teams. Then there are people who have their own personal lucky routines. Footballer Andy Cole said he always wanted to be the last player on the pitch. It might seem a bit silly, but if it works …

Track 2.25

W=Woman, M=Man

W: Your little brother spends so much time on the computer …

M: What? No, he doesn't … no more than any of his friends … Anyway, he's 14 … he's not so little…

W: True … but you know, it's not good for children … I read an article recently … it was on about computer classes for two-year-olds!! It's unbelievable what some parents do.

M: Computer classes for two-year-olds? Seriously?

W: Yes, I am totally serious. Apparently, it's a growing trend … special colleges which offer computer classes for toddlers … aged two and three. I'm sorry, but I think that's ridiculous!

M: Well, hang on a minute, it might not be so bad.

W: I remember the woman in the article. I think she was the director of technology in a college. Well, she claimed that some of their students sat the national school exams aged seven. I mean, what's the point?!

M: OK, but that's not toddlers.

W: Oh, I know, but she explained that the success of those exams led them to start children earlier and earlier. She said that the parents are really keen on their children getting a head start and denied having any problems. In fact, she denied that there were any negative effects at all …

M: Well, she would say that I suppose.

W: Yes, and she admitted feeling pleased that the parents gave her really positive feedback. I'm amazed. She actually admitted that it made her feel good. If you ask me, it's all about making her feel good, and making money, of course.

M: Yes, money. I'm sure that comes into it.

W: Well, yes, and without thinking about the effect on the children. As I remember from the article, she actually suggested encouraging toddlers to do homework too, you know, she suggested that parents should help them do more 'practice' on the computer at home.

M: Well, most kids don't need much encouragement!

W: That's right.

M: It doesn't sound like a very balanced article.

W: Well, it did have two parts actually. There was another person. I can't remember his name … but he was an educational psychologist, and of course, he confirmed what I feel. He confirmed that studies show too much time on computers is bad for young children.

M: Mmm. I'm sure I read something about one study which warned people not to let their children on a computer for more than an hour a day.

W: Exactly! Er … How long's your brother been sitting there?

M: Erm, oh, about two and half hours.

W: Two and half hours!! What?! Will you remind me to get that article for you? I think you should read it.

Track 2.26

Thank you so much for returning all the surveys to us. We have now had a chance to look at all your responses and here are the collated results. So, first, for question 1 … 13 out of 20 people admitted spending three or more hours a day on the computer, which adds up to over 20 hours a week. The majority claimed to use the computer largely for studying, although 75 percent of the group also said that they used the computer for fun, doing things like playing games and communicating with friends. Moving on to question 2 … for this one, everyone suggested restricting the number of hours that children spend on the computer. Most people said that an hour a day was the maximum amount of time that children under the age of 12 should be sitting in front of a computer. However, nearly half the group admitted that it was quite difficult to enforce this, and that many children had to do homework using a computer. Nobody thought that children should never use a computer at home. OK, so, now question 3 … computer classes for children under the age of five … for this one, only a small minority were in favour of computer classes for toddlers … The vast majority confirmed my own feelings on this one, and that is, that very young children should not use computers at all, and should be encouraged to be active and play with their friends. This leads us on to question number 4, and the link between obesity and computer use in children. Reports have warned us about the link and most people who answered the survey seemed to agree. 80 percent confirmed that they thought there was a definite link, and that the longer children spent in front of a computer, the more likely they were to be overweight. A few people, however, disagreed, saying that obesity is a complex issue with a number of contributing factors.

Track 2.28

E=Eliot, C=Caroline, P=Polly

E: For me, erm, Richard Branson would be someone I consider a success, considering he started off with a small company, and basically turned it into a huge multinational, erm, corporation, erm. How would you define success, would you agree with that statement?

C: Mm, yeah, I think I … I have similar, erm, ideas about success, erm, yeah I think it's definitely to do with your wealth and how far you progress in your career, erm, I think the best thing is probably when you attain the goals that you've set yourself which usually end up in success.

P: Well, erm, I kind of agree with you that, erm, it's about how … how well you do and, erm, how much you progress, but not necessarily about your wealth so, erm, Richard Branson has been really successful and because of the nature of his business that's made him really wealthy but you could have, erm, say, erm, I don't know, erm, an artist who, erm, had a huge talent and made fantastic paintings and therefore they were successful but, erm, maybe they weren't gonna make any money until after their death. So they still have, erm, had a huge achievement but not be that wealthy, but maybe still as successful as someone who's made lots of money.

C: Mm, yeah you're right. I mean another, erm, means of success, obtaining success – success I suppose is, erm, through your family, erm, having loyal friends and, erm, a big family some people consider that being successful.

E: I think it's good to have, erm, strong relationships that you surround yourself with, erm, regardless of your social status or how well you do in a career, erm, for some people you know they're quite happy just to have a strong marriage or a strong personal relationship with a close knit of people. And money and, erm, social status really doesn't come into it.

Track 2.29

M=Man, W=Woman

M: Did I tell you about this really funny lawyer story that a friend of mine sent me on email the other day?

W: No, go on.

M: Well … the way it goes is that … there's this lawyer in the US … North Carolina or somewhere … and he buys this box of really rare and very, very expensive cigars.

W: OK.

M: And because they're so expensive he decides to insure them … against fire, amongst other things.

W: Fair enough.

M: Yes … except that, within a month, the lawyer made a claim against the insurance company, having smoked his complete collection of these fantastic cigars! You know, without having paid the premium … he hadn't even made his first payment to the insurance company … he made a claim against them.

W: What on earth for?

M: Well, in his claim, the lawyer stated that the cigars were lost in a series of small fires.

W: How ridiculous!

M: And unsurprisingly, the insurance company refused to pay for the obvious reason that the man had smoked the cigars in the normal way. But then, the lawyer sued the insurance company … and won! When he gave his decision, the judge agreed with the insurance company that the claim appeared ridiculous BUT … concluded that the lawyer had a policy from the company in which it said that the cigars could be insured against fire, without defining exactly what did or did not count as 'fire'. And so the company would have to pay the claim.

W: No! You're kidding!

M: But that's not all! You see, the insurance company wanted to sort the claim out quickly so they accepted the decision and paid $15,000 to the lawyer for his loss of the valuable cigars in the 'fires'. But now comes the best part!

W: Go on … I can't wait …

M: Then … after cashing the cheque, the lawyer was arrested! The insurance company had him charged with 24 counts of arson! With his own insurance claim and evidence from the previous case being used against him, the lawyer was convicted of deliberately burning his insured property and so – can you believe it? – he was sentenced to 24 months in jail and a $24,000 fine.

W: No! Is that really true?

M: Cross my heart! My friend said he got it from a real newspaper.

W: How amazing!

Track 2.30

first, evidence, suspects, next, sentenced, punishments, products, scientist, insurance, clients, context, against

Track 2.31

M=Man, W=Woman

M: Well, what do you think?

W: Hmm, it's a hard one, I don't know, erm, well, the park ranger sounds quite sure. He must have a good reason to be so sure.

M: He might not be certain who it was. I mean, he says he knows who was lying, but he doesn't say that was definitely the person who committed the crime.

W: True, but they probably are. So, who then?

M: OK, well, the brothers, Jan and Marek, they were rather tongue-tied it says … that's a bit suspicious. But they had been hiking for two days, and then they'd spent the whole day fishing, so they couldn't have committed the crime.

W: What do you mean? It might be a big lie! You're too trusting. If you want to be a detective, you've got to spot clues, not just believe everything you hear!

M: Well, OK, I don't know. They might have done it, I suppose, but I'm not sure. What clues are there? He says that he asked them if they had fished in the rain. Do you think that's significant?

W: Yes probably, but it sounds a bit dodgy, and you can't prove anything. Let's think about the next lot of suspects, Adam and Jean. They're a middle-aged, well-dressed couple, it says.

M: OK, well, as you say, a middle-aged couple, they must be innocent, don't you think? I mean, they can't be guilty. A middle-aged couple wouldn't do that sort of thing. You know, they can't have stolen food, and vandalised a park ranger's cabin. Surely, they wouldn't do that!?

W: What?! There you go again! That is so prejudiced! You haven't got any idea what they would or wouldn't do just because of their age, honestly! You've got to look at proper clues, not just prejudices and things people say.

M: Proper clues? Well, what clues are there here then?

W: OK, well, they said they took shelter in a small cave when it started raining. I suppose that's possible …

M: Yes, and they set up camp the previous night. I can't see anything wrong with that.

W: No. OK, what about the last people, Lara and Pia?

M: Well, they sound very suspicious to me. Oh, no, wait, I shouldn't judge too quickly!

W: That's right. OK, they do sound a bit suspicious. I mean, firstly they parked in the wrong place … but that doesn't prove anything really.

M: No, but having a brand-new campervan, not in their name, that's a bit strange.

W: Hmm, true … it is a bit weird, but they do offer an explanation, and also their friend's phone number. Oh, I don't know. I'm sure it's really obvious. We're probably missing something really simple. Either that or it's something really far-fetched and we'll never get it.

M: Mmm. Are there any other details that we've missed? It's all in the detail, you know, when you're a detective!

W: Oh, I see, you're a professional now, are you?!

Track 2.32

1 When you were a child, were you ever caught red-handed doing something you shouldn't?

2 In what situations have you found yourself tongue-tied?

3 Between what ages is someone 'middle-aged' do you think?

4 What things do you have in your house which are colour-coded?

5 How often do you get things gift-wrapped professionally in shops?

6 Has anyone ever told you a story that was really far-fetched?

Track 2.33

W=Woman, M=Man

W: Did you see these photos in the paper?

M: Mmm?

W: Basically, they are pictures of a burglar … he broke into someone's house and he's in the middle of stealing that person's computer equipment … He was caught completely red-handed because they managed to take pictures of him in the middle of the crime …

M: Really? So, how did they manage to do that?

Track 2.34

M: Really? So, how did they manage to do that?

W: I'm not sure, I suppose they must have fixed up some kind of security camera.

M: What … inside their own house?

W: Yeah. Let's see … mmm … actually it says here that the householder had been burgled before so he set up a webcam

which would start recording as soon as it detected movement in the room.

M: Hmm, that's a good idea. But the burglar can't have realised that he was being filmed, otherwise wouldn't he just steal the camera too?

W: Well, it says that he did take the computer and the camera, but that the homeowner had already thought of that.

M: Oh? So what did he do?

W: Well, the particularly clever thing in this case was that even though the burglar stole the computer and webcam, the images had already been sent via the Internet to a private email address …

M: Oh, that's very good, he really was caught red-handed …

Track 2.35

I=Interviewer, S.H.=Sherlock Holmes

I: Mr Sherlock Holmes, I must ask you first … How is it that you have the same name as Sherlock Holmes, the great detective from London?

S.H: Please, call me Holmes – that's what my friends and family call me – well, you see, my parents were great fans of the original Conan Doyle stories. They were the kind of parents who would spend hours reading to me … and my father, especially, would spend hours reading the Sherlock Holmes adventures to me – even as a child.

I: Really!?

S.H: Yes … and when I was born, they discussed a number of first names. They wanted to give their son a name that was uncommon – but also that represented something special. They didn't take long to decide on Sherlock Holmes as he was their favourite literary figure – and they knew no one would forget me once they'd heard my name. And boy, were they right!

I: So, how do people in general react when you introduce yourself to them?

S.H: Well, I get all kinds of reactions really – everything from the usual 'Where's Dr Watson' type comments to people just thinking I'm being funny.

I: I can imagine … And do you mind?

S.H: No, not at all. I'm a pretty easy-going person and I've never minded … no. I think, the best reaction was when I was in San Francisco one time. I went into an electronic store to buy a TV. The clerk behind the counter was a young lady about eighteen or so. After noticing the name on my credit card, she stared at it for about ten full seconds. Then, she slowly lifted her face to look at me and she said, in all sincerity, 'I didn't know you were real! Wait 'til I tell my friends I saw the real Sherlock Holmes!'

I: No!

S.H: Yes! It may sound far-fetched, but it's absolutely true … You could have knocked her over with a feather. The expression on her face was as if she'd seen a ghost. It was very amusing.

I: Given your name, do you feel that you have any special talent or ability to solve mysteries in everyday life?

S.H: Well, I will say that having such a name does mean that people often turn to me if anything unusual happens. For example, if I'm watching TV with a friend or family member and a magician comes on and does some kind of trick – all eyes turn to me to explain how it's done.

I: Really? How funny!

Track 2.36

W=Woman, M=Man

W: So what do we have to decide?

M: We have to decide which of these crimes is the least serious and which is the most serious.

W: Right OK. Mm.

M: So, why don't we start by talking about them individually perhaps, first?

W: Yes that's a good idea. OK, erm, right shall we … shall we start with Paolo?

M: Let's go for it, yeah. Any thoughts?

W: I think this is quite a serious crime, hacking into somebody's bank account. Erm, for me that would rate quite highly on the scale of being one of the most serious crimes … and I haven't seen the others yet, but …

M: And it's not mitigated at all by the fact that he's unemployed? The man's desperate?

W: Not really, not in my opinion. No.

M: And I suppose thousands of euros' worth I suppose …

W: I'd like to suspend judgement until we've gone through the, you know, the other three.

M: So, moving on to Jenny who's 35 and married with two children. Sounds like it's gonna make a difference.

W: Well, if she's married then she's obviously got a husband who supports them.

M: Well presumably. I guess we don't know.

W: So why is she shoplifting, that's the … that's the question, erm …

M: Kleptomania perhaps, erm …

W: Shall we … shall we come back to this one? Let's come back to this one later.

M: Erm, yeah that's, ah … I'm wildly dubious. Akio.

W: Akio.

M: Erm, a graffiti artist, a young graffiti artist. Well …

W: For me this is not really a crime.

M: Really? Not at all?

W: No.

M: But the … depending on the type of graffiti, I suppose.

W: Oh I suppose, so if it's offensive, then that's a different matter.

M: His graffiti apparently is well done and quite artistic but, ah, beauty in the eye of the beholder and what not, so.

W: Mm, it is art though.

M: You think all graffiti is art?

W: Not all graffiti, not the offensive graffiti but if it's as it says here, erm, well done and quite artistic it can actually lift the urban environment.

M: Interesting.

W: So for me that's probably going to be one of the least crimes.

M: Yeah I probably … yeah I think I'd be inclined to agree. So Teresa, the successful doctor, erm, this to me, erm …

W: She's been spe- … speeding every day, my goodness.

M: Doesn't … ah. I guess in a 30, 40, 45 and a 30 zone I guess is pretty significant, it's certainly irresponsible but …

W: Well, it depends, I mean if she's going to an emergency case then, then I'd say it's quite alright for her to d- to speed, however, it does say every day.

M: Yeah.

W: Or most days, most days, so I'm sure she doesn't have emergencies most days.

M: Yeah, yeah. Maybe you need a little more context perhaps, but … bom, bom, bom, bom, boh … I mean doctors generally aren't responding to emergencies in their own cars are they?

W: No.

M: So, to me it seems pretty irresponsible, whether it's a terrible crime, yeah. So …

W: Oh let's come back to that one later. I'd like to go back to, um, Jenny.

M: Uhuh, OK, erm, Jenny, so we're thinking isn't too bad, then?

W: No.

M: Maybe the least, and then after that I would probably say, ah, Akio is the least … oh so probably Akio is the least offensive we would say followed by Jenny …

W: It really … it really depends doesn't it on people's opinion, I mean for me Akio is the least offensive, followed by Jenny. Erm …

M: Followed by … Teresa.

W: Teresa possibly.

M: And then probably Paolo …

W: I think Paolo is the most serious crime.

M: Probably no great excuses for what he's done. Erm, good.

W: So what else do we have to decide? I think we've agreed on everything.

M: I think that's it. Yeah.

Track 2.38

I=Interviewer, W=Woman, M=Man
Dialogue 1

I: How do you feel about Derren Brown?

W: Well, I reckon he's probably genuine myself. It sounds as if audiences love him. Whether it's magic or not, all his TV shows are completely compelling viewing – and you can't say that about much TV these days. So even if we don't really understand how he does it, if you ask me, it doesn't really matter. He must be doing something right! I think Derren Brown gives us real entertainment and there's nothing wrong with that. Some people want to know how everything works, but I'm in favour of just enjoying it as entertainment, and not analysing things too much!

Dialogue 2

I: What are your views on mind-reading and illusionists? Do you have any strong feelings about that kind of thing?

M: Yes, I do. I've always believed that people like Derren Brown are just good showmen. To my mind, it's all rubbish – he's just good at talking and charming people, and also filming things so they look spectacular. But, I have my doubts about how much mind-reading he actually does. I mean, what's the point of pretending to predict lottery numbers when really he's filmed himself picking out every number and then they've edited the correct ones together at the last minute? I'm sceptical that any of it is real and I'm against people paying for a show which is really just a con. I mean, I doubt anything he does is real … it's just clever filming.

Dialogue 3

I: What do you think of mind-reading by people like Derren Brown?

M: From my point of view, I have to say that when I went to one of his shows, I thought it was fantastic. I loved every minute of it. I mean, at the beginning I was quite open-minded about it all but having seen him in action, I'm convinced that he really does have some kind of power. As I say, I've seen this man in action with my own eyes. He's a magician, I can tell you. Right in front of me, with absolutely NO special effects or pre-

filming, he did mind-reading on me. He predicted my answers to every question he asked me. It was amazing and almost a bit scary. In fact, I suspect that a lot of people don't believe he's doing anything just because they are quite scared about the whole thing.

Track 2.39

I=Interviewer, E=Expert

I: Welcome to *Modern World*. On the programme today, we're talking to Jo Carlson about the power of persuasion. All around us, there are images on television, jingles on the radio, adverts in magazines, sound bites on the news, offers in the shops. They're all hard at work – trying to make us believe something or persuading us to buy something. Fear not, Jo Carlson is here to reveal their secrets and show us how to resist all this persuasion! Hello, Jo.

E: Hello.

I: First, persuading people is big business, isn't it? I mean, supermarkets and politicians, advertisers and salespeople, they all take it very seriously, don't they?

E: Yes. They spend a lot of money on marketing and on working out the best psychological tricks to guarantee that even the most cautious among us are open to manipulation.

I: Let's take supermarkets then. How do they make us buy things we don't necessarily want? What are some of their tricks?

E: Well, firstly, most supermarkets have a 'transition zone' as you enter the shop. You might have noticed that the entrances of most supermarkets are quite small and crowded …

I: Yes … ?

E: Well, this is a deliberate effort to slow people down. The supermarkets want you to stop rushing around and take longer with your shopping …

I: That's interesting …

E: Yes, and … they also try to relax you by playing music and by pumping the smell of fresh bread into the store. Studies have shown that the smell makes people buy more.

I: I know I've done that without even thinking about it …

E: Exactly … most of the time, we are completely unaware of what's happening. It's subconscious persuasion …

I: There are also endless tricks when it comes to pricing, aren't there?

E: Yes … there's the old one of putting the price at £3.99, or £9.99, or whatever … Of course, we know about the trick, but it still works, because every time we see a price of £9.99 we are manipulated into thinking that it's a lot cheaper than £10 … In our heads, we think £9.99 is £9 but in fact, of course, it's £10.

I: Yes … it's simple, but it works …

E: And, another trick which is used more and more is putting the produce, let's say, apples … in bags of different sizes … So, for example, they put the ordinary apples in a bag costing, say, £1.80 and the organic ones in a bag costing say, £1.90.

I: So, supposing you're a customer, you might think, oh, organic apples aren't so much more expensive – I'll have those.

E: Yes … but what you might not realise is that the bag of ordinary apples contains six apples and the bag of organic ones contains only five … so really, they are more expensive than you think.

I: Mmm, and unless you're really good at doing maths in your head, you won't want to work out the price of each apple all the time … it's just too difficult and time-consuming.

E: That's right …

I: And what about sales … I mean, shops are always trying to attract customers by cutting prices, especially during end of season sales …

E: Yes, and if there are large discounts on offer, customers will come to the shops in huge numbers. Shops know that people are tempted by lower prices … even if you end up spending more in the end. You certainly wouldn't have spent as much if you had stayed at home and not bought anything!

I: Shops rely on customers' greed …

E: Yes, people will buy something as long as it looks like a bargain … though often they don't really want or need it at all.

I: So, what about the advertising industry? In what ways do they persuade us to buy particular products?

E: Well, adverts on TV in commercial breaks, or on posters, or in magazines … all follow the same principles and basically, there are two types of ads … those that appeal to the thinking part of our brain and those that appeal to the emotional part.

I: So, for what type of products would they advertise by appealing to the thinking part of our brain?

E: Well, they are mostly used for things which have little emotional appeal, for example, cleaning products. They give us information about the product and try to influence us that way. However, if an advert targets our emotions, it's likely to be much more successful. You don't have to believe the hype … provided that you respond emotionally … you know, on a subconscious level, you'll probably want to buy the product …

I: So, what kinds of emotions are used?

E: Well, adverts for different brands of clothes often want to make us feel that we belong, for example by showing us how to buy the right clothes to fit in with our friends. And adverts for insurance play on our need to feel safe. For example, they might show a family happily spending their insurance money buying new things when their house has been burgled.

I: Celebrities are used a lot too, aren't they?

E: Yes, that's very popular. Celebrities are often used as a quick way of getting the message across. Their success and familiarity makes them feel safe, interesting, cool … whatever … If we see our favourite pop star drinking a particular fizzy drink, we're immediately persuaded to buy it!

Track 2.40

Dialogue 1
A=Anna, Z=Zoë

A: Hi Zoë … ?

Z: Oh, hi, Anna … How are you? Are you OK?

A: Oh, yes, I'm fine … I'm just phoning because, well, I need some advice …

Z: Mmm? Advice? What about?

A: Oh, nothing major … it's just that I've just been looking at phones … and I'm trying to decide what to do … I mean, there's a really nice phone I want … and … you've probably seen the adverts on telly … You know, when all those people are running around trying to grab the phone.

Z: Oh yes, I know the one ... It looks really good ...

A: Yeah, well, I've just been looking at it in the shop ... and I really like it. But, you know, I don't really need a phone ...

Z: Oh, but you've had your phone for ages ... it's pretty out-of-date now, isn't it? Go on ... treat yourself!

A: Do you think I should?

Z: Yes, you should just do it. Don't worry about things so much. Is it really expensive or something?

A: Well, it's more than I'm paying at the moment. You know, I'm on a contract, so it would be a little bit more every month ... but you get the phone itself free, if you go on the contract...

Z: Well, go for it then! If it's only a bit more money ... well, it's not a huge deal, is it?

A: Mmm ...

Z: I mean, supposing you don't get it, how will you feel? If I were you, I'd just do it!

A: Yeah, maybe I should ...

Z: Definitely ... you deserve it! I'm sure you won't regret it.

A: OK then. I will. Thanks, Zoë.

Dialogue 2
J=Jamie, A=Alex

J: So ... Alex, what do you think ... I mean, there's so much on that I want to see at the moment ... We're spoilt for choice really!

A: Yeah, true ... erm ... well, let's look at the list ... OK ...screen 1, there's some kids' film ... I've seen the trailer for that one, and it looks really ridiculous. I mean, I like some kids' animations, but that one looks a bit stupid ... from what I've seen, anyway.

J: OK, what about screen 2?

A: Erm ... there's some boring romantic comedy ... I'm not that keen on films like that...

J: OK, so, screen 3 then?

A: Screen 3? Oh, there's the new Woody Allen film.

J: Yes, that's right. I haven't seen a Woody Allen film for years.

A: Well, let's see that then. I haven't seen a trailer, but I did read a good review though.

J: Oh, I don't know. I don't usually go for psychological dramas. It looks a bit weird.

A: It's a comedy. Don't be so negative! Anyway, what do you mean, it looks a bit weird? You haven't seen anything about it yet! I'm sure you'll enjoy it.

J: I'm not so sure ...

A: Well, there's nothing else, unless you want to get a DVD?

J: No.

A: Well, what have you got to lose? Come on ... it'll be fun ... It might cheer you up a bit!

J: Oh, alright then. Let's go!

Pearson Education Limited
Edinburgh Gate
Harlow
Essex CM20 2JE
England
and Associated Companies throughout the world.

www.pearsonelt.com

© Pearson Education Limited 2012

The right of Araminta Crace and Richard Acklam to be identified as authors of this work has been asserted by them in accordance with the Copyright, Designs and Patents Act 1988.

First published 2012

ISBN: 978-1-4082-6723-3
Book with ActiveBook and MyEnglishLab pack

Set in MetaPlusBook-Roman
Printed in Slovakia by Neografia

The publishers would like to thank the following people for their feedback and comments during the development of the material:

Martina Medica, Australia; Keiby Caro, Daniel Boderick, Colombia; Allison Dupuis, Denise Donnio, John Fayssoux, France; Tom Windle, Japan; Kasia Witek, Konrad Brzozowski, Poland; Svetlana Tretyakova, Russia; David Corp, Cristina Sanz, Isabel Simancas, Anna Pastor Peidro, Spain; Ömer Faruk Cantekin, Yelda Eryilmaz, Turkey; Hayden Berry, Helen Samuels, UK

We are grateful to the following for permission to reproduce copyright material:

Extract in unit 1 adapted from 'Meet the Boehmers,' Official site of the Boehmer Family, www.tbfj.com/main.html, reproduced with permission of the Boehmer Family; Extract in unit 1 from "Birth Order Affects Career Interests, study shows" by Jeff Grabmeier, http://researchnews.osu.edu/archive/birthwrk.htm, copyright © Jeff Grabmeier, ResearchNews; Extract in unit 4 adapted from "Work: the daily grind we just can't do without", *Focus Magazine*, pp.72-75, June 1995 (Chorlton, W.), copyright © BBC Focus; Extract in unit 4 adapted from "The old man of Chandigarh", *The Observer*, 03/01/1988, pp.62-65 (Gerrard, N.), copyright © Guardian News & Media Ltd 1988; Extract in unit 6 from *The Memory Box*, published by Chatto and Windus (Margaret Forster) p.69, Reprinted by permission of The Random House Group Ltd and The Sayle Literary Agency; Extracts in unit 9 adapted from *The Return of Heroic Failures* Rogers, Coleridge and White (Stephen Pile, 1989) copyright © 1989 Stephen Pile. Reproduced by permission of the author c/o Rogers, Coleridge & White Ltd., 20 Powis Mews, London W11 1JN; Extract in 9 adapted from "The Green Bay Backpackers" by Hy Conrad, originally appeared on MysteryNet.com: "The Online Mystery Network", copyright © 1996-2010 MysteryNet.com; Extract in unit 9 adapted from "Sherlock Holmes and Dr. Joseph Bell", http://www.siracd.com/work_bell.shtm, copyright © Marsha Perry; Interview in unit 9 adapted from "An interview with the Rev. Sherlock Holmes" by Raffiel Alexander, http://www.sherlock-holmes.co.uk/news/reverend.html, copyright © The Sherlock Holmes Museum; Extract in unit 10 adapted from "The Persuaders", *Focus magazine*, pp.23-27, February 2004 (Jo Carlowe), copyright © Jo Carlowe.

In some instances we have been unable to trace the owners of copyright material, and we would appreciate any information that would enable us to do so.

The publisher would like to thank the following for their kind permission to reproduce their photographs:
(Key: b-bottom; c-centre; l-left; r-right; t-top)

Action Plus: Glyn Kirk 109tl (B); **Alamy Images:** Alex Segre 43c, Andrew Fox 46cl, CJG - Technology 140tr, David Hancock 141cl, David Tipling 106bc, Eddie Linssen 56c (B), Eitan Simanor 32cl, Jochen Tack 58b, Mark Harvey 128br, Michael Zegers 151tl, Michael Zegers 151tl, Oleksiy Maksymenko 41/B, Oleksiy Maksymenko Photography 88 (D), Rachael Bowes 31br, Robert Harding Picture Library Ltd 91cl; **Animal Photography:** Sally Anne Thompson 98bl; **Art Directors and TRIP Photo Library:** Tibor Bognar 26br; **Bridgeman Art Library Ltd:** Peasants planting potatoes (pencil and chalk on paper), Millet,

Jean-Francois (1814-75) / Private Collection 50br; **Buzz Pictures:** Tim McKenna 18tc/B; **Camerapress:** Gianni Muratore 129t; **Corbis:** Alfred / epa 91t, Andreas Gebert 105tl, Ariel Skelley 81tr (c), Artiga Photo 157tr, Catherine Karnow 7cl, cultura 30tr, H. Armstrong Roberts 43t, Helen King 7t, 7bl, Helen King 7t, 7bl, Image Source 156br, image100 69tl (D), Jon Feingersh 29br/C, Keith Brofsky 144tr/A, Larry Williams 112r, Michael T. Sedam 77cl, Nicky Niederstrasser 17tr, Patrick Ward 88t, Radius Images 21bl, Ragnar Schmuck 79br, Richard T. Nowitz 29tc, Rudy Sulgan 35t, The Francis Frith Collection 77tl, Vittoriano Rastelli 29bl, YM YIK / epa 95 (A); **Dinodia Photo Library Pvt Ltd:** Dinodia Photo Library 53t, 53cr, 54bl, Dinodia Photo Library 53t, 53cr, 54bl; **DPPI:** Benoit Stichelbaut 64tc, Jacques Vapillon 64bl; **Eye Ubiquitous / Hutchison:** 22tr; **Fotolia.com:** Aaron Amat 41/C, Andrey Khrobostov 88 (B), Gary 35tl, hugy 35bl, Marc Dietrich 41/D, Miqul 41/G, Monkey Business 49cl, Nolte Lourens 88 (A), Paul Liu 35cl, Pier95 49bl, TebNad 74tr, Thomas Hansson 67tr, Tinu 147tr; **Getty Images:** Adrian Pope 152br, AFP 49tl, 95 (E), AFP 49tl, 95 (E), Alan Thornton 111c, Annie Marie Musselman 144br/C, Archive Photos 77bl, Bernhard Lang 153tr, Brand New Images 91tl, Buda Mendes / LatinContent 105t, Car Culture 77t, Chabruken 60tr, Chris Mueller 128b (Teresa), Christopher Robbins 8-9, Connor Walberg 21tl, Dream Pictures 55bl, Emmanuel Faure 16bl, Erin Patrice O'Brien 128tl (paolo), George Shelley Productions 18tr/C, Greg Ceo 31bl, Henthorn Derek / STOCK4B 128 (Jenny), Hill Street Studios 116 (F), Hummer 98tr, James Whitaker 143tr, Jim Bourg 137c/C, Jim Cummins 105bl, Jonathan Wood 68tr (C), Joos Mind 56bl (C), Jose Luis Pelaez 83tr, Jun Takahashi 128 (Akio), Leon Neal 155tr, LWA 150bl, Mitchell Funk 139tl, Peter Adams 25tc, Peter Cade 81tr (a), Regine Mahaux 50cl, Robert Abbott Sengstacke 133cl, Robert Abbott Sengstacke 133cl, Ron Chapple 119cl, Samba Photo 49t, Sarah Ashun 41/A, Steve Cole 55c, Steve Peixotto 116 (D), Susanne Kronholm 116 (A), Sylwia Duda 63t, Tom Hanley / Redferns 96br, Ty Milford 21t; **Ronald Grant Archive:** Columbia Pictures 147cr, Hammer Film Productions Ltd 126tr; **Guardian News and Media Ltd.:** Sam Frost 78t; **Image courtesy of The Advertising Archives:** 95 (C), The Advertising Archives 137tr/B, 138br; **Imagestate Media:** E. Sampers / Explorer / Hoa-Qui 39tl; **J. Cede Prudente:** 22cr; **Judy Boehmer:** 11tl; **Kobal Collection Ltd:** 20TH CENTURY FOX 127tr, UNIVERSAL 70tr; **Masterfile UK Ltd:** CRed 10bl, Noel Hendrickson 108br, Sarah Murray 97cr; **Panos Pictures:** Robert Wallis 39tr, Sven Torfinn 38br; **Pearson Education Ltd:** Eben Maasdorp 81tl; **Penguin Books Ltd:** (c)Eric Blair,1949.The estate of the late Sonia Brownwell Orwell 1987. 155cl, Chatto & Windus 1999,Penguin Books 2000,(c) Margaret Forster. 84tr; **Photolibrary.com:** A Chederros 141tl, Angela Cameron 15tc, Asia Images Group 102tc, Axel Schmies 45tr, bilderlounge / Alessandro Ventura 97br, Christian Mang 63cl, Comstock 97tr, Frank Chmura 51br, Gonzalo Azumendi 26bl, Hangen 116 (E), Jan Greune 68tc (B), Jim Wark 74cr, Jochen Tack 63bl, JTB Photo 45bl, Kablonk 56t, Keith Levit 21cl, LLC - 5 / 5 116 (C), Marc Dozier 63tl, Monkey Business Images Ltd 114cl, Norbert Michalke 50t, Patrick Forget 102tr, Pedro Coll 133bl, Peter Frank 83cr, Radius Images 105cl, RiccardoLombardo 32tr, Robert Lawson 137/A, Robert Llewellyn 116 (B), Roger Leo 111b, SGO 136br, Splashdown Direct 119tl, Stefan Wackerhagen 32cr, Stephan Gabriel 154br, Steve Vidler 32tl, Stockbroker 102tl, Templer 91bl, Walter Hodges 83br; **Press Association Images:** AndrewCornaga / PA 109tr/C, DPA 119t; **Rex Features:** 20thC. Fox / Everett 37tl, 95cl (D), CBS / Everett 120tl, 120tr, CBS / Everett 120tl, 120tr, Dreamworks / Everett 147cl, F1 Online 68tl (A), Geraint Lewis 134cl, Image Source 38cr, ITV 121tl, John Powell 7tl, Jonathan Hordle 88 (E), 134br, Jonathan Hordle 88 (E), 134br, KPA / Zuma 70br, Nils Jorgensen 98br, OJO Images 144cr/B, Peter Brooker 8ocl, 95 (B), Peter Brooker 8ocl, 95 (B), RD / Keystone USA 8ocr, Rex Features 92cl, 125cl, 125cr, 125bc, Rex Features 92cl, 125cl, 125cr, 125bc, Rex Features 92cl, 125cl, 125cr, 125bc, Sam Tinson 133tl, Sipa Press 74tl, 159tr, Sipa Press 74tl, 159tr, Steve Rapport / 41/E, Tom Hoenig 41/E, Warner Br / Everett 71tl, 72tl, 72tr, Warner Br / Everett 71tl, 72tl, 72tr, Warner Br / Everett 71tl, 72tl, 72tr; **Science Photo Library Ltd:** Carol & Mike Werner, Visuals Unlimited 133t, Mehau Kulyk 119bl; **TIPS Images Ltd:** Alexis Platoff 98c; **TopFoto:** 18tl/A, 46t, Topham / ProSport 109tr/A

Cover images: *Front:* Alamy Images: Maros Markovic

All other images © Pearson Education

Every effort has been made to trace the copyright holders and we apologise in advance for any unintentional omissions. We would be pleased to insert the appropriate acknowledgement in any subsequent edition of this publication.

Illustrated by Beach, Ian Mitchell, Kveta, Roger Penwill, Peter Richardson, Stephanie Strickland and Teresa Tibbetts.